KAREN BROWN'S

Italy

Charming Inns & Itineraries

Karen Brown Titles

KAREN BROWN'S
Italy
Charming Inns & Itineraries

Written by

CLARE BROWN

Illustrations by Barbara Tapp
Cover Painting by Jann Pollard

Travel Press
Karen Brown's Country Inn Series

Editors: Karen Brown, June Brown, Clare Brown, Nicole Franchini, Iris Sandilands
Technical support: William H. Brown III, Aide-de-camp: William H. Brown
Illustrations: Barbara Tapp; Cover painting: Jann Pollard; Cover design: Tara Brassil
Maps: Susanne Lau Alloway—Greenleaf Design & Graphics; Cover photograph: Elaine Eisenberg
Written in cooperation with Carlson Wagonlit/Town & Country Hillsdale Travel, San Mateo, CA 94401

Distributed USA & Canada: The Globe Pequot Press
Box 833, Old Saybrook, CT 06475, tel: (860) 395-0440, fax: (860) 395-0312
Distributed Europe: Springfield Books Ltd., tel: (01484) 864 955, fax: (01484) 865 443
Norman Road, Denby Dale, Huddersfield HD8 8TH, W. Yorkshire, England
Distributed Australia & New Zealand: Little Hills Press Pty. Ltd.
1st Floor, Regent House, 37-43 Alexander St, Crows Nest NSW 2065, Australia
tel: (02) 437-6995, fax: (02) 438-5762
A catalog record for this book is available from the British Library

Library of Congress Cataloging-in-Publication Data

Brown, Clare.
     Karen Brown's Italy : charming inns & itineraries / written by
Clare Brown ; sketches by Barbara Tapp ; cover painting by Jann
Pollard
        p. cm. -- (Karen Brown's country inn series)
  Previously published : Karen Brown's Italian country inns &
itineraries . 1995.
      includes index.
      ISBN 0-930328-40-X (pb)
      1. Bed and breakfast accommodations--Italy--Guidebooks.
2. Hotels--Italy--Guidebooks. 3. Italy--Guidebooks.   I. Brown,
Karen. II. Title. III. Series.
  TX907.5.173B78 1996
  647.9445' 03--dc20

95-41057
CIP

As Always
to
My Best Friend, Bill
With Love and Gratitude for
Many Miles of Memories

Contents

ITINERARIES (continued)

 # Introduction

Of all the countries in the world, there is none more magical than Italy: it is truly a tourist's paradise—a traveler's dream destination. No one could be so blasé, that within Italy's narrow boot there would not be something to tantalize their fancy. For the archaeologist, there are some of the most fascinating and perfectly preserved ancient monuments existing today—just begging to be explored. For the gourmet, there is the finest food in the world. For the outdoors person, there are towering mountains to conquer and magnificent ski slopes to enjoy. For the lover of art, the museums are bursting with the genius of Italy's sons such as Michelangelo, Leonardo da Vinci, and Raphael. For the architect, Italy is a school of design—you are surrounded by the ancient buildings whose perfection has inspired the styles of today. For the history buff, Italy is a joy of wonders—her cities are veritable living museums. For the wine connoisseur, Italy produces an unbelievable selection of wine whose quality is unsurpassed. For the adventurer, Italy has intriguing medieval walled villages tucked away in every part of the country. For the beach buff, Italy's lakes and islands hold the promise of some of the most elegant resorts in the world. For the religious pilgrim, Italy is the cradle of the Christian faith and home of some to the world's most famous saints. The miracle of Italy is that all these treasures come packaged in a gorgeous country of majestic mountains, misty lakes, idyllic islands, wonderful walled villages, and gorgeous cities. In addition, the climate is ideal and the people warm and gracious. Italy is truly a perfect destination.

About This Guide

This guide is written with two main objectives: to describe the most romantic small hotels throughout Italy and to tie these hotels together with itineraries that include enough details so that you can plan your own holiday. This introduction explains how to use the guide and also touches upon what to expect while traveling. After the introduction the main part of the guide is divided into three sections: itineraries, hotel descriptions, and maps. The itinerary section outlines itineraries with sightseeing suggestions along the way; the hotel descriptions section gives a comprehensive list of recommended lodgings (appearing alphabetically by town); the map section has 14 maps to help you pinpoint each town where we suggest a place to stay. The pertinent regional map number is given at the right on the *top line* of each hotel's description. To make it easier for you, we have divided each location map into a grid of four parts, a, b, c, and d, as indicated on each map's key.

We have personally inspected each place that we recommend and describe its ambiance and merits in our write-up which is followed by an illustration and practical information such as address, telephone and fax numbers, rates, etc. **None of the places to stay ever pays to be included**—our choices are strictly based on hotels we think you would most enjoy. Frequently we hear, "I don't care where I stay—I'm rarely in my room except to sleep." If this is your true philosophy, then this book is *not* for you. To our way of thinking, where you stay weaves the very fabric of your trip and your choice of hotels is of absolutely prime importance. Not that the hotel needs to be expensive: a moonlit dinner on the terrace of a simple inn can be as memorable as dining at a fancy hotel— sometimes even more so because the owner is there to pamper you. The recommendations in our guide vary tremendously: some are grand hotels—fit for a king and priced accordingly; others are simple, inexpensively priced hotels tucked away in remote hamlets. We include them all if they have personality, romantic charm, and antique ambiance.

About Itineraries

In the itinerary section of this guide you'll be able to find an itinerary, or portion of an itinerary, that can be easily tailored to fit your exact time frame and suit your own particular interests. If your time is limited, you could certainly follow just a segment of an itinerary. In the itineraries we have not specified the number of nights at each destination, since to do so seemed much too confining. Some travelers like to see as much as possible in a short period of time. For others, just the thought of packing and unpacking each night makes them shudder in horror and they would never stop for less than three or four nights at any destination. A third type of tourist doesn't like to travel at all—the destination is the focus and he uses this guide to find the perfect resort from which he never wanders except for daytime excursions. So, use this guide as a reference to plan your personalized trip.

Our advice is do not rush. Part of the joy of traveling is to settle in at a hotel that you like and use it as a hub from which to take side trips to explore the countryside. When you dash too quickly from place to place you never have the opportunity to get to know the owners of the hotels and to become friends with other guests. Look at the maps in the back of this guide to find the hotels in the areas where you want to travel. Read about each hotel in the hotel description section of this book and decide which places to stay sound most suited to your taste and budget, then choose a base for each area you want to visit.

MAPS

With each itinerary there is a map showing the routing and suggesting places of interest along the way. These are an artist's renderings and are not intended to replace a good commercial map. To supplement our generalized routings, you definitely need a set of detailed maps that indicate all of the highway numbers, expressways, alternate little roads, expressway access points, and exact distances. Our suggestion is to purchase a comprehensive set of city maps and regional maps before your departure, and with a highlight pen mark your own personalized itinerary and pinpoint your city hotels. If you live in a metropolitan area, you should have no problem buying maps in a travel bookstore or else your local bookstore should be able to place a special order. Our personal preference for Italy are the Rand McNally *Hallwag* maps (there are Rand McNally stores in many major cities, so these maps are readily available). Depending upon your itinerary, you need either the *Southern Italy* or *Northern Italy* map—or both (don't purchase the map that covers the whole of Italy—it is too general). Each map comes with a small index booklet to help you find the towns you are seeking. Almost every town in our guide can be found on these two maps. A superb complement to the *Hallwag* maps is a series of three atlases published by the *Touring Club Italiano*. These can be purchased in Italy in the shops located in service stations along the main expressways. Each volume, *North*, *Central*, and *South*, can be purchased individually. They are expensive, but highly recommended. They are so detailed and well-indexed that it makes finding your way very easy.

SIGHTSEEING

Ideas on what to see and do are suggested throughout the six itineraries. However, we just touch upon some of the sightseeing highlights. There is a wealth of wonders to see in Italy, plus, of course, many local festivals and events. Before you leave, check with the tourist office for further information targeted at exactly where you plan to travel. And, once on the road, make it a habit to always make your first stop the local tourist office to pick up maps, schedules of special events, and sightseeing. Even more important, before you drive out of your way to see a particular museum or place of interest, check when it is open. As a general guideline, most museums are closed on Mondays and for a couple of hours in the middle of the day. Small museums are usually open only in the morning. Outdoor museums usually open at 9 am and close about an hour before sunset. Most monuments and museums close on national holidays—see HOLIDAYS on page 14.

About Hotels

BASIS FOR SELECTION

This guide does not try to appeal to everyone. It is definitely prejudiced: each hotel included is one we have seen and liked. It might be a splendid villa elegantly positioned overlooking one of Italy's romantic lakes or a simple little chalet snuggled high in a mountain meadow. But there is a common denominator—they all have charm. Therefore, if you too prefer to travel spending your nights in romantic old villas, appealing chalets, dramatic medieval castles, ancient monasteries, converted stone cottages, and gorgeous palaces, we are kindred souls. Follow the paths we have suggested and each night will be an adventure.

For some of you, cost will not be a factor if the hotel is outstanding. For others, budget guides your choices. The appeal of a simple little inn with rustic wooden furniture beckons some, while the glamour of ornate ballrooms dressed with crystal chandeliers and gilded mirrors appeals to others. What we have tried to do is to indicate what each hotel has to offer and describe the setting, so that you can make the choice to suit your own preferences and holiday. We feel if you know what to expect, you won't be disappointed, so we have tried to be candid and honest in our appraisals.

CREDIT CARDS

Almost all hotels in this guide accept credit cards. Those hotels that do accept plastic payment are indicated in the hotel description section using the following abbreviations: AX–American Express, MC–MasterCard, VS–Visa, or simply, all major. *NOTE:* When calculating how much cash you will need, be aware that some hotels will accept a credit card to guarantee the reservation, but will not let you pay your bill by credit card.

DECOR

It is difficult to find hotels in Italy furnished in a simple style. Italian hotels frequently reflect a rather formal opulence and tend toward a rather fussy decor. There are some exceptions. In a few instances (which we note in the hotel descriptions) the hotels are decorated with a more rustic ambiance using country antiques, but this is not the norm. When antiques are used, they are very often the fancy, gilded variety.

GROUPS & AFFILIATIONS

There are two well-known groups of hotels to which many of the hotels in this guide belong. The *Romantik Hotels* group is an affiliation of charming small hotels that are managed by the owner and are usually located in a historic building. You can recognize the hotels that belong to this group because they have the word *Romantik* preceding their name. The *Relais & Chateaux* group is an affiliation of luxurious small hotels that are very expensive, with extremely high standards of excellence. You can tell which of the hotels in our guide belong to this group because we have indicated "Relais & Chateaux" in the hotel's information description.

RATES

In the hotel reference section in the back of the book each hotel shows a rate that reflects the approximate nightly cost for two persons including tax, service, and Continental breakfast during the high season of 1996. There are a few hotels where breakfast and one other meal (either lunch or dinner) are included in the rate and, if so, this too is noted. Please use the rates given only as a general guide because each hotel has such a wide range of price possibilities that it is impossible to project with complete accuracy. In addition, sometimes rates increase after this book goes to print. However, the lire price quoted helps you anticipate the approximate cost. When you plan your holiday, check the current exchange rate with your bank to convert lire into your currency.

HOW TO ECONOMIZE: The price for a room in Italy has soared in the last few years. However, if you study carefully the rates given in the back of this guide, you can still find a few bargains available and can plan your trip using one of the less expensive hotels as your hub from which to venture out each day. We also publish *Karen Brown's Italy: Charming Bed & Breakfasts* which makes an ideal companion to this guide. The maps in both are similar, making it easy to choose a place to stay from either book. Not only can you save money by sometimes choosing a bed and breakfast for a night's accommodation, but you can also enjoy the experience of staying where you have the opportunity to know your host and fellow guests. We highly recommend choosing a combination of places to stay from both books.

For those of you who want to squeeze the most value out of each night's stay, we have several other suggestions:

1) Travel off season—spring and fall are usually lovely in Italy and the hotels often have less expensive rates.

2) Ask for a room without an en-suite bathroom—some hotels have very nice rooms, usually with a washbasin in the room, but with a shared bathroom down the hall.

3) Ask if there is a weekly rate—frequently hotels offer a price break for guests staying a week or more. If traveling with children, ask if there is a special family suite at a lesser price than separate rooms.

5) Ask about rates with meals included. For a stay of three days or longer, many hotels offer a special rate including meals: MAP (Modified American Plan) means two meals a day are included, AP (American Plan) means three meals a day are included.

6) Last, but not least, is the most important way to save money: stay in the countryside instead of in the cities. We cannot stress enough how much more value you receive when you avoid the cities—especially the tourist centers such as Rome, Florence, Milan, and Venice. Of course stay right in the heart of town if you are not watching your budget, but if you are trying to squeeze the greatest value from your lire, choose hotels in the countryside and take side trips to visit the pricey tourist centers.

RESERVATIONS

People frequently ask, "Do I need a hotel reservation?" The answer really depends on how flexible you want to be, how tight your time schedule is, in which season you are traveling, and how disappointed you would be if your first choice is unavailable.

It is not unusual for the major tourist cities to be completely sold out during the peak season of June through September. Be forewarned: hotel space in Rome, Florence, Milan and Venice is really at a premium and unless you don't mind taking your chances on a last-minute cancellation or staying on the outskirts of town, make a reservation as far in advance as possible. Space in the countryside is a little easier. However, if you have your heart set on some special little hotel, you certainly should reserve as soon as your travel dates are firm. Reservations are confining. Most hotels want a deposit to hold your room and frequently you cannot get a refund if you change your plans. So it is a double bind: making reservations locks you into a solid framework, but without reservations you might be stuck with accommodations you do not like. During the height of the tourist season, some small hotels accept reservations only for a minimum of three or more nights. However, do not give up, because almost all of the hotels that have this policy take a last-minute booking for a shorter period of time if you call along the way and there is space available. For those who like the security blanket of having each night pre-planned so that once you leave home you do not have to worry about where to rest your head, several options for making reservations are listed on the following pages.

Introduction–About Hotels

FAX: If you have access to a fax machine, this is a super-efficient way to reach a hotel. The majority of hotels in Italy have fax numbers which we have noted in the back of the book under each hotel listing. Clearly state the following: number of people in your party; how many rooms you desire; whether you want a private bathroom; date of arrival and date of departure; ask the rate per night and if a deposit is needed. Do not forget to include your fax number for their response. When you receive a reply, send the deposit requested and ask for a receipt and a map. *NOTE:* When corresponding with Italy, be sure to spell out the month. Do not use numbers since in Europe they reverse the American system—e.g., 6/9 means September 6, not June 9. Although most hotels can understand a letter written in English, at the end of this introduction we provide a letter written in Italian with an English translation. Photocopy it and use it when you fax your reservation request.

LETTER: If you start early, you can write directly to the hotels and request exactly what you need. Again, be sure to be specific as to your arrival and departure dates, number in your party, and what type of room you want (see the paragraph above). For convenience, use photocopies of the sample reservation-request letter. Allow six weeks for an answer—mail to Italy is *very* slow.

TELEPHONE: Another way to make a reservation is to telephone. You can have your answer immediately, and if space is not available, you can then decide on an alternative. The cost is minimal if you direct-dial—ask your local operator when to call for the lowest rates. Also consider what time it is in Italy when you call (even the most gracious of owners are sometimes a bit grouchy when awakened at 3 am). If you are dialing from the United States, the system is to dial 011 (the international code), then 39 (Italy code), then the city code (dropping the 0 in front of the city code), and then the telephone number. Almost all of the hotels have someone who speaks English. The best chance for finding the owner or manager who speaks English is to call when it is late afternoon in Italy (Italy is six hours ahead of New York). Be aware that Italy's telephone numbers are constantly changing, so if you cannot reach a hotel, ask for operator assistance.

TRAVEL AGENT: A travel agent can be of great assistance, particularly if your own time is limited. A proficient agent can expertly handle all the details of your holiday and tie them together for you in a neat package—including hotel reservations, airline tickets, boat tickets, train reservations, ferry schedules, and theater tickets. For your airline tickets there is usually no service fee (unless you are using some kind of discount coupon), but the majority of travel agencies do charge for their other services. Talk with your agent. Be frank about how much you want to spend and ask exactly what he or she can do for you and what the charges are. If your travel agent is not familiar with all the small places in this guide (many are so tiny that they appear in no other major publications), you can loan him or her your book—it is written as a guide for travel agents as well as for individual travelers.

UNITED STATES REPRESENTATIVE: Some hotels have a United States representative through whom reservations can be made. Many of these representatives have a toll-free telephone number. This is an extremely convenient and efficient way to secure a reservation and you can often book accommodations at several hotels with just one telephone call. However, you might find it less expensive to make the reservation yourself since sometimes representatives make a charge for their service, reserve only the more expensive rooms, or quote a higher price to protect themselves against currency fluctuations and administrative costs. Nevertheless, if you understand that it might cost you more, contacting the hotel representative is an easy way to make a reservation. If a hotel has a representative, his name and telephone number are listed under the hotel's description. In the back of the book there is information on Hidden Treasures of Italy (HTI), a company specializing in travel arrangements in Italy which, for a fee, makes hotel reservations.

These various hotel booking services are given solely as a source of information for you. We are in no way affiliated with any of the hotel representatives and cannot be responsible for reservations made through them or money sent as deposits or prepayments.

About Italy

The following pointers are given in alphabetical order, not in order of importance.

CURRENT–ELECTRICITY

You need a transformer plus an adapter if you plan to use an American-made electrical appliance in Italy. The voltage is usually 220, but sometimes it is 115 or 125. Check with the manager before plugging anything into an outlet if you have any question. It is very embarrassing to have the electricity go out all over the hotel because you were drying your hair. *NOTE:* Many hotels have hair dryers in the room or else can loan you one.

DRIVING

DRIVER'S LICENSE: A current license from your home country is valid for driving throughout Italy if you are on holiday. However, if you are renting a car, certain age limits apply. Please check on the age limit policy with the car rental company.

DISTANCES: Distances are indicated in kilometers (one kilometer equals 0.621 mile), calculated roughly into miles by cutting the kilometer distance in half. Distances between towns are also indicated in orange alongside the roads on the Touring Club Italiano maps. Italy is a compact country and distances are relatively short, yet you will be amazed at how dramatically the scenery can change in an hour's drive.

GASOLINE: Gasoline (petrol) is very expensive so plan ahead and budget this cost as part of your trip if you are driving. Most of the service stations located on the main expressways accept credit cards.

ROADS: The Italian roads are nothing short of spectacular, including some of the finest highways in the world. In fact, the Italians are absolute geniuses when it comes to their engineering feats (which actually is not such a surprising fact when you consider what a fantastic road system the Romans built 2,000 years ago). Nothing seems to daunt the

Italian engineers: you would think the mountains are made of clay instead of solid rock, the way the roads tunnel through them. Sometimes a roadway seems endlessly suspended in mid-air as it bridges a mountain crevasse.

ROAD SIGNS: Before starting on the road prepare yourself by learning the international driving signs so that you can obey all the rules of the road and avoid the embarrassment of heading the wrong way down a small street or parking in a forbidden area. There are several basic sign shapes: triangular signs warn that there is danger ahead; circular signs indicate compulsory rules and information; square signs give information concerning telephones, parking, camping, etc. Yellow signs are for tourists and indicate a site of historical or cultural interest, hotels, and restaurants.

TOLL ROADS: Italy has a network of super expressways that makes any spot in the country an easily manageable destination by car. Once you are on the toll roads, the kilometers slip by and you can go quickly from almost any area of Italy to another. However, be forewarned—these toll roads are very expensive. It seems that about every half hour a toll station appears and you must pay again. However, every cent is well spent when you consider the alternative of creeping along within a maze of trucks and buzzing motorcycles, taking forever to go only a few kilometers. Use the toll roads for the major distances you need to cover, and then choose the small roads when you wish to meander leisurely through the countryside. Toll roads are mystifying until you learn the system—even then it is confusing because just when you think you have the operation down pat you find it varies slightly. This is the most common routine: first follow the green expressway signs toward the toll road. Sometimes these signs begin many kilometers from the expressway, so be patient and continue the game of follow-the-sign. Each entrance to the expressway handles traffic going in both directions. As you enter into the toll gate there is usually a red button you push and a card pops out of a slot. After going through the toll station you choose the direction you want to go. As you leave the expressway there is a toll station where your ticket is collected and you pay according to how many kilometers you traveled.

FOOD and DRINK

It is almost impossible to get a bad meal in Italy. Italians themselves love to eat and dining is a social occasion to be with family and friends. Restaurants are bustling not only with tourists, but also with the Italians who dawdle at the tables long after the meal is over, chatting and laughing with perhaps a glass of wine or a last cup of coffee.

You soon get in the spirit of the game of deciding which kind of restaurant to choose for your next meal. The selection is immense, all the way from the simple family trattoria where mama is cooking in the kitchen to the most elegant of gourmet restaurants with world-renowned chefs. Whichever you choose, you won't be disappointed. The Italians are artists when it comes to pasta, seen on every menu and prepared in endless, fascinating ways. Delicious green salads are always on the menu.

Wine, of course, is offered with every meal. You rarely see an Italian family eating without their bottle of wine on the table. Unless you are a true wine connoisseur we suggest the regional wines and if you ask your waiter to assist you with the choice, you flatter him and discover many superb wines.

Some of the most popular wines which you see on the Italian menus are: Chianti, a well-known wine produced in the Tuscany area south of Florence; Marsala, a golden sweet wine from Sicily (a favorite of Lord Nelson); Soave, a superb light white wine produced near Venice; Orvieto, a semi-sweet wine from the Umbria region near Assisi, and Est Est Est, a beautiful semi-sweet wine produced near Rome. The story that we heard about Est Est Est is lots of fun and perhaps even true. It seems that many years ago a wealthy nobleman was traveling south. Being a true gourmet both of food and drink, he sent his servant before him to pick out all the best places to eat and drink along the way. When the servant neared Rome he discovered such a divine wine that all he could relay back to his master was "Est, est, est," meaning "Yes, yes, yes." Today you will think the same about most of the wines you enjoy in Italy—the answer is still "Yes, yes, yes!"

HOLIDAYS

It is very important to know Italian holidays because most museums, shops, and offices are closed. National holidays are listed below:

New Year's Day (January 1)

Epiphany (January 6)

Easter (and the following Monday)

Liberation Day (April 25)

Labor Day (May 1)

Assumption Day (August 15)

All Saints' Day (November 1)

Christmas (December 25)

Santo Stefano (December 26)

In addition to the national holidays, each town has its own special holiday to honor its patron saint. Some of the major ones are listed below:

Bologna–St. Petronio (Oct 4)

Florence–St. John the Baptist (June 24)

Milan–St. Ambrose (December 7)

Palermo–Santa Rosalia July 15

Rome–St. Peter (June 29)

Venice–St. Mark (April 25)

The Vatican in Rome has its own schedule. The museums are closed every Sunday, except the last Sunday of each month when admission is free.

INFORMATION SOURCES

If you have questions not answered in this guide or need special guidance for a particular destination, the Italian Government Travel Offices can assist you. These offices are usually open from 9 am–5 pm, Monday through Friday.

UNITED STATES

Chicago: Italian Government Travel Office, 401 N. Michigan Ave., Suite 3030, Chicago, IL 60611 USA; tel: (312) 644-0990, fax: (312) 644-3019. (Mail, fax, or phone only.)

Los Angeles: Italian Government Tourist Board, 12400 Wilshire Blvd. Suite 550, Los Angeles, CA 90025, USA; tel: (310) 820-0098, fax: (310) 820-6357.

New York: Italian Government Travel Office, 630 5th Ave., Suite 1565, New York, NY 10111, USA; tel: (212) 245-4822, fax: (212) 586-9249.

CANADA

Montreal: Italian Government Travel Office, 1 Place Ville Marie, Suite 1914, Montreal, Quebec H3B 3M9, Canada; tel: (514) 866-7667, fax: (514) 392-1429.

GREAT BRITAIN

London: Italian State Tourist Office, 1 Princes Street, London WIR 8AY, England; tel: (0171) 408-1254, fax: (0171) 493-6695.

ITALY

Rome: E.P.T. (Ente Provinciale per il Turismo) (Rome Tourist Office), Via Parigi, 11, Rome 00185, Italy; tel: (06) 48.81.851, fax: (06) 48.19.316.

AUSTRALIA AND NEW ZEALAND

These areas are covered by the Tokyo office—Italian Government Travel Office, Itaria Seifu Kanko Kyoku (ENIT) Lion's Building -1-1-2, Moto Akasaka Minato-Ku, Tokyo 107 Japan; tel: (3) 3478-2051, fax: (3) 3479-9356.

PROVINCES

Italy is divided into Provinces. These provinces appear in abbreviated form in addresses and are shown on license plates—it is fun to watch the cars to see where they are from. Some of the provinces you are likely to see and their abbreviated codes are as follows:

AL	*Alessandria*	AN	*Ancona*	AO	*Aosta*	AR	*Arezzo*
AP	*Ascoli Picino*	AT	*Asti*	BA	*Bari*	BL	*Belluno*
BG	*Bergamo*	BO	*Bologna*	BZ	*Bolzano*	BS	*Brescia*
BR	*Brindisi*	CZ	*Catanzaro*	CO	*Como*	FI	*Firenze*
FO	*Forli*	GE	*Genova*	GO	*Gorizia*	GR	*Grosseto*
LU	*Lucca*	MN	*Mantova*	MI	*Milano*	MO	*Modena*
NA	*Napoli*	NO	*Novara*	PD	*Padova*	PR	*Parma*
PV	*Pavia*	PG	*Perugia*	PS	*Pesaro*	PI	*Pisa*
PT	*Pistoia*	PZ	*Potenza*	RA	*Ravenna*	SA	*Salerno*
SV	*Savona*	SI	*Siena*	TA	*Taranto*	TR	*Terni*
TO	*Torino*	TN	*Trento*	TV	*Treviso*	VE	*Venezia*
VC	*Vercelli*	VR	*Verona*	VI	*Vicenza*	VT	*Viterbo*

REGIONS

In addition to provinces, Italy is divided into 20 regions. A map showing the location of each region is found in the back of the book in the map section. Below is a list of the regions and their capital cities.

REGION	*CAPITAL CITY*	REGION	*CAPITAL CITY*
Abruzzo	*L'Aquila*	Apulia	*Bari*
Basilicata	*Potenza*	Molise	*Campobasso*
Calabria	*Catanzaro*	Piedmont	*Torino*
Campania	*Naples*	Sardinia	*Cagliari*
Emila-Romagna	*Bologna*	Sicily	*Palermo*
Friuli-Venezia Giulia	*Trieste*	Tuscany	*Florence*
Lazio	*Rome*	Trentino-Alto Adige	*Trento & Bolzano*
Liguria	*Genova*	Umbria	*Perugia*
Lombardy	*Milan*	Valle d'Aosta	*Aosta*
Marches	*Ancona*	Veneto	*Venice*

SECURITY WHILE TRAVELING

The Italians are wonderful hosts. They are friendly, outgoing, gregarious and merry—no one is a stranger. In fact, it seems every Italian has a brother or cousin in the United States, and so the warmth of camaraderie is further enhanced. In spite of the overall graciousness of the Italians, there are instances where cars are pilfered or purses snatched, but this happens all over the world. Just be cautious. Watch your purse. Don't let your wallet stand out like a red light in your back pocket. Lock your valuables in the hotel safe. Use travelers' checks. Don't leave valuables temptingly exposed in your car. Never set down luggage in train stations, even for a minute. In other words, use common sense. Unfortunately, we have heard of incidents of groups of gypsy children who flock to you, usually in congested tourist areas, and attempt to steal your wallet or purse. If this should happen to you, shoo them away and call for the police. *NOTE:* Whenever you travel to any country, it is wise to make a photocopy of the pages of your passport showing your picture, passport number, date, and where issued. With this photocopy in hand it is much easier to get a replacement passport.

SHOPPING

Italy is definitely a shopper's paradise. Not only are the stores brimming with tempting merchandise, but their displays are beautiful, from the tiniest fruit market to the most chic boutique. Each area has its specialty. In Venice items made from blown glass and handmade laces are very popular. Milan is famous for its clothing and silk-wear (gorgeous scarves, ties, and blouses). Florence is a paradise for leather goods (purses, shoes, wallets, gloves, suitcases) and also for gold jewelry (you can buy gold jewelry by weight). Rome is a fashion center—you can stroll the pedestrian shopping streets browsing in some of the world's most elegant, sophisticated shops. You can buy the latest designer creations and, of course, religious items are available, especially near St. Peter's. Naples and the surrounding regions (Capri, Ravello, Positano) offer delightful coral jewelry and also a wonderful selection of ceramics.

For purchases over 300,000 lire an immediate cash refund of the tax amount is offered by the Italian government. Goods must be purchased at an affiliated retail outlet with the "tax-free for tourists" sign. Ask for the store receipt **plus** the tax-free shopping receipt. At the airport go to the customs office where they will examine the items purchased and stamp both receipts, and then to the "tax-free cash refund" point after passport control.

TELEPHONES—HOW TO MAKE CALLS

CALLING HOME: Calling overseas is very expensive from Italy. In addition, hotels usually add a hefty surcharge to telephone calls charged to your room. The best bet is to use one of the many available international telephone cards. With these you can make a local call within Italy and be connected with your home operator. When you arrive home, the cost appears on your telephone bill. Ask your local telephone company what access number to use. In the United States all of the long-distance phone companies including AT&T, MCI, and Sprint offer this option.

CALLING WITHIN ITALY: Most telephones in Italy take either 100-or 200-lire coins. Becoming more common are the telephones that take a telephone credit card called a *scheda*. These credit cards can be purchased at tobacco stores or telephone offices and are extremely handy. You choose a card costing 5,000 or 10,000 lire and use the card until the credit is used up by the calls you made. It is very simple. The instructions are on the telephone demonstrating how to use them. There are a few telephones still remaining that take only special tokens. These can usually be purchased at a vending machine near the telephone.

Dial 113 for emergencies of all kinds—24-hour service nationwide.

Dial 116 for Automobile Club for urgent breakdown assistance on the road.

TRANSPORTATION

TRANSFERS INTO CITIES: Travelers from abroad normally arrive by plane in Milan, Rome, or Venice and pick up their rental car at the airport. However, if your first destination is the city and you plan on picking up your car after your stay, approximate transfer rates are as follows:

MILAN

From Malpensa to city by taxi (70 min)	Lire 125,000
From Malpensa to city by bus	Lire 18,000
From Linate to city by taxi (20 min)	Lire 45,000
From Linate to city by bus	Lire 2,500

ROME

From Da Vinci to city by train (1 hour)	Lire 15,000
From Da Vinci to city by taxi (45 min)	Lire 80,000

VENICE

From airport to city by waterbus (1 hour)	Lire 15,000
From station to city by waterbus (15 min)	Lire 4,000
From station to city by private watertaxi	Lire 85,000

TRAINS: Italy has an excellent network of trains. The major express trains are usually a quick, reliable way to whip between the major cities. In contrast, the local trains stop at every little town, take much longer, and are frequently delayed. Each train station is well organized. There is almost always an information desk where someone speaks English who will answer any questions and advise you as to the best schedule. There is another counter where you purchase your tickets. Still a third counter is where seat reservations are made. We strongly recommend purchasing your train tickets in advance: it is quite time consuming to stand in two lines at each train station, only to find—particularly in summer—that the train you want is already sold out. You can purchase open tickets in the United States. However, it is almost impossible to purchase seat reservations in advance (except for major European routes). Go ahead and buy the open tickets, and then you can either purchase your seat reservations locally, or else pay the concierge at your hotel to handle this transaction for you. Seat reservations cannot be made just before getting on the train—it is best to make them as far in advance as possible. *NOTE*: A new policy has just been established by the country's national train network—your ticket must be stamped with the time and date **before** you board the train, otherwise you will be issued a 40,000-lire fine. Tickets are stamped at small and not very obvious yellow machines near the exits to the tracks. Unstamped tickets may be reimbursed with a 30% penalty.

The very popular Eurailpass is valid in Italy. This pass allows travel for varying periods of time on most trains throughout Europe. However, if you are going to travel exclusively in Italy, buy instead an Italian Rail Pass. These bargain passes which must be purchased outside of Italy include the *Tourist Pass,* available for unlimited travel for a period of 8, 15, 21, or 30 days and the *Flexi Railcard* where you can arrange your own travel time as follows: the *9-Day Pass* is valid for travel for any 4 days during a 9-day period, the *21-Day Pass* is valid for travel for any 8 days of a 21-day period, the *30-Day Pass* is valid for travel on any 12 days of a 30-day period. All of the Italian passes can be bought for either first- or second-class travel. You can purchase these passes through your local travel agent or, in the United States, from the Italian State Railways, 342 Madison Avenue, Suite 207, New York, NY 10173, telephone: (212) 697-2100, fax: (212) 697-1394 or the Italian State Railways, 6033 West Century Boulevard, Los

Angeles, CA 90045, telephone: (310) 338-8616 or (310) 338-8620, fax: (310) 670-4269. *NOTE:* In the summer when rail traffic is very heavy, unless you make dining car reservations in advance you might not be able to have the fun of eating your meal en route. If you have not made these reservations, as soon as you board the train, stroll down to the dining car and ask to reserve a table.

BOATS: Italy has gorgeous islands dotting her shorelines, a glorious string of lakes gracing her mountains to the north, and romantic canals in Venice. Luckily for the tourist, the country's boat system is excellent.

All of Italy's islands are linked to the mainland by a wonderful maritime network. The many outlying islands sometimes have overnight ferries that offer sleeping accommodations and facilities for cars. The closer islands usually offer a choice—the hydrofoil that zips quickly across the water or the regular ferry that is slower.

Italy has an enchanting selection of lakes. One of the highlights of traveling in Italy is to explore these wondrous lakes by hopping on one of the ferry boats that glide romantically between little villages clustered along the shorelines. Again, there is usually a choice of either the hydrofoil that darts between the hamlets, or the ferry that glides leisurely across the water and usually offers beverage and food service on board. The boat schedules are posted at each pier, or you can request a timetable from the Italian tourist office. *NOTE:* These little boats are punctual, to the minute. Be right at the pier with your ticket in hand so you can jump on board during the brief interlude that the boat stops at the shore. If at all possible, try to squeeze in at least one boat excursion—it is a treat you will long remember.

WEATHER

Italy is blessed with lovely weather. However, unless you are a ski enthusiast following the promise of what the majestic mountains have to offer in the winter, or must travel in summer due to school holidays, we highly recommend traveling in spring or fall. Travel at either of these times has two dramatic advantages: you miss the rush of the summer tourist season when all of Italy is packed and you are more likely to have beautiful weather. In spring the meadows are painted with wildflowers. In fall the forests are a riot of color and the vineyards are mellow in shades of red and gold. Although the mountains of Italy are delightfully cool in summer, the rest of the country can be very hot, especially in the cities. *NOTE:* Many hotels are not air conditioned, and those that are, frequently charge extra for it.

WHAT TO WEAR

During the day informal wear is most appropriate, including comfortable slacks for women. In the evening, if you are at a sidewalk café or a simple pizzeria, women do not need to dress up nor men to wear coats and ties. However, Italy does have some elegant restaurants where a dress and coat and tie are definitely the proper attire. A basic principle is to dress as you would in any city at home. There are perhaps a few special situations: the churches are still very conservative—shorts are definitely inappropriate as are low-cut dresses. Some of the cathedrals still insist that women have their arms covered. It is rare that a scarf on the head is required, but to wear one is a respectful gesture. If you have an audience with the Pope, then the dress code is even more conservative.

The layered effect is ideal. Italy's climate runs the gamut from usually cool in the mountains to frequently very hot in the south. The most efficient wardrobe is one where light blouses and shirts can be reinforced by layers of sweaters that can be added or peeled off as the day demands.

Florence

HOTEL RESERVATION REQUEST LETTER IN ITALIAN

HOTEL NAME & ADDRESS—clearly printed or typed

Vi prego di voler riservare:
I would like to request:

   Numero delle camere con bagno o doccia privata   _____
   Number of rooms with private bath or shower

   Numero delle camere senza bagno o doccia   _____
   Number of rooms without private bath or shower

   Data di arrivo _____   Data di partenza _____
   Date of arrival   *Date of departure*

Vi prego inoltre de fornirmi le seguenti informazioni:
Please let me know as soon as possible the following:

   Potete riservare le camere richieste? Si / No
   Can you reserve the space requested? Yes / No

   I pasti sono compresi nel prezzo?   Si / No
   Are meals included in your rate?   Yes / No

   E necessario un deposito?   Si / No
   Do you need a deposit?   Yes / No

   Prezzo giornaliero   _____
   Price per night

   Quanto e necessario come deposito? _____
   How much deposit do you need?

Ringraziando anticipatamente, porgo distinti saluti,
Thanking you in advance, I send my best regards,

YOUR NAME & ADDRESS—clearly printed or typed

ITINERARIES

Highlights by Boat & Train-or Car

Romantic Hilltowns of Tuscany & Umbria

Mountain & Lake Adventures

Rome to Milan via the Italian Riviera

Highlights of Southern Italy

Exploring the Wonders of Sicily

25

Colosseum, Rome

Italian Highlights
by Train & Boat-or Car

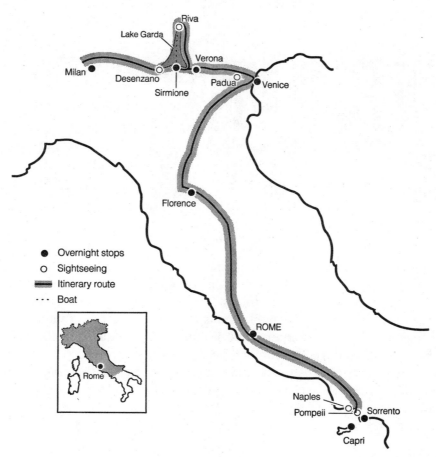

Riva

Lake Garda

Verona

Milan

Desenzano

Padua

Sirmione

Venice

Florence

● Overnight stops
○ Sightseeing
▬ Itinerary route
--- Boat

Rome

ROME

Naples

Pompeii

Sorrento

Capri

Italian Highlights by Train & Boat—or Car

Island of Burano, near Venice

If you delight in the freedom of following a whim to explore a back road, this itinerary can easily be duplicated by car. However, the thought of Italian expressways sometimes intimidates even the bravest breed of tourist, so we have given you the formula to see the highlights of Italy either way—by public transportation or by car. An aversion to driving does not mean that your *only* alternative is the confining structure of a package tour. Italy can be seen splendidly by train and boat. This is a glorious way to travel and has many advantages: everyone can watch the scenery instead of the road, a glass of wine can be enjoyed with lunch, and you arrive rested and ready to enjoy the sights. Perhaps the best advantage of all is that while using public transportation you make friends. Perhaps there is just a smile at first, then maybe the sharing of a piece of fruit, and later comes the admiration of each other's family photographs. Somehow barriers break down on a long journey and the universal warmth of friendliness—at this the Italians are masters—spans any language barriers. Please be aware however, that if you choose to travel this way, you must travel lightly—when burdened by heavy suitcases, the charm of public transportation quickly diminishes!

This itinerary covers some of the most famous destinations within Italy. For a short holiday it is impossible to include all the places of interest. However, following this pathway easily provides you with a glimpse of some of the highlights of Italy and will tempt you to return quickly to delve more deeply into the wonders that Italy has to offer. This itinerary is woven around towns that are conveniently linked by public transportation. Of course, if your time is extremely limited, this itinerary lends itself well to segmentation. If you cannot travel with us all the way, then choose what fits into your schedule and what most appeals to you.

In the following itinerary approximate train and boat times have been included. Please note that these are given only as a reference to show you how the pieces of this itinerary tie together. Schedules are constantly changing, so these must be verified. Also, many boats and some trains are seasonal, so be very meticulous in making your plans.

ORIGINATING CITY MILAN

This highlight tour begins in **Milan,** a most convenient city since it is the hub of airline flights from many cities in Europe, plus non-stop air service from the eastern United States. Also, Milan is strategically located for trains arriving from all over Europe— trains rush into its busy station via the Gotthard, Simplon, and Bernina passes. However, it is not location alone which makes Milan an ideal starting point. Although frequently bypassed as an enormous industrial city of little tourist interest, Milan has, at its core, a truly charming old section. Be forewarned: not only is this a major city, but it also hosts many merchandise fairs, so hotel space is limited and rates very expensive.

While in Milan you must not miss visiting the **Duomo**, the third-largest cathedral in the world. Facing a massive square, the Duomo is a gingerbread fantasy adorned with 135 spires and over 2,000 statues.

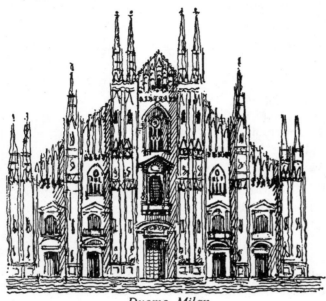
Duomo, Milan

Milan's other great claim to fame is **La Scala**, one of the world's most famous opera houses. In addition to wonderful opera, other performances are given here. If it is opera season, try your best to go to a performance; if not, try to get tickets for whatever is playing. It is such fun to watch the lights go down and the curtains go up in this fairy-tale-like theater with row upon row of balconies rising like layers on a wedding cake. Tickets are sold in the ticket office located around the left-hand side of the theater.

Between the Duomo and La Scala theater is one of the world's most beautiful arcades, the forerunner of the modern shopping mall, but with far more style. Even if you are not a shopper, stop to browse and have a cup of tea in the **Galleria Vittorio Emanuele**. In this Victorian-era fantasy, there are two main, intersecting wings, both completely domed with intricately patterned glass. Along the pedestrian-only arcades are boutiques and beautiful little restaurants with outside tables for people-watching. Milan also has its share of museums, but I would save the museums and churches for Venice, Florence, and Rome.

The train for Desenzano (the station you want for your destination of **Sirmione**) usually departs from Milan's Central Station. However, sometimes the trains leave instead from the Porto Garibaldi station, so it is vital that schedules be checked very carefully.

12:10 pm depart Milan Central Station by train
1:24 pm arrive Desenzano

When the train arrives in the ancient port of **Desenzano**, you can take a taxi to the pier where hydrofoils, steamers, and buses leave regularly for Sirmione. However, although more expensive, we suggest you splurge and take a taxi directly to Sirmione (only about 10 kilometers away). This is definitely the most convenient means of transportation since you are taken directly to your hotel.

Sirmione is a walled medieval village fabulously located on a tiny peninsula jutting out into **Lake Garda**. This peninsula seems more like an island because it is connected to the mainland by just a thread of land. To enter the ancient town, you first cross over a moat, and then enter through medieval gates. Unless you are one of the lucky ones with a hotel confirmed for the night, you cannot take your automobile inside the town walls, since only pedestrians are allowed through the entrance. But if you have hotel reservations, stop near the entrance at the information office where you are given a pass to enter in your car or taxi.

There are several hotels in the heart of Sirmione, but the most glamorous choice, the **Villa Cortine Palace Hotel,** is located in a parklike estate on the outskirts of town. The entrance is absolutely Hollywood. You must ring a bell at the impressive gates which then slowly swing open, allowing you to wind your way up through the truly beautiful park to the hotel crowning the small hill. Previously, this was a sumptuous private villa. Now a new wing has been built which doubles the original size. Although the newer wing looks a bit sterile from the outside, the rooms are delightful and most have better views than those in the old section. Demi-pension (breakfast and dinner) are required if you are staying at the Villa Cortine Palace. In addition, reservations are usually taken only for stays of at least three nights. Neither should prove a problem—you will never want to leave such a romantic setting.

From the Villa Cortine Palace Hotel it is an easy walk to the wharf in the middle of town. There study the posted schedule to decide which boat you want to take for your day's excursion. You can glide around the lake all day and have a snack on board, or get off in some small jewel of a town and enjoy lunch at a lakefront café. There is a choice of transportation: either the romantic ferry boats or the faster hydrofoils.

There are also some **Roman Ruins** on the very tip of the Sirmione peninsula which can be reached either on foot, or, if you prefer, by a miniature motorized train that shuttles back and forth between the ruins and the village.

NOTE FOR TRAVELERS BY CAR: The Villa Cortine Palace Hotel is an excellent hotel choice if you are traveling by public transportation. However, if you are traveling by car, consider staying in **Gargnano, Gardone**, or **San Vigilio**—these towns are also located on Lake Garda and offer wonderful places to stay.

DESTINATION II   VERONA

There are trains almost every hour that cover the half-hour journey between Desenzano and Verona. But if it is a beautiful day, it is much more romantic to incorporate sightseeing into your transportation and take a boat and bus instead of the train. If this appeals to you, the following gives an idea of how this can be done.

9:50 am depart Sirmione by ferry
1:25 pm arrive Riva

You can have lunch on board the ferry or else you can wait until you reach the medieval town of **Riva**, located on the northern shore of Lake Garda. The outdoor terrace overlooking the lake at the **Hotel Sole** (located just across from where the ferry docks) provides a serene luncheon setting. The interesting ancient core of Riva is small, so it doesn't take long to stroll through the old city.

After lunch and a walk through the old part of town, leave Riva by bus for Verona (buses run every 15 minutes in summer), tracing a scenic route along the eastern shore of the lake.

When you arrive in **Verona,** you are in for a treat. This is a town that is all too frequently bypassed by the tourist, but what a prize it is. This medieval gem is the perfect city to explore on foot. Buy a detailed map and be on your way.

Definitely not to be missed is the **Roman Amphitheater**, one of the largest in Italy. This dramatic arena, dating from the 1st century, has perfect acoustics and hosts operatic performances in summer. As you continue to wander through Verona's enchanting streets, you discover many delights, including the **Piazza delle Erbe** (Square of Herbs), which is the old Roman forum where chariot races used to take place. Follow your map to nearby 23 Via Cappello to find the 13th-century **Capulets' Palace** and the balcony where Juliet met Romeo. Another colorful square, the **Piazza dei Signori,** has a stature of Dante in its center and 12th- and 13th-century buildings. The **Castelvecchio** (Old Castle), built by Congrande I Scaligerbuthe in the 14th century, houses an art museum with paintings, sculptures, jewelry, and armaments. The 14th-century **Ponte Scaligero** (Scaliger Bridge) links the Castelvecchio with the opposite side of the river. The **cathedral**, dating from the 12th century, is well worth a visit to see its fine red marble columns and richly adorned interior. Just across the river from the heart of the old city, visit the old **Roman Theater** where performances are still held in summer.

Verona has several good hotels to complement her marvelous sights. A favorite in the heart of the city is the **Hotel Gabbia d'Oro**, which is brimming with charm and conveniently located near all the places of interest. If you are traveling by car, you have the option of choosing a hotel in the countryside outside of Verona where you get more value for your money. Hotels we suggest in the area are: in **Pedemonte** and **Gargagnago**.

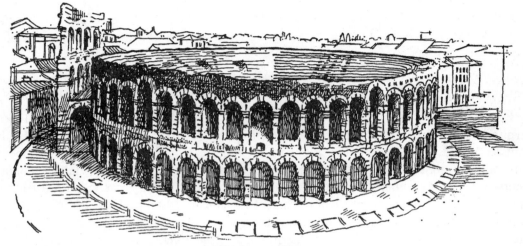

Amphitheater, Verona

DESTINATION III   VENICE

When you are ready to leave Verona, there is frequent train service to **Venice** so the following departure time is just a suggestion. *NOTE:* As you approach Venice, be sure not to get off the train at the Venice Mestre station, but instead wait for the next stop, the Santa Lucia station (about ten minutes further).

    2:27 pm depart Verona Porto Nuova station by train
    3:52 pm arrive Venice, Santa Lucia station

As you come out of the front door of the train station, you find that the station is directly on the **Grand Canal**. It is a few short steps down to where you can board a boat to take you to your hotel. The **vaporetti** are the most popular means of transportation and are a very inexpensive means of getting about the city. They are like boat buses that constantly shuttle back and forth from the train station to St. Mark's Square. The Number Two ferry makes only major stops while the Number One ferry pauses at every stop to exchange passengers. Much more expensive, but a little faster, are the **motoscafi** (water-taxis) which deliver you right to the door of your hotel, provided there is a motor-boat dock.

St. Mark's Square, Venice

The third choice is a **gondola**, but these are much slower and very expensive, so save your gondola ride for a romantic interlude rather than a train connection.

Venice has many fine hotels in every price range. Look in the back of this guide for various suggestions of places that we recommend. If you want to splurge, consider the very expensive, very sumptuous, **Gritti Palace**, a former home of the immensely wealthy Doge Andrea Gritti. If you are on a more limited budget, the intimate, family-operated **Hotel Flora** is a gem in its category. Note the closest boat stop so that you know where to disembark if you take the vaporetti from the train station.

Venice has so many sights: marvelous restaurants, beautiful boutiques, and fascinating little alleyways to explore, that you could happily stay for weeks.

Of course, you must savor the incomparable ambiance of **Piazza San Marco** (St. Mark's Square). Late afternoon is especially romantic as music wafts across the enormous square, courtesy of the tiny orchestras entertaining guests as they enjoy an aperitif. A colonnaded walkway encloses the square on three sides, forming a protected path while window-shopping at the beautiful boutiques and fancy cafés. The fourth side of the square is dominated by the **Basilica di San Marco** (St. Mark's Cathedral), richly endowed with gold and mosaics. The church dates back to the 12th century when it was built to house the remains of St. Mark. Next to the church rises the 99-meter-tall **Campanile** (bell tower) where in the 15th century priests were suspended in a cage to repent their sins. If you are in the plaza on the hour, watch the two Moors strike the hour with their huge bronze hammers as they have done for 500 years. To the right of the basilica is the **Palazzo Ducale** (Doge's Palace), a sumptuous fantasy of pink and white marble—open now as a museum. The Palazzo Ducale faces on to the **Piazzetta**, a wide square opening onto the Grand Canal. The square's nickname used to be the *Piazzetta Il Broglio* (Intrigue) because in days of yore, only nobles were allowed in the square between 10 am and noon, at which time the area buzzed with plots of intrigue. Adorning the center of the square are two granite columns, one topped by the **Lion of St. Mark** and the other by a statue of **St. Theodore**.

Glass Blowing, Island of Murano

There is no better way to get into the mood of Venice than to join the crowd at the St. Mark's dock as they climb aboard one of the ferries that ply the city's waterways. It is a real bargain to board the vaporetto and enjoy the many wonderful palaces bordering the Grand Canal. In addition to exploring the canals that lace Venice, you can take ferries to the outlying islands. Go either on your own or on a tour to the three islands: **Murano** (famous for its hand-blown glass), **Burano** (famous for its colorfully painted fishermen's cottages and lace making), and **Torcello** (once an important city but now just a small village with only its lovely large church to remind you of its past glories).

Another all-day outing by boat is to take the **Il Burchiello,** named for a famous 17th-century Venetian boat. From April to November, this boat departs Tuesdays, Thursdays, and Saturdays at 8:45 am from the Pontile Giardinetti pier near St. Mark's Square and travels the network of rivers and canals linking Venice and Padua. (The schedule might change, so verify dates and times.) This little boat, with an English-speaking guide on board, stops at several of the exquisite palaces en route. Lunch is served and there is time for sightseeing in **Padua** before returning to Venice by bus. Reservation Office: Siamic Express, Via Trieste 42, Padua, Italy, telephone: (049) 66 09 44, fax: (049) 66 28 30.

A favorite pastime in Venice is wandering—just anywhere—exploring the maze of twisting canals and criss-crossing back and forth over some of the 400 whimsical bridges. One of the most famous, the **Rialto Bridge**, arching high over the canal, is especially colorful because it is lined by shops. Also much-photographed is the **Bridge of Sighs,** so named because this was the bridge prisoners passed over before their execution.

Although all of Venice is virtually an open-air museum, it also has many inside museums. Two excellent ones are both easy to find near the Accademia boat stop. The **Galleria dell'Accademia** abounds with 14th-to 18th-century Venetian paintings. Within walking distance of the Galleria dell'Accademia is the **Peggy Guggenheim Museum**, featuring 20th-century art. The paintings and statues were the gift of the now-deceased wealthy American heiress, Peggy Guggenheim. The lovely museum was her canal-front home.

When leaving Venice, there are several direct trains each day from Venice to Florence: however, in summer, space is at a real premium, so be sure to reserve a seat in advance. Some of the express trains must have prior seat reservations and require a supplemental fee. *NOTE:* During the busy season, if you want to dine on the train it is necessary to make advance reservations when you buy your ticket.

   2:42 pm depart Venice, Santa Lucia station (reservations obligatory)
   5:27 pm arrive Florence

When you arrive in **Florence**, take a taxi to your hotel unless you have chosen **Mario's**, a moderately-priced hotel close enough to the train station to walk. There are outstanding places to stay in Florence in every price range. If you want to be right on the Arno with a balcony overlooking the Ponte Vecchio, the **Lungarno Hotel** is fabulous. For tasteful

Ponte Vecchio, Florence

luxury, the **Hotel Helvetia and Bristol** is a small jewel. For old-world ambiance, the **Torre di Bellosguardo** stars. For price and location, the **Loggiato dei Serviti** is excellent. We recommend these and many other hotels in and around Florence—study the descriptions in the back of the guide and you are sure to find one that is perfect for your taste.

Be generous with your time and do not rush Florence—there is too much to see. You must, of course, pay a visit to **Michelangelo's David** in the **Galleria dell'Accademia** located just off the **Piazza San Marco**.

During your explorations of Florence, you will cross many times through the **Piazza della Signoria**, located in the heart of the old city. Facing this characterful medieval square is the 13th-century **Palazzo Vecchio**, a stern stone structure topped by a crenellated gallery and dominated by a tall bell tower. It was here that the *Signoria* (Florence's aristocratic ruling administrators) met for two months each year while attending to government business. During this period they were forbidden to leave the palace (except for funerals) so that there could not be a hint of suspicion of intrigue or bribery. Of course, you cannot miss one of Florence's landmarks, the **Ponte Vecchio.** Spanning the Arno in the heart of Florence, this colorful bridge is lined with quaint shops just as it has since the 14th century.

Palazzo Vecchio in Piazza della Signoria, Florence

Don't miss the fantastic museums and cathedrals—the world will probably never again see a city that has produced such artistic genius. Florence's **Duomo** is one of the largest in the world. The cathedral's incredible dome (over 100 meters high) was designed by Brunelleschi. The **Battistero** (the baptistry) has a beautiful mosaic dome, but is even more famous for its incredible bronze doors by Lorenzo Ghiberti and his son Vittorio Ghiberti. The main door shows scenes from the life of John the Baptist, the north door shows the life of Jesus, and the east door shows stories from the prophets of the Old Testament. The **Uffizi Museum** (housed in a 16th-century palace) is undoubtedly one of the finest museums in the world. Also, do not miss the **Pitti Palace** with its fabulous art collection, including paintings by Titian and Raphael.

Be sure to buy a guidebook and city map at one of the many magazine stalls and study what you want to see. We just touch on the many highlights. Florence is best appreciated by wandering the historic ancient streets: poke into small boutiques; stop in churches that catch your eye—they all abound with masterpieces; sit and enjoy a cappuccino in one of the little sidewalk cafés and people-watch; stroll through the piazzas and watch the artists at their craft—many of them incredibly clever—as they paint portraits and do sculptures for a small fee. End your day by finding the perfect small restaurant for delicious pasta made by mama in the back kitchen.

DESTINATION V   ROME

There is an excellent train service from Florence to Rome. It is probably best to take one of the mid-day trains—a choice that allows you to enjoy lunch as you soak in the beauty of the Tuscany hills flowing by your window. Remember that you need both seat and dining reservations.

   12:02 pm depart Florence via train
    1:55 pm arrive Rome, Termini station

As the train pulls into **Rome**, you feel overwhelmed by its size and confusion of traffic, but once you settle into your hotel, you realize that Rome is really not as cumbersome as it looks. The ancient part of the city is manageable on foot—a fabulous city for walking with its maze of streets and captivating boutiques just begging to be explored. We recommend many places to stay in this expensive city. If you are looking for a well-located small deluxe hotel, the **Hotel d'Inghilterra** is a superb choice near the bottom of the Spanish Steps. The super-deluxe **Hotel Hassler**, just at the top of the Spanish Steps, is also a very popular choice. But you do not need to splurge—there are many less expensive places to stay

"She Wolf" with Romulus and Remus

recommended in the hotel description section that are excellent and equally well-located (such as **La Residenza** and the **Hotel Gregoriana**).

According to legend, Rome was founded in 753 B.C. by Romulus, who, along with his twin brother, Remus (whom he later conveniently did in), was suckled by a "she wolf." Although a far less colorful story, historians concur that it was the Etruscans who first settled here and gave the city its name. By the time Christ was born, Rome controlled the entire Italian peninsula plus many areas around the Mediterranean.

Rome is bursting with a wealth of fantastic museums, ancient monuments, spectacular cathedrals, gourmet restaurants, beautiful boutiques, colorful piazzas, whimsical fountains, inspiring statues, theater, and opera—the city itself is virtually a museum. You cannot possibly savor it all. Either before you leave home or once you arrive in Italy, purchase a comprehensive guidebook and decide what is top priority for your special interests. There are many stalls along the streets as well as bookstores throughout Rome where guidebooks are available and every hotel has brochures available that tell about sightseeing tours. If there are several in your party, a private guide might be money well spent since he will custom-tailor your sightseeing—with a private guide you squeeze much more sightseeing into a short period of time.

To even begin to do justice to Rome's many wonders, this entire book would need to be devoted to its sightseeing possibilities. However, we cannot resist mentioning a few places you must see.

Vatican-Swiss Guard

You cannot go to Rome and miss seeing the **Vatican City** with **St. Peter's Basilica**, the largest church in the world. The original construction was begun in the 4th century by Emperor Constantine over the site of St. Peter's tomb. In 1506 Pope Julius II began plans for the new cathedral, which took over 100 years to build. It is no wonder the complex is so breathtaking—all of Italy's greatest Renaissance artists were called upon to add their talents—Bramante, Raphael, Sangallo, and Michelangelo, to name just a few.

The Vatican is a miniature nation tucked within the city of Rome. It is ruled by the Pope, has its own flags, issues its own postage stamps, has its own anthem, mints its own coins, and even has its own police force—the Swiss Guard who still wears the costume designed by Michelangelo.

Fronting the cathedral is the **Piazza San Pietro,** a breathtaking square designed by Bernini. It is so large that it can hold 400,000 people (making the square a favorite place for the Pope to address large audiences). A double semicircle of columns encloses the square, so perfectly designed that the columns fade into each other, giving the illusion that there is a single row. In the center of the square is a towering ancient Egyptian obelisk—adorned, of course, by a Christian cross. As you stand at a distance, the Piazza San Pietro forms a visual frame for the cathedral.

To fully appreciate all the Vatican City has to offer, you could easily spend two days, one in St. Peter's Basilica and one day in the **Vatican Museums**. The Basilica is a virtual museum. Not only is the structure magnificent, but the works of art inside are almost unbelievable: imagine gazing at such masterpieces as the **Pietà** (the ethereal sculpture of Mary holding Jesus in her arms after the crucifixion, carved by Michelangelo when he was only 25) and the **Baldaccchino**, the bronze canopy over the papal altar created by another master, Bernini. Also, be aware when you gaze up at the double columned dome, that this too was designed by Michelangelo.

St. Peter's Basilica, Rome

The **Sistine Chapel** alone is well-worth a trip to Rome just to savor the breathtaking beauty of its ceiling painted by Michelangelo. In addition to St. Peter's Basilica and the Vatican museums, the gardens and the rest of the Vatican can be visited, but only on guided tours. If you are interested, inquire at the *Ufficio Informazioni Pellegrini et Turisti* in St. Peter's Square. *NOTE:* The Vatican museums are closed on Sundays, except for the last Sunday of the month when they are open free of charge.

The Vatican City, as spectacular as it is, is just one small part of what Rome has to offer. You cannot miss seeing the gigantic **Colosseum**, the entertainment center for the citizens of ancient Rome. Here 50,000 people gathered to be entertained by flamboyant spectacles that included gladiatorial contests, races, games, and contests where Christian martyrs fought against wild beasts.

Another landmark is the **Forum**. It is difficult to make out much of this site because it is mostly in ruins, but at one time this was the heart of Rome. Once filled with elegant palaces, government buildings and shops, it teemed with people from throughout the known world.

My favorite building in Rome is the **Pantheon.** It is difficult to imagine that this perfectly preserved jewel of a temple dates back to 27 B.C. Step beyond the heavy bronze doors which open into a relatively small, beautifully proportioned room lit only by light streaming in from an opening in the top of the dome.

No trip to Rome would be complete without a stroll down the **Via Veneto**, lined by fancy hotels and luxury boutiques. There are also many outdoor restaurants where a cup of coffee costs almost as much as a meal in a simple trattoria. However, along with your coffee, you are paying the price for the fun of people watching along one of Rome's most elite avenues.

While walking the back streets of Rome, you find many picturesque squares, usually enhanced by a fountain adorned with magnificent sculptures. Especially popular is the **Trevi Fountain** where tourists go to throw a coin—assuring that they will return to Rome.

The **Spanish Steps** are definitely a landmark of Rome. Topped by the twin spires of the Church of the Trinity of the Mountains, the wide avenue of steps leads down to the **Piazza di Spagna** (Spanish Square). This large square is highlighted by the **Fountain of Baraccia** (Fountain of the Boat), a masterpiece by Bernini. The steps are usually crowded both with tourists who come to capture the moment on film and vendors who lay out their wares to sell.

Leading from the Piazza di Spagna, the **Via Condotti** is an avenue lined by shops selling the finest of merchandise. Branching off the Via Condotti are the narrow lanes of **Old Rome**, again featuring exquisite small boutiques.

When you are ready to relax, walk to the **Villa Borghese,** a splendid large park in the center of Rome that originated in the 17th century as the private gardens of the Borghese family. Stroll through the park watching the children at play. If you are not saturated with sightseeing, there are many

Spanish Steps, Rome

museums to see in the park. One of the loveliest is the **Museo di Villa Giulia** a museum in a pretty villa that features artifacts from the Etruscan era.

You could spend weeks discovering the museum that is Rome, but if you have time to add a few more highlights, include Sorrento and Capri. There is frequent train service from Rome to Naples and from there it is a short hydrofoil ride to Capri. However, for the adventurous it is fun to include Pompeii and Sorrento en route to Capri. Please be advised that this makes a long day of travel and takes some manipulating of schedules, but the rewards are great.

You need an early start to accomplish a tour of Pompeii on your way to Sorrento, but this is a must. How could you be so close without visiting this intriguing city of the Romans that was destroyed, yet preserved forever by the ashes of Vesuvius?

   9:15 am depart Rome, Termini station
  11:58 am arrive Pompeii, Main station

You arrive in **Pompeii** at the Main station, but you depart from Pompeii at the Villa d'Misteri station, located just across from the main entrance to the archaeological site. Since it's no fun to lug your suitcases around while you do your sightseeing, take a cab from the Main station to the Villa d'Misteri station where there is a place to check luggage, then just walk across the street to the main gate of Pompeii. There is a nice terrace restaurant by the entrance and also a café inside. If you want to do your own touring, you can buy a guidebook in English from a stall, or else you can negotiate with one of the licensed guides for a personal tour. You may have heard that the earthquake of 1980 destroyed much of Pompeii. It is true that many of the sites were damaged, but now almost everything has been reconstructed.

An aura of mystery lingers in the air as you wander the streets of Pompeii. All visitors are touched by this ancient city of an estimated 25,000 inhabitants, which in one day became frozen for all time. Probably there is nowhere else in the world where you can so vividly step back in time. Much of what you see today has been reproduced, but the reality is pure. Plaster was poured into molds formed by the lava that demolished the buildings and buried so many families that fateful day. Thus it became possible for latter-day archaeologists to reconstruct houses and make reproductions of people and pets. Walk through the town along the sunken streets crossed by high stepping-stones, strategically placed so that pedestrians did not get their feet wet on rainy days. Be sure not to miss some of the reconstructed villas which allow you a glimpse into the daily life of long ago. The **Casa del Fauna**, a fine example of how the wealthy lived, has two inner courtyards and several dining rooms. The **Casa del Poeta Tragico**, a more modest home, has a sign in mosaic saying *Cave Canem* (beware of the dog). At the **Villa di Giulia Felice** you see the example of an entrepreneur—in addition to being a private villa, the owner rented out rooms, had shops on the ground floor, and operated an adjacent bathhouse. If traveling with children, you might want to go alone into the **Lupanare** (Pompeii's brothel) where there are erotic paintings on the walls. At the **Terme Stabiane** you see a sophisticated underground water-heating system.

There are many more places to visit than those listed above. As you explore Pompeii, there is no need to watch the time. There is a narrow-gauge train departing from the Pompeii Villa d' Misteri station about every 20 minutes for the half-hour scenic journey to Sorrento.

When you arrive in **Sorrento**, stay at the **Grand Hotel Excelsior Vittoria**, a romantic old villa at the center of town in a prime cliff location overlooking the harbor. The hotel's once-perfect grandeur is perhaps a bit faded, but as you sit on the terrace in the evening and watch the sun turning the bay to shades of red and gold, the atmosphere is perfect. There is also a pool for relaxing and sunning. If within your budget, splurge and ask for a deluxe room with a view.

When it is time to leave Sorrento there is excellent service by either hydrofoil or ferry to Capri. The following schedule is a suggestion:

  3:45 pm depart Sorrento by hydrofoil
  4:10 pm arrive Capri

Your hydrofoil arrives at the **Marina Grande**, a small harbor filled with colorful boats and edged by brightly painted shops. When the boat docks, you find hotel porters on the pier along with carrier services that go to all of the hotels. They relieve you of your luggage and take it directly to the hotel of your choice, freeing you to take either a mini-bus or the funicular to the main town of Capri which is located on a flat saddle of land high above the sea.

There are many charming places to stay on **Capri**. Since this is a very popular tourist destination, the hotels are generally speaking expensive, but the ones we recommend are all special. Some are located in the heart of town, others a short stroll away—read our descriptions and choose one that suits you.

Capri has many wonders. The most famous is its submerged cave, the **Blue Grotto**, which can be reached by boat when the seas are calm. Large boats begin leaving the harbor every morning at 9 am for the short ride to the entrance to the grotto, where you are transferred into tiny rowboats. The excursion is an adventure in itself. As your little boat approaches the tiny cave opening it seems impossible that there is adequate room, but suddenly the sea surges forward and in you squeeze. Like magic, you see it—the mysterious, stunning blue light reflecting from some hidden source that illuminates the grotto.

Capri is a superb island for walking. As you stroll the trails, all your senses are treated by the fragrant flowers, the gorgeous vistas of the brilliant blue waters, and the sound of birds luring you ever onward. There are many spectacular walks. Follow the trail winding down the cliffs to the small harbor **Marina Piccola,** located on the opposite side of the island from the ferry dock.

Marina Grande, Capri

At the Marina Piccola there are lovely views of the shimmering aqua waters as you make your way to the small beach where you can enjoy a swim before your return. Instead of walking back up the hill, take the little bus that delivers you quickly back to the main square. *NOTE:* On our last visit to Capri, the romantic walking path to Marina Piccolo was closed for repairs, but hopefully it will be back in operation by the time you arrive. If not, you can take the bus in both directions.

Another absolutely spectacular walk—although a long one of at least 45 minutes each way—is to Emperor Tiberius's Palace, **Villa Jovis**, perched high among the trees on the cliffs on the western tip of the island. This is the grandest of the palaces left by Tiberius. Although mostly in ruins, you can easily appreciate its former magnificence as you climb about exploring the ruins of the terraced rooms. From the palace there are stunning panoramic vistas: you have an overview of the whole island and can watch the ferries shuttling back and forth to the mainland. A much shorter walk, but one equally as beautiful, is to the **Cannone Belvedere**. This path guides you near delightful private villas hidden behind high walls (you get glimpses through the gates) and on to a promontory overlooking the sea.

Another excursion is to **Anacapri**, the only other town on the island, to visit the **Villa San Michel**, a lovely villa overlooking the sea that was the home of the Swedish scientist Axel Munthe. His residence is now open as a museum. Anacapri is bit too far to walk easily—buses leave regularly from the main square in town.

During the day, Capri is swarming with tourists who descend like a hoard of locusts from the constant stream of hydrofoils and ferries on package tours. You might surmise that in the evening the activity subsides, but it isn't so. The tour groups leave at dusk but then a new group of people emerges from the secreted villas and fancy hotels. Guests in chic clothes and fancy jewelry stroll the streets—both to see and be seen. The joy of over-nighting in Capri is that you can relax during the heat of the day when the tourist scene is at its height, then enjoy the magic of the balmy evenings.

When the real world calls and you must leave Capri, there is frequent ferry or hydrofoil service back to Naples. From Naples, you can take a train to Rome or a plane to your next destination.

Romantic Hilltowns
of Tuscany and Umbria

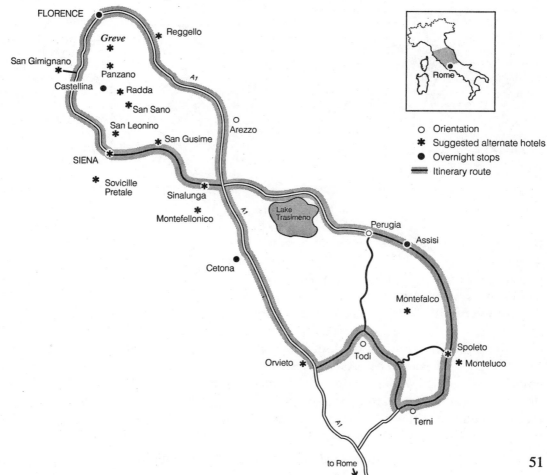

FLORENCE

Greve

Reggello

San Gimignano

Panzano

A₁

Castellina

Radda

San Sano

San Leonino

San Gusime

Arezzo

SIENA

Soricille
Pretale

Sinalunga

A₁

Montefellonico

Lake
Trasimeno

Perugia

Assisi

Cetona

Montefalco

Orvieto

Todi

Spoleto

Monteluco

Terni

A₁

to Rome

○ Orientation
∗ Suggested alternate hotels
● Overnight stops
━━ Itinerary route

Rome

51

Romantic Hilltowns of Tuscany & Umbria

Assisi

Nothing can surpass the exquisite beauty of the countryside near Florence in the spring—it is breathtaking. But it is not only in the spring that this region is beautiful: if you meander into the hilltowns of Tuscany and Umbria any time of the year, all your senses are rewarded with the splendors that this enchanting area of Italy has to offer. Almost every hillock is crowned with a picture-perfect walled town; fields are brilliant with vibrant red poppies; vineyards in all their glory and promise lace the fields; olive trees dress the hillsides in a frock of dusky gray-green; pine forests unexpectedly appear to highlight the landscape. As if these attributes were not enough, tucked into the colorful villages are a treasure-trove of some of the finest small hotels in all the world. If this is still not sufficient to tempt you away from the normal tourist route, be reminded that the food and wines of Tuscany and Umbria are unsurpassed.

When planning your trip to Italy, allow time to treat yourself to a unique adventure. Save at least a few days to slip away from the cities and into the country. Perhaps you won't have time to follow this entire itinerary, but at least sneak in a few days in Umbria and Tuscany. You will be well rewarded with a wealth of memories that will linger long after you return home. The following itinerary makes a southern loop from Florence. Along the way are three suggested stops—one in Umbria, one in the southern region of Tuscany, and one in the northern region of Tuscany. If possible, stay several days in each of these hubs and make excursions into the countryside.

ORIGINATING CITY   FLORENCE

Your journey begins in **Florence**. Allow enough time to savor this marvelous city but, if you are reluctant to leave, be consoled: there are many treats in store for you in the delightful hilltowns that surround it. Magnificent art is not confined to the city limits of Florence and you will see impressive cathedrals and beautiful works of art throughout the neighboring areas. On pages 38–40 we offer a few sightseeing suggestions for Florence.

DESTINATION I   ASSISI

The traffic around Florence is congested. Follow signs in town that lead to the expressway A1 to Rome which you take as far as the turnoff for **Arezzo**, located about 10 kilometers east of the highway. You might want to bypass Arezzo since, although it has a rich history dating back to the Etruscan era, it is a large city and not as quaint as some of its smaller neighbors.

Following the main road 71 south from Arezzo, you soon arrive at **Cortona**. This is a beautifully situated walled town climbing up a steep hillside covered with olive trees. Stop to enjoy the atmosphere of this medieval town: its narrow twisting streets, jumble

St. Francis of Assisi

of small squares, and colorful buildings are delightful. A mighty castle stands guard dramatically over the town.

Leaving Cortona, continue south toward **Lake Trasimeno**. Just before you reach the lake, take the four-lane expressway that skirts the lake's northern shore heading east to **Perugia**, a large medieval city surrounded by ramparts. An important Umbrian city since Etruscan days, the heart of the old city is the **Piazza IV Novembre**, a beautiful square with an appealing fountain, the **Fontana Maggiore**, built in the late 13th century.

It is only a short drive farther east from Perugia to **Assisi**. Built up the steep slopes of Mount Subasio, this magical city is a tribute to St. Francis. Although he was born into a family of wealth, after several visions in which Christ appeared to him, St. Francis left his privileged life. Obviously a person with a deep poetic soul, his tender teachings of reverence for the beauties of nature and kindness to all animals and birds still appeal to us today.

Even if it were not for the lingering memory of the gentle St. Francis, Assisi would be a "must see" for it is one of the most spectacular hilltowns in Umbria. Perhaps there are a few too many souvenir shops, but this is a small price to pay for such a very special place. The town walls begin on the valley floor and completely enclose the city as climbs the steep hillside, climaxing in an enormous castle. Assisi with its maze of tiny streets is a marvelous town for walking (you must wear sturdy shoes). It is great fun as you come across intriguing little lanes opening into small squares. When you stop to rest, there are marvelous vistas of the breathtaking Umbrian fields stretching out below.

To truly appreciate the beauty of Umbria, it is best to spend several nights in the area. Luckily, there are good hotel choices—not only in Assisi, but also in nearby towns (see Map 9 for other towns with recommended hotels). If you prefer to stay right in Assisi, consider the **Hotel Umbra**. Superbly located in the heart of town, it is a most appealing small, family-run hotel that is highly recommended for those who don't expect the height of luxury. The **Hotel Subasio**, a larger hotel that receives more tour groups, is also recommended. It is beautifully situated with one of its walls forming a section of the Piazza of the St. Francis' Basilica. The Subasio is not a deluxe hotel, but has much to entice the tourist. Perhaps its most impressive attribute is the view from the vine-covered dining terrace over the undulating Umbrian fields which glow with a special mellow golden radiance.

In Assisi you must see **St. Francis' Basilica**. You cannot miss this enormous structure whose massive supporting arches soar from the valley floor. The basilica, which also houses a monastery, faces onto a large square bound by columns forming vaulted covered walkways. In addition to the monastery, there are two basilicas—upper and lower. Both are adorned with excellent frescoes. Do not miss in the upper basilica the 28 scenes depicting the life of St. Francis. Also while in Assisi, be sure to visit **Santa Chiara** (St. Clara's Church). Clara, a close friend of St. Francis, founded the Order of St. Clares. In the church view the lovely frescoes of St. Clara and her sisters. Hike up to the **Rocca Medioevale**, an enormous 14th-century fortress, perched on the hillside above the city. From here you have a magnificent bird's-eye view of the city and surrounding landscape.

While staying at Assisi, take a side trip to nearby **Torgiano** where there is a splendid wine museum. You would never dream that such a tiny town could boast such a stunning museum, but it is not a coincidence: the Lungarotti family owns the vineyards for many kilometers in every direction. Signore Lungarotti furnished the museum with artifacts pertaining to every aspect of the production of wine from the earliest days. The collection is interesting and beautifully displayed, worthy of a detour by anyone interested in wines. The family also own a delightful hotel in the center of town, **Le Tre Vaselle**. A charming spot for lunch or overnight stay, Le Tre Vaselle has the ambiance of a lovely country manor house.

DESTINATION II   CETONA

Get an early start this morning because it is going to be difficult to squeeze in all of the enchanting hilltop towns en route. Driving south on 3 from Assisi, you soon come to **Spoleto**, an intriguing town. Not only is medieval Spoleto dramatically perched atop a hill, but it also has an almost unbelievable bridge dating from Roman times. This **Ponte delle Torri**, spanning the deep ravine between Spoleto and the adjoining mountain, was built over an aqueduct existing in the 14th century. This incredible engineering wonder, 230 meters long and 81 meters high, is supported by a series of ten Gothic arches and has a fort at the far end as well as a balcony in the center. The 12-century **cathedral** in Spoleto is also so lovely that it alone would make a stop in this charming town worth a detour. The exterior of this very old cathedral, with its beautiful rose window and intricate mosaics, is truly charming. In the town of Spoleto, we recommend the **Hotel Gattapone**, strategically perched on the side of the cliff overlooking the Ponte delle Torri.

Before leaving the vicinity of Spoleto, if you are a St. Francis enthusiast, make the short detour to visit **Monteluco**, where the saint lived as a hermit. You'll appreciate why he chose Monteluco for his meditations after you twist to the top of the mountain and enjoy the glorious view of the surrounding hillsides covered with olive trees. *NOTE:* On the road leading to the top of Monteluco, you can spot on your left the **Eremo delle Grazie**, a charming hotel, almost hidden in the dense woods.

From Spoleto you can take either the 418, a short cut that twists west over the hills to the BIS 3, or the longer route that loops south toward **Terni**. About 4 kilometers past Terni, watch for and take the BIS 3 north. Watch carefully for the turnoff to the west to **Todi**, located just off the main road. Take time to park and explore this truly picture-perfect hilltop walled village. Stop for a cappuccino in one of the sidewalk cafés. However, do not linger too long in Todi because the next town, Orvieto, is the real prize.

Whereas Todi is a small, easily managed village, **Orvieto** is a city spread across the top of a hill that drops down on every side in steep volcanic cliffs. You wonder how the town could ever have been built. Drive as far as you can up to the city, park your car, and proceed on foot. Have a good map handy because you pass so many churches and squares that it is difficult to orient yourself. Continue on to Orvieto's center where a glorious **Duomo** dominates the immense piazza.

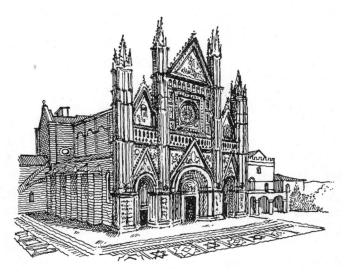

Duomo, Orvieto

You may think you have seen sufficient stunning cathedrals to last a lifetime, but Orvieto's Duomo is truly special—brilliantly embellished with mosaic designs and accented by lacy slender spires that stretch gracefully into the sky. Also of interest in Orvieto is **St. Patrick's Well**, hewn out of solid volcanic rock. Pope Clement VII took refuge in Orvieto in 1527 and to ensure the town's water supply in case of siege, he ordered the digging of this 62-meter-deep well. What makes it unusual are the 70 windows which illuminate it and the two spiral staircases which wind up and down without meeting.

After seeing Orvieto, head directly north on the A1 for about 40 kilometers to the turnoff for your night's destination, **Cetona**. As you exit the freeway, follow the signs that wind circuitously into Cetona. Go through the village and follow signs for Convento San Francesco, the convent where your suggested hotel, **La Frateria di Padre Eligio**, is located in a 16-hectare forest. After spending time in Assisi, it is most appropriate to stay in a 13th-century convent founded by St. Francis. This idyllic hideaway is well suited as a base from which to explore the wealth of places to see in this lower region of Tuscany.

From Cetona make daily forays into the beautiful countryside. One day visit **Pienza**—a jewel of a tiny walled village crowning a hilltop. Stop for lunch here and then continue taking the back roads for about 35 kilometers to **Abbazia di Monte Oliveto Maggiore**, serenely situated among the cypress forest. Of special interest in this abbey are the beautiful terra cottas adorning the entrance (created by the famous artist, Luca della Robbia) and the charming frescoes in the cloisters portraying the life of St. Benedict.

Take an all-day excursion from Cetona to **Siena**, another of the strategically built walled hilltowns. This is an entrancing city and deserves many hours to savor all its attributes. The ramparts are perfectly preserved with a series of massive gates guarding a meticulously maintained medieval stronghold. Drive as close as you can to the main square, park your car, and set out to explore on foot. The giant **Piazza del Campo** is a sight in itself: it is immense and, instead of being square, is fan shaped. Eleven streets surrounding the square converge into it like spokes of a massive wheel. It is in this gigantic piazza that the colorful *Palio delle Contrade* takes place in July and August every year. The horse race is only a part of a colorful spectacle of medieval costumes, wonderful banners, and parades. You can check for the exact dates, but the festivities extend beyond the actual date of the races. Monopolizing one side of the Piazza del

Campo is the 13th-century Gothic **Palazzo Pubblico** (Town Hall) whose graceful arches are embellished with Siena's coat of arms. The Palazzo Pubblico is open as a museum where you can stroll through the governor's living quarters. Also visit Siena's 12th-century **cathedral,** facing the Piazza del Duomo, just a short walk from the Piazza del Campo. Save time to visit the interior of this fabulous cathedral with its bold patterns of black and white marble because within is an excellent museum of antique religious art and sculptures.

NOTE: While Cetona is suggested as the hub from which to explore this southern portion of Tuscany, look at Map 9 in the back of this guide to see other choices nearby. There is a marvelous selection of places to stay in this region, any one of which would make an excellent base for your explorations.

DESTINATION III   CASTELLINA IN CHIANTI

Your next destination is **Castellina,** in the heart of Chianti country. Here you find the **Tenuta di Ricavo,** a cluster of charming stone cottages deep in the pine forest. The entire village has been converted into a romantic small hotel with tastefully decorated rooms. For a choice of other towns in the Chianti region where we recommend places to stay, study Map 8. Any one of the recommended hotels would make an ideal hub for exploring this part of Tuscany.

Of all the beautiful areas of Tuscany, picture-perfect Chianti is the most special. It lives up to every dream—hills crowned by walled villages, straight rows of towering cypresses, romantic villas, ancient stone farmhouses, vast fields of brilliant poppies, forests of pine trees, vineyards stretching to the horizon. In Chianti the sightseeing is mostly just meandering through the countryside, stopping at quaint hamlets, wandering through perched villages. Do not be too structured. Take a detailed map so that if you get lost you can find your way home, but otherwise, just explore. Enjoy the freedom to discover your own *perfect village*, your own favorite restaurant.

During your adventures, the one town you must not miss is **San Gimignano**. What is so dramatic about San Gimignano is that at one time this walled town was surrounded by 72 towers. During the Middle Ages it was a status symbol for noble families to build personal towers for protection—the higher the tower, the greater the image of wealth and importance. It is amazing that 14 of the original towers are still standing. They make a striking silhouette, soaring like skyscrapers. On a clear day you can see them on the horizon from far away. San Gimignano is truly a jewel—plan to spend at least a day here. There are many shops and marvelous restaurants tucked along the maze of streets. *NOTE:* If you want to spend the night, we highly recommended the **L'Antico Pozzo**, a charming hotel in the center of town. **Hotel La Cisterna** on the main square and **La Mangiatoia** near L'Antico Pozzo both serve excellent food.

When it is time to complete your loop, Florence is about an hour's drive away.

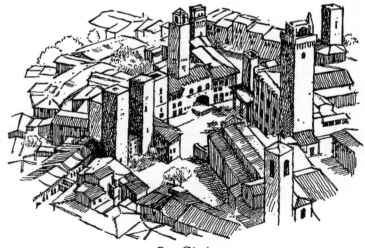

San Gimignano

Mountain & Lake Adventures

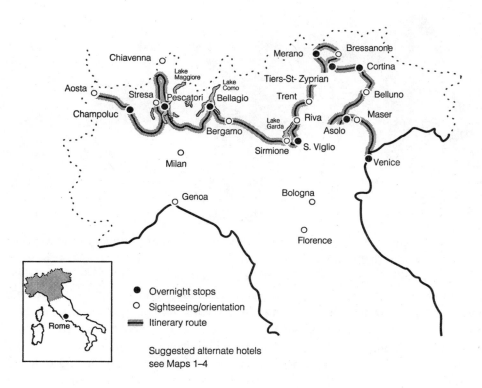

Chiavenna

Merano · Bressanone
Cortina

Lake
Maggiore

Tiers-St- Zyprian

Lake
Como

Aosta
Stresa · Pescatori · Bellagio · Trent · Belluno

Champoluc · Riva · Maser

Lake
Garda · Asolo

Bergamo · Sirmione · S. Viglio

Milan · S. Viglio · Venice

Genoa · Bologna

Florence

● Overnight stops
○ Sightseeing/orientation
▰▰▰ Itinerary route

Rome

Suggested alternate hotels
see Maps 1–4

Mountain & Lake Adventures

Santa Maria Rezzónico, Lake Como

For the traveler who wants to combine the magic of seeing some of the world's most splendid mountains with the joy of visiting Italy's scenic northern lakes, this itinerary is ideal. Contrasts will heighten the impact of visual delights as you meander through lovely mountain passes. Along the way you pass lush green meadows splashed with wildflowers and giant mountains piercing the sky with their jagged granite peaks. Farther on you come to lazy blue lakes whose steep shorelines are decorated with villages wrapped in misty cloaks of siennas and ochres. This itinerary can stand alone. However, it is also perfect for the traveler arriving in or departing from neighboring countries. We show detours for the tourist who will be leaving or entering from Austria, Switzerland, or France. All too often the tourist thinks he has finished Italy when his tour ends in Venice, and he rushes north into Austria or Switzerland. What a waste—a very picturesque region still remains. Please linger to enjoy the mountains and lakes that truly are some of Italy's greatest natural treasures.

ORIGINATING CITY   VENICE

This itinerary begins in **Venice,** one of the most romantic cities in the world. Her many narrow waterways are criss-crossed by story-book bridges and shadowed by majestic palaces whose soft hues reflect warmly in the shimmering water. Black gondolas quietly glide through the narrow canals as the gondolier in his red-and-white-striped shirt softly serenades his passengers with an operatic selection.

Venice is not a traditional city with streets and automobile traffic, but rather an archipelago of 117 islands glued together by 400 bridges. There is a wealth of things to do here: pick up a guidebook at one of the tourist stalls to give you an idea of what you want to see. On pages 35–37 we give brief sightseeing suggestions.

DESTINATION   ASOLO

You need not rush your departure this morning. Venice is a city that should be enjoyed slowly and since your journey today is short, you can certainly have the luxury of a last leisurely breakfast before embarking on your countryside adventure.

Since all the "streets" in Venice are canals, you will need to take a boat to your car. It will probably be at the **Piazzale Roma** where most of the car rental companies are located. Also in the Piazzale Roma there are overnight car parks for storing your car if you drive into Venice. The choice of conveyance will depend upon your budget and your inclination. The **vaporetti** are the most reasonable: similar to river buses, the vaporetti leave regularly from St. Mark's Square for the approximately half-hour ride to the

Piazzale Roma. The Number One service stops at most of the little docks along the route whereas Number Two is an express boat that stops at only a few major points. The **motoscafi** are motorboats that duck through the back canals and usually take about 15 minutes to the Piazzale Roma. The Motoscafi are like private cabs and are much more expensive than the "bus," but can be very convenient, especially if your hotel has a private motor-boat landing. The most deluxe mode of transportation is by private **gondola**: however, these are very expensive and usually take about an hour to reach the Piazzale Roma.

Once you have retrieved your car from the parking garage, head north from Venice toward **Treviso**, which requires about an hour's drive. If time allows, stop here. Stroll through this picturesque city spider-webbed with canals and surrounded by 15th-century ramparts—perhaps have a cup of coffee or a bite of lunch. Treviso is famous for its arcaded streets, churches lavishly decorated with frescoes, and painted houses. You might want to climb the ramparts for a view of the Alps beckoning you on. From Treviso it is approximately another hour north to Asolo. However, just a few kilometers before you reach Asolo you see signs for the town of **Maser** where the **Villa di Maser** (some of your books might use the name of **Villa Bararo**) is located. This is a splendid villa designed by Palladio and fabulously decorated with frescoes by Paolo Veronese. It also has a very interesting museum of old carriages and antique cars. This elegant villa has erratic days and hours when it is open to the public—usually in late afternoons on Tuesdays, Saturdays, and Sundays. However, it is only about 1½ kilometers out of your way, so it is well worth a detour to investigate.

Your prize tonight is **Asolo**, a gem of a medieval village snuggled on the side of a hill with exquisite views of the countryside. As you drive toward Asolo, the terrain does not seem to hold much promise—just modern towns and industry. Then a side road winds up a lovely hillside and into the intimate little town. Although definitely a tourist destination, Asolo maintains the atmosphere of a *real* town with colorful fruit stands, candy shops, and the neighborhood grocer for those lucky few who live here. In addition, there are boutiques with exquisite merchandise for the tourist. Of course, a castle adorns the hill above the village—mostly in ruins but setting the proper stage. Naturally, there is a wonderful cathedral dominating the square, just as it should. You will find all this plus vineyards and olive trees on the hillsides and the scent of roses in the air.

Villa Cipriani, Asolo

No wonder Robert Browning fell in love with Asolo and chose it as his home. It might not be possible for everyone to live here, but at least you have the marvelous option of staying at the **Villa Cipriani**, an enchanting villa that was once Browning's home. Here you can dream on the peaceful terrace in the evening and watch the soft lights paint the distant villa-dotted hills in mellow shades of gold. *NOTE:* A less expensive alternate choice is the **Hotel Duse**, located on the main square.

DESTINATION II   CORTINA D'AMPEZZO

There are a couple of towns that are worth seeing before leaving the Asolo area. If brandy holds a special interest for you, visit **Bassano del Grappa**, an old town famous for its production of grappa (or brandy). The town is also a pottery center. However, it is rather large and, in our estimation, much less interesting than **Marostica**, a tiny town just a few kilometers farther on. If you are in this area in September, check your calendar and consider a stop in Marostica. Here, during the first part of September (in alternate years) the central square is transformed into a giant chess board and local citizens become the human chess pieces. Even if it isn't the year of the chess game, you will enjoy this picturesque little medieval town encircled by ramparts, its pretty central square enclosed by colorful buildings and castle walls. There is also a second castle guarding the town from the top of the hill.

As you head north into the **Dolomites** there are various routes from which to choose. The major highway heads north through Feltre and Belluno and then on to Cortina d'Ampezzo.

If the day is nice and your spirit of adventure is high, there is really nothing more fun than taking the back roads through the mountains. Journey through tiny hamlets and gorgeous mountain valleys far from the normal tourist path; always keeping a map accessible so that you don't wind up hopelessly lost.

You might want to travel casually and stop in a village that captures your heart as you drive through the picturesque valleys of the Dolomites. But if you are making reservations (and in the summer season this is highly recommended), a good choice for an overnight stop is **Cortina**

The Dolomites

d'Ampezzo. This is not a small town—it has grown into a large tourist center due to its excellent skiing facilities. However, its location is truly breathtaking—the town spreads across a sunny meadow ringed by gigantic granite peaks. Our choice for a place to stay on the outskirts of town is the **Hotel Menardi,** whose history dates back far before the skiing craze. It used to be a simple farmhouse, but today it is a proper hotel where the guests sleep in comfortable beds with fine linens and down comforters.

Although the true allure of Cortina d'Ampezzo is its beauty, there are a few places you can go if you want to do some sightseeing—see the beautiful frescoes in the Romanesque **Church of SS Filippo e Giacomo,** visit the stadium where the Olympic ice skating competition was held in 1956, go to see the geological display and the contemporary art exhibition, both housed in the **Museo Ciasa de Ra Regoles.**

DESTINATION III   TIERS–ST. ZYPRIAN (Tires–San Cipriano)

When it is time to leave Cortina, take the Old Dolomite Road, originally used by the merchants of Venice on their way to Germany, heading west from Cortina toward Bolzano. Quite frankly, we think this is one of the most stunning regions of Italy—the mountains are truly breathtaking. Our favorite adventure is exploring the tiny back roads in the **Dolomites** in an effort to add a wider choice of places for you to stay. Look on map 2 in the back of this guide to find our selection of hamlets where we have discovered small inns. Read about each of them and decide where you want to spend the night—any one of them would make a good base for walking and soaking in the beauty of these soaring, saw-toothed mountain peaks. Before leaving Cortina, buy a very detailed map of the region because this is a confusing area for driving. Adding to the confusion of finding your way is the fact that most of the towns have two names: one Italian and one Austrian. Before World War I this section of Italy belonged to the Austrian Empire, and most of the towns have retained their original names along with their new ones.

From Cortina follow the highway S48 as it leaves the valley floor and climbs over a windswept, barren pass surrounded by towering granite peaks. The road then drops into a valley before climbing again to conquer the **Pordoi Pass** and then down into the Fassa valley. About 12 kilometers beyond Canazei, highway S48 splits off to the south. At this point, keep to your right and continue west on S241 which goes through Vigo di Fassa. From the turnoff onto S241, it is about 10 kilometers farther to where you turn right on the road leading to Bolzano by way of Tiers (Tires). This road loops over the mountains and then drops down to an idyllic meadow where **St. Zyprian** (San Cipriano) is located. We suggest an overnight sojourn in this especially scenic village just a few kilometers from Tires (Tiers). As you drive into town, you will see a signpost on your right indicating the **Pensione Stefaner,** a simple chalet-style inn run by the gracious young Villgrattner family.

If you enjoy the outdoors, plan to spend at least several days in the Dolomites so that you can enjoy the splendor of the mountains. Join other travelers from throughout Europe who come to trek the well-marked trails which feather out into the hills. (At gift shops or tourist offices, you can purchase detailed hiking maps that show every little path.)

DESTINATION IV   MERANO

When you leave St. Zyprian, follow the road signposted to Bolzano. Before you reach Bolzano, watch for signs to the E6. Get on the expressway heading north in the direction of the Brenner Pass. Soon after getting on the expressway, there is an exit for **Bressanone**—try to allow time to stop in here. This medieval walled town ringed by mountains has much to offer including a charming village square and a river (lined on both banks by promenades) meandering through its center. Bressanone hides another treasure, the **Hotel Elefant.** This inn is famous for its exquisite cuisine. In its beautiful dining rooms only the freshest foods and wines are served—usually from the hotel's own farms and vineyards. The hotel also has an intriguing history. In 1550, King John III of

Portugal sent, as a special gift, an elephant to Emperor Ferdinand of Austria. It seems this gift grew weary of walking by the time it arrived in Bressanone and so was housed at the local inn—you guessed it, the Elefant. The story alone merits a stop, but the joy is that the Elefant also retains so much character and serves such excellent food.

From Bressanone continue north for a short distance on the expressway toward the Brenner Pass. Then near Vipiteno, exit and head southwest along a twisting road that maneuvers along the **Monte Giovo Pass** as it twists its way through the mountains. It then drops down into the valley to follow the River Passiria as it winds a path into Merano. *NOTE:* If your destination is Austria, then at Vipiteno continue north on the expressway for the short drive to the Brenner Pass which leads into Austria.

In **Merano** the **Castel Freiberg** is an enchanting fairy-tale castle that majestically dominates all of the surrounding countryside from its romantic hillside perch. This fabulous castle truly has everything: setting, view, stunning architecture, gourmet food, beautiful rooms, priceless antiques, pool, tennis, and an efficient, friendly management. Since this is a luxury hotel, you might want to consider the **Hotel Castel Labers** (just below the Castel Freiberg) or the mountain-top **Hotel Vigiljoch** in nearby **Lana** as alternatives. You will find a write-up of both of these less expensive hotels in the hotel descriptions section at the back of this guide.

DESTINATION V   LAKE GARDA

It is a short drive south from Merano to Bolzano. Here you again join the expressway (E7), but this time heading south toward Trent. **Trent** is best known as the town where the Catholic Council met in the 16th century to establish important articles of faith that emphasized the authority of the Catholic church.

Northern Italian Lake District

Leave the freeway at Trent and head west on 45 toward the small, but lovely, green **Lake Toblino** which is enhanced by a superb castle on its north shore where you can stop for lunch. From Toblino head south on the pretty country road, lined with fruit trees and vineyards, heading directly south toward Lake Garda, Italy's largest lake. When you come to Arco, the road splits. Take the road to the left and continue south to Lake Garda and then follow 249 as it curves along the eastern shore of the lake.

Allow several nights in the **Lake Garda** area so that you can leisurely enjoy several excursions on the lake and a side trip to nearby **Verona**. On Map 3 you can find many towns where we recommend places to stay in every price range that are on or close to the lake. However, we cannot resist sharing with you one or our favorites, **Locanda San Vigilio.**

Locanda San Vigilio, Lake Garda

As you follow 249 which traces the eastern shore of Lake Garda, continue about 4 kilometers beyond the town of Torri d'Benaco. Turn right when you see San Vigilio signposted. There is a gate where you will be stopped by an attendant who will want you to pay for parking (**San Vigilio** is also a park). Say you are a guest at the hotel and you will be allowed to pass. Drive as far as you can and then park your car. Walk down the path, turn left at the stately villa (glimpsed through tall gates), and follow the lane until it dead-ends at the Locanda San Vigilio, a 16th-century stone building, so close to the water's edge that waves lap beneath the windows. With such a setting, it is not surprising that Winston Churchill used to come here to paint. Inside, you will not be disappointed. The rooms are tastefully decorated with country antiques complemented by color-coordinated fabrics. If you want to splurge, ask for a suite overlooking the lake, but no matter which room you choose, they are all most appealing. There is a romantic dining room where you can eat in your own little niche by a window overlooking the lake.

When you are ready to sightsee, drive a few kilometers farther south along the lake to **Garda**. Park your car and take one of the ferries or hydrofoils that ply the lake. If you have the time, choose a different destination each day—perhaps planning to have a bite of lunch at an enticing little lakeside café. If you have time for only one adventure, visit **Sirmione.** This is a wonderful walled village at the south end of Lake Garda positioned at the end of a miniature peninsula. During the summer this town is absolutely bursting with tourists, but you can easily understand why: this is another one of Italy's "stage setting" villages, almost too perfect to be true. If you take the ferry or hydrofoil to Sirmione, your boat will dock in the center of the town. From here you can stroll through the little boutiques, perhaps have lunch at one of the beautiful terrace cafés overlooking the lake, and explore the tiny island-like village. If you want to go to the tip of the peninsula, there are small motorized trams that take you there.

If time permits, take the ferry to **Riva** on the northern shore of the lake. Although much of the town is of new construction, it has at its medieval core the **Piazza III Novembre** and 13th-century **Tower of Apponale.** A good place to eat lunch is on the terrace of the **Hotel Sole,** located directly across from the boat dock.

Another excursion is by car to **Gardone Riviera** (on the western shore of the lake) to see a nearby museum, the **Vittoriale,** once the home of Gabriele D'Annunzio, the celebrated Italian poet. (For those of us who love stories of romance, **D'Annunzio** is also famous for his love affair with Eleanora Duse.) While there, if you enjoy gourmet food, try the pink and white **Villa Fiordaliso,** a well-known restaurant located right on the lake. The

Villa Fiordaliso also has a tidbit of historical romance—this was once the hideaway of Mussolini and his mistress, Claretta. For a simpler meal, just a few kilometers farther north along the lake at **Gargnano-Villa,** you can enjoy a wonderful seafood lunch on the sun-drenched deck of the **Baia d'Oro.**

It might be easier to leave the Lake Garda knowing that beautiful Lake Como awaits your arrival.

Bergamo

On your way from Lake Garda to Lake Como, stop at **Bergamo**, about an hour's drive west on the A4. As you approach Bergamo, the congested city doesn't appear to be worth a stop— but it is. The shell of the city is deceiving because it hides a lovely kernel, the **Cita Alta**, or high city. The lower part of Bergamo is modern and a bit dreary, but the old medieval city snuggled on the top of the hill holds such treasures as the **Piazza Vecchia**, the **Colleoni Chapel**, and the **Church of St. Mary Major**. Should you want to time your stop in Bergamo with lunch, there are several excellent restaurants. One suggestion would be the **Agnello d'Oro**, a cozy, charming, 17th-century inn in the Cita Alta.

From Bergamo it is a short drive on to **Bellagio**, a medieval fishing village located at the tip of a peninsula. This peninsula divides the lower section of Lake Como into two lakes, Lake Como on the west and Lake Lecco on the east. Bellagio makes an excellent base for exploring beautiful Lake Como. In the hotel description section we list three hotel suggestions in various price ranges. The **Grand Hotel Villa Serbelloni**, found behind gates opening onto the main square of Bellagio, is a large, imposing, old-world palace. It offers everything you could wish for in a lakeside interlude—tennis, swimming pool, boat excursions, private beach, and more. It is very ornate, still retaining its glory of bygone days with soaring, intricately painted ceilings, heavy chandeliers, and a fabulous sweeping staircase. The setting of the Villa Serbelloni is superb and overshadows what might be perceived as the slightly faded elegance of the hotel's decor. Just outside the gates of the Villa Serbelloni, with a prime location across from the lake, the **Hotel Florence** is also very highly recommended. This moderately priced small hotel is more intimate than the Villa Serbelloni and offers the warmth of welcome found only at family-run hotels. If you are on a really tight budget, consider **Il Perlo Panorama,** a simple hotel on the hill overlooking the town.

Bellagio, Lake Como

Bellagio is a delightful town. Not only can you meander through its quaint medieval streets, but you can walk to the pier for one of the boats that will take you to all corners of the lake. **Lake Como** is absolutely beautiful—especially the lower eastern branch of the lake called **Lake Lecco** where cliffs enclose the shorelines like gorgeous walls and give a fjord-like beauty to the area. There are numerous romantic steamers that glide in and out of the picturesque, softly hued little hamlets dotting the lake shore. You can settle onto a steamer equipped with bar and restaurant and from your armchair lazily enjoy the constantly changing, but always intriguing shoreline as the boat maneuvers in and out of the colorful little harbors, past elegant private villas, by postcard-pretty villages. From Bellagio you can also step on board one of the swift hydrofoils that will whisk you about the lake or put your car right on the ferry to either **Varenna** on the eastern shore or **Cadenabbia** on the western shore to visit the **Villa Carlotta**, a fairy-tale-like 18th-century palace—worthy of the Prussian Princess Carlotta for whom it was named. You reach the villa, which is encircled by its own gorgeous park of terraced gardens, by a short drive from the ferry landing along the beautiful tree-lined Via del Paradiso.

DESTINATION VII   ISOLA DEI PESCATORI

NOTE: If you plan to leave Italy and head into Switzerland, this would be an excellent point to begin your journey. Head north along Lake Como and on to Chiavenna where you then turn east for the short drive (only about 10 kilometers) to the Swiss border. From there it is a lovely drive through the Engadine Valley to St. Moritz.

Continuing on toward Lake Maggiore, take advantage of the expressways to make your drive as easy as possible because there is usually heavy traffic in this part of Italy. It is best to head directly south from Bellagio to pick up the freeway in the direction of Milan. Keep on the bypass that skirts the north of Milan and follow the freeway northwest to **Lake Maggiore**. When you reach the lake continue along the western shore to Stresa. It seems only suitable that for a "mountain and lake adventure" one of your hotels should be located on an island in a lake—so we have chosen for you one of the **Borromean Islands, Isola dei Pescatori** (Fisherman's Island), in Lake Maggiore. This is an enchanting little island with twisting, narrow, alley-like streets and colorful fishermen's cottages. As the name implies, this is still an active fishing village. During the tourist season the island teems with people and the streets are lined with rather tacky souvenir shops, but it is hard to dull the charm of this quaint town.

Isola Bella, Lake Maggiore

Isola dei Pescatori can be reached by ferry from Stresa, Baveno, or Pallanza, but the most convenient of these is **Stresa** from where there are frequent scheduled departures to the island. Be sure to take one of the scheduled public ferries—these are very reasonable in contrast to the very expensive private speedboats whose captains will attempt to take you to the island. Your best choice for a place to stay here is the **Hotel Verbano.** This is not a deluxe hotel, but its setting is superb, and over the years (since our first visit) the decor of this most romantic hotel has improved enormously. The bedrooms are pleasantly decorated, but lovely vistas are their most enchanting feature. The view from the terrace, where guests enjoy dining while overlooking the lake, is also outstanding. The food is delicious, and the service of the Zacchera family, who own and manage the Verbano, is warm and gracious. How smug you will feel as you settle into your room then sip a drink on the lovely terrace while watching the last of the tourists hustle onto the boat for shore, leaving you to enjoy the sunset.

This tiny archipelago consisting of **Isola Bella** (Beautiful Island), Isola dei Pescatori, and Isola Madre (Mother Island) is world-famous for its dramatic palaces and spectacular, fragrant gardens. Isola Bella is the closest island to dei Pescatori—be sure to allow enough time to visit its sumptuous palace and glorious terraced gardens before returning to the mainland.

DESTINATION VIII   CHAMPOLUC

NOTE: If your next destination is Switzerland, then it is time to leave Italy by heading north in the direction of Domodossolo. About 16 kilometers beyond Domodossolo you arrive at Iselle where you drive your car piggyback-style onto the train and ride in your car as you zigzag through the fabulous **Simplon Tunnel** and emerge about 20 minutes later in Brig.

From Isola Bella, take the ferry back to pick up your car and drive south to the main freeway and head west toward Turin. Before reaching Turin watch for the signs and take the branch of the expressway heading toward Aosta. When you come to Verres, leave the highway and take the small road north to Champoluc, an hour's drive. The road follows the Evancon river as it cuts its path through the mountains. At first the valley is quite steep and narrow and then opens up into wide meadows lazily stretching out on both sides of the river. In early summer the meadows are truly lovely, blanketed in brilliantly colored wildflowers.

Just before the road leaves **Champoluc** you see a marker for the Anna Maria. At this sign turn to the right and follow the road for a very short drive up the hill until you see the hotel. It is beautifully located amid pine trees and has views in every direction of the spectacular mountains. The **Villa Anna Maria** is a small chalet-style inn. Its dining room is cozy and inviting with gay red-checked curtains at the windows and rustic Alpine-style carved wooden chairs. The bedrooms, although small, all have private bathrooms and are very appealing with paneled walls and a country flavor.

When it is time to leave Champoluc you have two options if you want to travel into Switzerland. First you must drive back to the main expressway and head west. In about a half-hour you will come to Aosta at which point you can leave the expressway for the road leading north to the **San Bernardino Tunnel** and into Switzerland's Rhone valley. Or, by continuing on the expressway west through the village of Courmayeur, you arrive at the **Mont Blanc Tunnel**. This delivers you briefly into France, and then on to Geneva via the main highway. Of course, by taking the short drive to Milan you can easily tie in with another Italian holiday suggested in this guide.

Villa Anna Maria, Champoluc

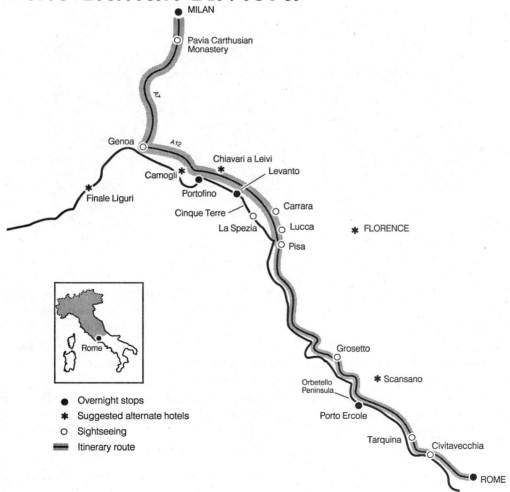

Rome to Milan via the Italian Riviera

● MILAN

○ Pavia Carthusian Monastery

N2

Genoa ○   *A12*

Chiavari a Leivi

Camogli ✱   ✱

Portofino

Levanto

✱ Finale Liguri

Cinque Terre

○ Carrara

La Spezia ○

○ Lucca

○ Pisa

✱ FLORENCE

Grosetto ○

Orbetello Peninsula

✱ Scansano

Porto Ercole ●

Tarquina ○

Civitavecchia ○

● ROME

Rome

● Overnight stops
✱ Suggested alternate hotels
○ Sightseeing
▬ Itinerary route

79

Rome to Milan via the Italian Riviera

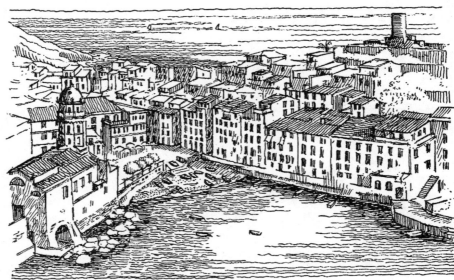

Vernazza, Cinque Terre

This itinerary traces the western coast of Italy as far as Genoa before heading north for the final stretch to Milan. To break the journey, stop first in Orbetello, a picturesque peninsula-like island joined to the coast by three spits of land. The next destination is Cinque Terre—a string of five tiny peninsulas along the coast that have not yet fallen prey to a great influx of tourists. As you follow the highway up the coast, it becomes a masterpiece of engineering—bridging deep ravines and tunneling in and out of the cliffs which rise steeply from the sea. Along the way you pass picturesque small towns snuggled into small coves. Then it's on to Portofino—one of the Italy's most treasured jewels—before the final destination of Milan.

ORIGINATING CITY ROME

This itinerary begins in **Rome**, a perfect introduction to Italy. The joy of Rome is that every place you walk you are immersed history. The whole of the city is a virtual museum—buildings over 2,000 years old, ancient fountains designed by the world's greatest masters, the Vatican, Renaissance paintings that have never been surpassed in beauty. On pages 41–45 we give just a few suggestions of places you must not miss, but we just touch on the wealth of sightseeing possibilities. Buy a guidebook at one of the many bookstores or magazine stands to plan what you most want to see and do. Also buy a detailed city map and mark each day's excursion. Most places are within walking distance—if not, consider taking the subway that stretches to most of the major points of interest.

Rome has a rich selection of places to stay. We suggest that you browse through the hotel section in the back of this guide where we describe hotels we think are especially appealing. Make a reservation in advance because space is very tight—particularly during the busy summer season. Plan to stay in Rome for several days. When you are saturated with the overwhelming number of sights and are ready to continue your journey, ask at the hotel desk for help in marking your map for the best route out of town.

DESTINATION I ORBETELLO–PORTO ERCOLE

From Rome follow the well marked signs for the expressway heading west toward the Leonard di Vinci airport. About 5 kilometers before you arrive at the airport, head north on A12 in the direction of Civitavecchia.

About 20 kilometers beyond **Civitavecchia**, turn off at **Tarquinia,** the Etruscan city that supposedly dates back to the 12th century B.C. Even if it is not quite that old, archaeologists have established that people were living here as early as 600 years before

Christ. Scattered on the windswept hill where the ancient city once stood are thousands of tombs with paintings showing the Etruscans' daily life. There is no way you can visit all the burial chambers, but one of the most popular is the **Tomb of the Leopards** where there is a well preserved banquet scene. If time allows, visit the **Museo Nazionale Tarquiniese** (housed in the 15th-century **Vitelleschi Palace**). This contains many Etruscan artifacts along with several reconstructed tombs.

After your brush with Etruscan civilization, continue north for approximately 50 kilometers to Scalo/Orbetello where you turn east. The road crosses 6 kilometers of lagoons on a narrow spit of land (going through the town of Orbetello) before reaching the large, bulbous peninsula dominated by Monte Argentario. Turn left when you reach the island and continue through the town of **Porto Ercole** following signs to the exquisite resort of **Il Pelicano**, romantically perched on the cliffs overlooking the sea. If time and pocketbook allow, settle in to relax for a few days in this hideaway of the rich and famous before heading north. Enjoy the romantic setting, the swimming pool, tennis courts, and excellent food. Also explore the small peninsula, admire the many splendid yachts in the harbor at Porto Ercole, then continue on to the picturesque old fishing village of **Porto San Stefano**.

NOTE: If Il Pelicano exceeds your budget, or catching a glimpse of the rural area of the southernmost part of Tuscany tempts you, the following is an alternate stopover suggestion. Instead of taking the exit for Orbetello, continue north on 1 for about 7 kilometers to Albinia, where you turn left and follow signs to Scansano on the 323. The narrow road weaves up into the mountains. Two kilometers west of **Scansano** is the **Attico Casale di Scansano**, a simple 200-year-old farmhouse which has been converted into a small inn. Horseback riding is a specialty here, along with exploring the many walled towns in the area.

When it is time to continue, return to highway 1 and head north. The A12 is scheduled to be completed all the way up the coast. However, as we go to press the expressway ends near Civitavecchia and doesn't pick up again until near Livorno (except for short four-lane stretches which are finished). So be patient and allow more time than usual because there are many trucks and slow-moving traffic on the road. Get an early start if you want to stop in Pisa, Lucca, and Carrara along the way.

Leaning Tower of Pisa

The next large town after Livorno is **Pisa**. Exit here and follow signs into the congested center of the old town. There is such a solid mass of tourists and souvenir shops during the summer season that you can hardly find a place to park before trying to squirm your way to the central piazza. Admittedly, Pisa's gleaming white **Duomo** with its companion **Leaning Tower** are impressive, and such a symbol of Italy that you should stop once to see it if you have never done so before.

Even more interesting and not nearly so touristy as Pisa is the extremely picturesque city of **Lucca**, only a few kilometers to the north. Lucca too is an ancient city, even more perfectly preserved than its neighbor, Pisa. Completely surrounding the city is an enormous wall—a wall so wide that it even shelters pretty, small parks and a road that runs along the top. Lucca is truly a jewel. Take time to wander through her maze of narrow streets, admiring characterful mansions and colorful squares

Leaving Lucca, return to the expressway A12 and head north to Genoa. Along the way you see what appears to be a glacier shimmering white in the mountains that rise to the right of the highway. This is not snow at all, but rather your introduction to the renowned white Italian marble. Unless it is too late in the day, detour to visit some of the marble quarries. Exit the highway at Carrara and take the winding drive up into the hills to the ancient village of **Colonnata**—famous through the ages for its marvelous white marble. As you wander this tiny town you're following the footsteps of Michelangelo, who used to come to here to choose huge blocks of marble from which to carve his masterpieces.

Take the small road from Carrara west to join the A12 and continue north for an entirely different kind of experience—exploring the five little isolated towns on the coast called **Cinque Terre**. This area is quickly becoming linked with civilization, so do not tarry if you love the thrill of discovering old fishing villages still untouched by time. En route you come to an exit to **La Spezia**, a large seaport and navy town. If you want to take a detour, go to La Spezia and from there take the short drive to the tip of the peninsula south of town to visit the old fishing village of **Portoverere** which clings to the steep rocks rising from the sea. This was one of Lord Byron's haunts when he lived across the bay at **San Terenzo**. Then return to the A12 and continue north and take the exit for Levanto. Because we could not find any suitable places to stay in any of the villages of the Cinque Terre so have chosen **Levanto** as a hub for your explorations. Levanto, at one time a prosperous fishing port, lacks the luster of chic resorts, yet a faded, somewhat bedraggled charm remains. There are no luxury resorts here, just a smattering of simple places to stay. Our recommendation, **Hotel Stella Maris**, is a basic two-star hotel which, like the town, harks back to past grandeur. The small hotel is found up a narrow staircase which leads to the second floor of a 17th-century palace, in its heyday a real showplace with manicured gardens stretching to the sea. Remnants of the past can be seen in frescoed ceilings, paneled walls, and antique furnishings. Although this is not a hotel for those who expect a decorator-perfect ambiance, the genuine hospitality really grows on you.

Cinque Terre

Along the Cinque Terre there used to be five completely isolated fishing villages dotted along the coast between La Spezia to the south and Levanto to the north. First only a footpath connected these hamlets, then a train was installed, and now civilization is encroaching, with a road under construction which will open them up to greater commercialism. Three of these little villages, (named **Riomaggiore**, **Monterosso**, and **Manorola)** are already accessible by road. Still completely cut off from car traffic are the fishing hamlets of **Vernazza** and **Corniglia**.

In Levanto you do not need to use your car. Instead, take a boat that connects the villages during the summer season. Alternatively, you can walk to the station and hop aboard one of the many trains in the direction of La Spezia. Most of these make stops at the Cinque Terre villages en route. Let your mood, the time, and the weather dictate your explorations: as well as hopping on and off trains to investigate each village and taking the small ferry between them, you can also hike the spectacular trails along the rocky coast which connect them to one another. Best yet, combine all these options.

If you have time to see only one of the scenic towns, Vernazza, which clings perilously to a rocky promontory that steps down to a tiny harbor, is the most picturesque. This colorful jewel has brightly painted fishermen's houses, quaint restaurants, a harbor with small boats bobbing in the clear water, and a maze of twisting narrow steps that lead up to the promontory overlooking the village.

DESTINATION III   PORTOFINO

After Cinque Terre, continue north beside the coast. Stop for lunch along the way in **Sestri Levante**, one of the most picturesque coastal villages en route. Continue along the small coastal road that goes through **Chiàvari** and on to **San Margherita** where you take the small road south for the short drive to the picture-book village of **Portofino**. This last section of the road, especially in summer, is jammed with traffic, but the plum at the end is worth the trials endured to reach it. Portofino is by no means undiscovered, but it is well deserving of its accolades. Without a doubt it is one of the most picturesque small harbors in the world.

Before you reach Portofino, watch on your right for the sign for the **Hotel Splendido**. From the main road, a small lane winds up the wooded hillside to the magnificent villa-style hotel. Be prepared: the deluxe Splendido is a super-expensive hotel whose prices include breakfast and dinner. But what a gorgeous setting! The hotel is perched in the hills above Portofino with breathtaking views of the sea and the harbor. A swimming pool and tennis courts nestle below the hotel and enchanting little paths thread their way through the gardens, offering strategically placed benches for quiet moments to savor the stunning view. It is an easy walk into Portofino if you can bear to leave this haven. *NOTE:* If you are on a tight budget, the **Hotel Eden**, located in the heart of town, is recommended. This basic, 12-room hotel is at the opposite end of the measure for ambiance and luxury, but has a great location and the warmth and caring of a family-owned small hotel.

Portofino is a national treasure—it truly is a jewel. Her tiny harbor is filled with glamorous yachts, small ferries, and colorful fishing boats. Enveloping the harbor are narrow fishermen's cottages, poetically painted in warm tones of sienna, ochre, and pink and all sporting green shutters. Bright flowerboxes accent the windows and the laundry flaps gaily in the breeze. Vivid reflections of these quaint little houses shimmer in the emerald water. In the center of town is a small square, lined with restaurants, that faces the harbor. Forming a backdrop to the town are heavily forested, forested hills that rise steeply to complete this idyllic scene.

Portofino

Rome to Milan via the Italian Riviera

NOTE: While staying in Portofino, if you appreciate gourmet dining, drive south to one of Italy's finest restaurants, the **Ca'Peo**, located in **Chiavari a Leivi**. You must make prior reservations because Franco and his wife, Melly, only take guests who call ahead since the food is specially prepared depending upon how many will be dining: telephone (0185) 319090. The Ca'Peo, whose origins date back to a very old farmhouse, is located high in the hills overlooking the coast. Be forewarned: the meals are VERY expensive. If you want to spend the night, there are moderately priced suites available.

DESTINATION IV   MILAN

NOTE: For those of you traveling to the French Riviera, we wish you farewell in Portofino. From Portofino continue to follow the coastal highway west to Genoa along the Italian Riviera into the principality of Monaco and then across the border to France.

For the rest of our group, after leaving Portofino, return to the A12 highway and continue west for about 30 kilometers to Genoa. As you circle the city, watch for the freeway A7 going north to Milan.

An interesting detour on the last leg of your journey is the **Pavia Carthusian Monastery** (*Certosa di Pavia*). Probably the simplest way to find it is to watch for the turnoff to Pavia (96 kilometers north of Genoa): take the road east to Pavia and from there go north about 10 kilometers to the monastery. Lavishly built in the 15th century, this splendid monastery is claimed by some to be one of the finest buildings in Italy. (Check carefully the days and hours open—the monastery is usually closed on Mondays and for several hours midday.) The outside of the building is lavishly designed with colorful marble and intricate designs. Inside, the small cloisters are especially charming with 122 arches framed by beautiful terra-cotta moldings. It also has a baroque fountain and several small gardens. Next to the monastery you find the **Palace of the Dukes of Milan** which is now a museum. After your tour of the monastery it is approximately 26 kilometers farther north to **Milan**.

The outskirts of Milan are not very inviting—frustrating traffic and modern commercial buildings. However, the heart of Milan has much to offer. If you enjoy shopping (and Milan has some of the finest in Italy), pay a visit to the splendid **Galleria Vittorio Emanuele**, one of the prettiest shopping arcades in the world. Even if you are not a shopper, you must take time to browse. Located between Milan's other two sightseeing stars, the Duomo and La Scala, the Galleria Vittorio Emanuele is the forerunner of the modern shopping mall, but with much more pizzazz. In this Victorian-era fantasy there are two main, intersecting wings, both completely domed with intricately patterned glass. Along the pedestrian-only arcades you find many boutiques and colorful restaurants with outside tables where everyone seems to stop for a cup of tea or an aperitif.

After a stroll through the arcade, you emerge into an imposing square dominated by the truly spectacular **Duomo**, the third-largest cathedral in the world. Not only is the size impressive, but this sensational cathedral has a multi-colored marble façade enhanced by over 100 slender spires piercing the sky. This spectacular cathedral faces onto an enormous square which is lined with cafés, office buildings, and shops. Stop to have a snack at one of the outdoor restaurants—you could sit for hours just watching the people go by.

Also, a "must-see" is Milan's opera house. Every opera buff knows about **La Scala**. Even if you have not been an opera enthusiast in the past, if you are going to be in Milan during the opera season (which usually runs from December to May), write ahead and try to get tickets. The theater is stunning and an experience not to be missed. When it is not opera season, there is usually some other performance or concert featured. If you haven't purchased seats in advance, you can try to buy them on the day of the performance (the ticket office is located down a flight of stairs to the left of the opera house).

Milan does not offer a wealth of charming places to stay: most are modern, commercial hotels, seemingly way overpriced, with minimal old-world appeal. Happily (if your budget can handle a deluxe hotel), there is an exception: the intimate, expertly managed **Hotel Pierre Milan,** which abounds in antiques and charm.

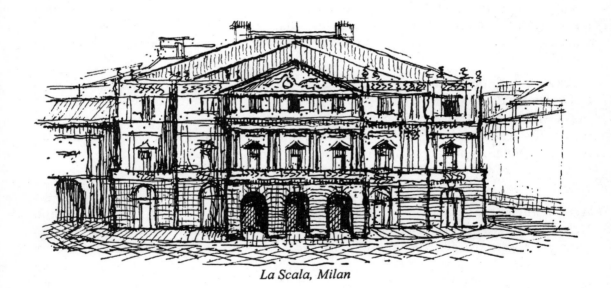

La Scala, Milan

Highlights of
Southern Italy

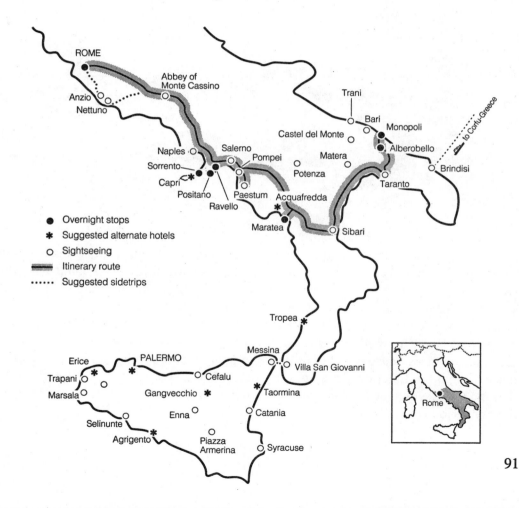

ROME

Abbey of
Monte Cassino

Anzio
Nettuno

Trani

Bari
Monopoli

Castel del Monte

Alberobello

Naples
Salerno
Pompei
Matera
Potenza

Sorrento

Capri
Paestum
Acquafredda

Positano
Ravello

Maratea
Sibari

Taranto

to Corfu-Greece

Brindisi

● Overnight stops

* Suggested alternate hotels

○ Sightseeing

▬ Itinerary route

····· Suggested sidetrips

Tropea

Messina

Erice
PALERMO

Trapani
Cefalu

Marsala

Gangvecchio

Villa San Giovanni

Taormina

Selinunte
Enna
Catania

Agrigento
Piazza
Armerina
Syracuse

Rome

Highlights of Southern Italy

Amalfi Coast

Having visited the famous trio of Rome, Florence, and Venice, most tourists think that they have seen Italy. Childhood history lessons call forth such names as Pompeii, Herculaneum, and Paestum, yet, all too frequently, the urge to visit these jewels of archaeological wonders is lost in the misconception that southern Italy is an uninteresting destination. What a mistake: southern Italy has fascinating ruins, gorgeous coastlines, beautiful medieval walled villages, lovely beaches, marvelous hilltowns, and some of the most unusual sights in Italy. So many visitors to Italy's south are amazed to discover that the Emerald Grotto on the Amalfi Coast rivals the Blue Grotto of Capri and that the Greek ruins of Paestum outshine many found in Greece, and they are haunted by the mysterious town of Alberobello.

Therefore, for those of you who have already seen the fantastic highlights of northern Italy, we take pleasure in presenting to you the best of southern Italy. This itinerary makes a circle of the south in order to suit the travel needs of a wide selection of tourists. Follow the entire route or select the portion best for you since this itinerary lends itself especially well for the traveler who wants to take only a segment. For instance, the journey from Rome to Brindisi is a popular one for the lucky tourists on their way to Greece, while the west coast is a popular drive for the tourist who wants to visit Sicily and then return to Rome by air or ferry. Most popular of all is the segment from Rome to the Amalfi Drive. This itinerary allows you to custom-tailor your journey and gives you tantalizing sightseeing along the way.

ORIGINATING CITY   ROME

Rome is a most convenient starting point to begin a tour of southern Italy, since its airport is the destination of planes from all over the world. In Rome you can immerse yourself in a wealth of history, art, architecture, museums, and monuments—and build a foundation for the sights that will be encountered on your journey southward. See pages 41–45 for suggestions of what to see and do in Rome.

There is a wide selection of accommodations in Rome in various price categories and locations. Choose the hotel that best suits your personality and budget from the hotel descriptions section in the back of this guide. You will find that Rome has many excellent hotels and, even though the city is large, most of the hotels are still within walking distance of both shopping and sightseeing highlights. If you do not like to walk, ask the concierge at your desk to call you a taxi or direct you to the nearest subway station. Rome's main subway line stretches across the city—conveniently connecting most of the places of interest for the tourist.

When leaving the city by car, bear in mind that Rome always has a monumental traffic problem. Within the city look for strategically placed signs indicating that there is an expressway ahead. It might be quite a distance, but be patient as these signs lead you to the outskirts of Rome to the highway that makes a ring around the city with various spokes going off to different destinations. Follow the ring and take the exit for the A2, the expressway heading south toward Naples. Continue south for approximately 128 kilometers to the exit for **Cassino** where you leave the expressway. Actually, you can spot your destination from several kilometers away—the **Abbey of Monte Cassino** crowns the top of a large mountain to the left of the highway as you drive south. The road that winds up to the summit of the mountain to the Abbey of Monte Cassino is clearly marked about midway through Cassino. This abbey, founded by St. Benedict in 529 A.D., is extremely interesting both religiously and historically. For war historians the abbey brings back many battle memories—this is where the Germans staunchly held out against the Allied forces for almost a year in World War II. When the mountain was finally conquered in May 1944, it opened the way for the Allies to finally move into Rome. As you read your history books it seems strange that one fort could hold out for so long, but when you see the abbey you understand: it is an enormous building on the crest of a precipitous mountain. In the siege the abbey was almost destroyed, but it has been rebuilt according to the original plans.

NOTE: For those of you who for sentimental or historical reasons are especially interested in World War II, there is another destination you might well want to visit in this day's journey. **Anzio** is a town on the coast about 56 kilometers south of Rome and could easily be included as a stop before Cassino. It was at Anzio that the British and Americans forces landed in January 1944. The emotional reminder of this terrible battle is a few kilometers south at **Nettuno** where 8,000 white crosses and stars of David range—row after row across the green lawn. There is a circular drive around the beautifully manicured, parklike grounds where you also find a memorial chapel and small war museum. For those who lost family or friends during the invasion, there is an information office to the right as you drive in where you can stop to find out exactly where your loved ones are buried—you will need help because the park is huge.

From Cassino return to the expressway and continue south for about 60 kilometers until you see the sign for **Pompeii**. Unless you have absolutely NO interest in archaeology you must see the city of your childhood history books. This is where time was frozen in 79 A.D. for the 25,000 people who were smothered by ashes from the eruption of **Mount Vesuvius**. If you are a dedicated student of archaeology, you must also visit the **National Archaeological Museum** in **Naples** where many of the artifacts from Pompeii are housed.

Time slips eerily back 2,000 years as you wander the streets of Pompeii and visit the temples, lovely homes, wine shops, bakeries, and public baths. There is probably no other place on earth where you can feel so strongly the pulse of ancient days. Many of the private homes have been reconstructed so you can marvel at the pretty inner courtyards, beautiful dining rooms in Pompeii-red with intricate paintings on the walls, fountains, servants' quarters, bathrooms, and gardens. At the entrance to Pompeii there are souvenir stands where you can purchase a guidebook to the city, or, if you prefer, you can hire a private guide at the entrance. Pompeii is so fascinating that you might well want to come back to spend a complete day visiting the city and the nearby ruins of **Herculaneum** which was also buried in the ashes of Vesuvius.

Leaving Pompeii, head to the coast in the direction of Sorrento where the **Amalfi Drive**, tracing one of the most beautiful stretches of shoreline in the world, begins. Be sure to make journey in daylight because you want to be sure to glimpse every magnificent vista as well as safely negotiate this extremely twisty and precipitous road.

It is hard to recommend our favorite town along the Amalfi Coast since each has its own personality: **Sorrento** is an old fishing town perched on a rocky bluff overlooking the

Positano

sea. It makes an especially convenient place to stay if you want to make a side trip to Capri by ferry or hydrofoil. **Ravello** is a tiny village tucked high in the hills above the coast with absolutely dazzling views down to the sea. **Positano** is an especially romantic town with picturesque whitewashed houses that terrace down an ever so steep embankment to a pebble beach that is dotted with brightly painted fishing boats.

There are many excellent choices for hotels along the Amalfi Drive—concentrated in just a few kilometers are some of the most splendid hotels in all of Italy. Study the various hotel choices in Sorrento, Ravello, and Positano in the hotel descriptions section to see what most appeals to you.

From whatever hub you choose as your hotel base, venture out to do some exploring. The traffic during the tourist season is staggering, with buses and trucks and cars all jockeying for position on the narrow twisting roads. Prepare for much shouting, waving of hands, honking, and general bedlam as long buses inch around the hairpin curves. The best advice is to relax and consider the colorful scene as part of the sightseeing. Also, begin your excursions as early in the day as possible to try to avoid the major traffic.

If you are not overnighting in **Ravello**, you must plan to take the narrow winding road up to this romantic clifftop town. When you arrive, leave your car in one of the designated parking areas, pick up a map at the tourist office, then walk along the well marked path to the **Villa Rufolo** and the **Villa Cimbrone**—both have beautiful gardens that are open to the public and enchanting views of the Bay of Salerno.

If you are not overnighting in **Positano**, by all means make this a day's excursion. The town is a photographer's dream—houses painted a dazzling white step down the impossibly steep hillside to a pebble beach that is lapped by brilliant blue water. To reach the small plaza dominated by a church with a colorful mosaic-tiled dome you have to climb one of the town's many staircases. Today Positano attracts artists and tourists from around the world, but in the 16th and 17th centuries it was an important sea port with tall-masted ships bringing in wares from around the world. When steamships came into vogue in the 19th century, Positano's prosperity declined and three-quarters of its population emigrated to the United States.

If you have not been able to include an interlude on **Capri** during your Italian holiday, it is easy to arrange an excursion to this enchanted island as a side trip from the Amalfi Coast. Steamers and hydrofoils depart regularly from Sorrento, Amalfi, and Positano. Ask at the tourist bureau or your hotel for the schedule. (When the seas are rough it is more difficult to leave from Positano since there is no pier, making it necessary to take a small boat from the shore to the ferry.) *NOTE:* If you have time, you could leave your car in Sorrento and spend several nights on Capri. See pages 48–50 for further information on what to see and do on Capri.

While exploring the Amalfi Coast, visit the **Emerald Grotto**, located between the towns of Amalfi and Positano. After parking, buy a ticket and descend by elevator down the steep cliff to a small rocky terrace. Upon entering the water-filled cave, you're rowed about the grotto in a small boat. Your guide explains how the effect of shimmering green water is created by a secret tunnel allowing sunlight to filter from deep below the surface. The cave is filled with colorful stalactites and stalagmites that further enhance the mysterious mood. There is also a nativity scene below the water that magically appears and then drifts again from view.

DESTINATION II   GULF OF POLICASTRO–MARATEA

When it is time to leave the Amalfi area, take the coastal road south as it twists and turns along the dramatic cliffs toward Salerno. At Salerno, join the expressway A3 for about 19 kilometers until the turnoff for **Paestum** which is located on a side road about a half-hour drive from the freeway. Magically, when you enter the gates of the ancient city you enter a peaceful environment of a lovely country meadow dotted with some of the world's best preserved Greek temples. As you walk the remains of streets criss-crossing the city, your senses are thrilled by the sound of birds singing and the scent of roses. Before leaving Paestum, stop for a snack at the **Marini Sea Garden**, a former villa set in a garden whose gates open onto the west side of the excavation.

From Paestum return to the A3 and continue south until you come to the Lagonegro Nord-Maratea exit. Do not be tempted by some of the short cuts you see on the map that lead to the coast, but stay on the main road 585. In about 25 kilometers the road comes to the sea where you turn north at Castrocucco, following signs to **Maratea**.

We have three hotel choices in this area, each lovely, each with its special merits. **La Locanda delle Donne Monache**, housed in an 18th-century convent, is snuggled in the hills above the quaint town of Maratea. The **Hotel Santavenere** has a prime location hugging high cliffs that drop down to the sea. The **Villa Cheta Elite**, located a short drive north of Maratea in **Acquafredda**, is a moderately priced hotel whose gracious owners welcome guests as friends.

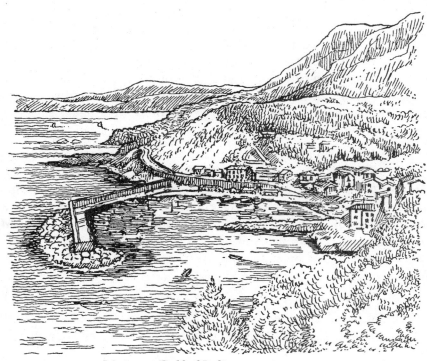

Maratea, Gulf of Policastro

If possible, spend several days in Maratea. Not well-know to foreigners, this lovely section of coast, known as the **Gulf of Policastro,** is a popular resort area for Italians. The loveliest section of the road is between Maratea and Sapri where the road traces the sea along a high corniche, providing lovely vistas of small coves and rocky promontories. This is not an area for intensive sightseeing, but provides a quiet interlude for several days to relax.

From the Gulf of Policastro, take road 585 back to the A3 and continue south for about 75 kilometers, turning east at Frascineto/Castrovillari toward the instep of Italy's boot. After about 25 kilometers you near the coast. Here you turn left on 106 to **Taranto**. Stop to see this ancient port which is connected by a bridge to the modern city. Even if you are not interested in ancient history, it is fun to see the Italian naval ships—giant gray monsters—sitting in the protected harbor.

From Taranto, take 172 north and continue on for about 45 kilometers following signs to Alberobello. If you are staying in **Alberobello**, follow signs to the **Hotel dei Trulli** in the trulli district of town (see below). If your chosen destination is **Monopoli**, do not go into town: instead, turn right and follow the ring road around Alberobello watching for the road signs to Monopoli, which is 23 kilometers farther. You arrive at **Il Melograno** before reaching Monopoli. Coming from Alberobello, turn left on a small road just before the four-lane road that bypasses the town. The hotel is a bit tricky to find, so when making your reservation, ask for detailed directions.

You are now in the province of **Apulia,** not a well-known destination, but all the more fun to visit because it is off the beaten path. With either Monopoli or Alberobello as your hub, venture out to explore the fascinating sights in the area. Some suggestions are listed below.

Trulli District: Trulli houses (whose origins date back to at least the 13th century) are some of the strangest structures in Italy—circular stone buildings, usually built in small clusters, standing crisply white with conical slate roofs and whimsical twisted chimneys. Outside ladders frequently lead to upper stories. Often several of these houses are joined together to form a larger complex. What a strange and fascinating sight—these beehive-like little houses intertwined with cobbled streets form a jumble of a small village that looks as though it should be inhabited by elves instead of *real* people. The heart of the

Trulli Houses, Alberobello

trulli region is Alberobello where there are so many trulli houses (more than 1,000 along the narrow streets) that the trulli district of town has been named a national monument.

Trulli houses are not confined to the town of Alberobello although this is where you find them composing an entire village. In fact, the trulli houses you see in the vicinity of Alberobello are sometimes more interesting than those in the town itself. As you drive along the small roads, you spot gorgeous villas cleverly converted from trulli houses which are now obviously the homes of wealthy Italians. Others are now farmhouses with goats munching their lunch in the front yard. Occasionally you spot a charming old trulli home nestled cozily in the center of a vineyard. But most fun of all are the trulli homes of the free spirits: their homes, instead of displaying the typical white exteriors, have been painted a brilliant yellow or pink or bright green with contrasting shutters.

Grotte di Castellana: As you are exploring the countryside near Alberobello, take the short drive north to see the Castellana Caves—the largest in Italy. In a two-hour tour you see many rooms of richly colored stalagmites and stalactites.

Coastal Villages: Be sure to include in your sightseeing some of the characterful towns along the coast. They look entirely different from the colorful fishing villages in the north of Italy. These are Moorish-looking, with stark-white houses lining narrow, alley-like streets. The Adriatic looks an even deeper blue as it laps against the white buildings, many of which rise from the sea with small windows perched over the water. Besides Monopoli, other coastal towns to see are **Polignano a Mare** and **Trani**.

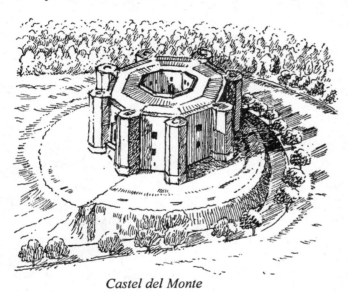

Castel del Monte

Castel del Monte: On the same day that you explore the coastal villages, include a visit to the 13th-century Castel del Monte. Built by Emperor Frederick II of Swab, it is somewhat of a mystery, having none of the fortifications usually associated with a medieval castle. Nevertheless, it is dramatic—a huge pastel-stone structure crowning the top of a hill with 8 circular towers that stretch 24 meters into the sky. There are stunning views in every direction. (Check with the tourist office before you go, since the castle is not open every day of the week.)

When it is time to leave Apulia, you can breeze back to Rome by an expressway. Or, if your next destination is Greece, it is just a short drive to **Brindisi** where you can board the ferry for Corfu, Igoumenitsa, or Patras. Best of all, if you can extend your holiday in Italy, join the following itinerary, *Exploring the Wonders of Sicily*.

Exploring the
Wonders of Sicily

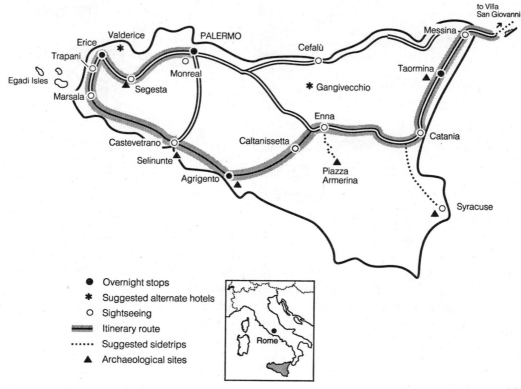

Exploring the Wonders of Sicily

Greek Theater, Taormina

Sicily, the largest island in the Mediterranean, is a wondrous destination. This triangular hunk of land jutting out from the tip of Italy's toe became the crossroads of the ancient world. Nowhere in your travels can you discover a more diverse archaeological treasure-trove. Stone-Age tools and figures carved in the Grotta di Addaura at Monte Pellegrino indicate people were living in Sicily during the Palaeolithic Age. About 1270 B.C. the island was invaded by a Mediterranean tribe called Siculians. But they were not the only settlers: excavations show the arrival of tribes from Asia. Beginning in the 10th century B.C., pioneering Phoenicians took a fancy to this fertile land, followed later by their descendants, the Carthaginians. However, the true dawn of Sicily's reign of glory began with the colonization by the Greeks whose enormous influence permeates Sicily today. However, the rich fabric of Sicily's heritage does not end with the Greek influence: later the Romans invaded, then the Normans, then the Spanish, and on and on. This resulting melting pot of cultures makes Sicily an absolute MUST for those who delight in the romance of archaeology. The true magic of Sicily is that most of the ruins are so natural in their setting. Frequently you discover you are alone—the only tourist walking through a field of wildflowers to gaze in awe at an exquisite temple.

As mentioned, the greatest age of glory for Sicily began when the Greeks founded their first colony here about 770 B.C. Apparently these early Greeks left their native country for economic and political reasons, but many were also undoubtedly motivated by pure curiosity—the desire to discover what awaited across the sea. Like the immigrants who came to America, the early settlers wanted a fresh start in a new land and an opportunity to establish a better life for themselves. And they did. Prospering enormously from the richness of the fertile soil, the early Greeks became extremely wealthy. As the *nouveau riche* tend to do, they flaunted their success, building great cities, elaborate houses, theaters, spas, and stadiums—all bigger and better than those they left at home. Syracuse, the mightiest city in Sicily, eventually became more powerful than Athens. The temples they built surpassed in size and splendor those left in their native land. Not losing their passion for sports, every four years the new colonialists sent their finest athletes back to Greece where they dominated the Olympic games.

ORIGINATING CITY   TAORMINA

Exploring the Wonders of Sicily makes a natural extension from the previous driving tour, *Highlights of Southern Italy*. After ending that itinerary, drive to the tip of Italy's toe and take one of the ferries that cross the narrow channel twice an hour from **Villa San Giovanni** to **Messina**, Sicily. After buying your ticket, go to the indicated lane and wait with all the trucks, campers, and other cars for the signal to drive onto the boat.

When on board, you may leave your car and go upstairs to the lounge area where snacks can be purchased while traversing the short channel. In 35 minutes the large ferry draws up to the pier in Messina and you drive off to begin your adventures.

If you prefer to fly to Sicily, just reverse this itinerary. Start in Palermo and finish in Taormina. Alternatively, you can take a ferry from Naples to Palermo (a ten-hour journey).

Taormina makes an ideal starting point for your introduction to Sicily. Whereas good hotels are scarce in most of Sicily, there are many to choose from in Taormina. We recommend the luxury-category **San Domenico Palace** (a museum-quality 15th-century monastery that has been converted into a world-class hotel) and also the moderately priced **Hotel Belvedere** (combining the charm of a family-run hotel with a stunning location overlooking the sea).

Picture-perfect Taormina, with the dramatic peak of **Mont Etna** as a backdrop, hugs the crest of a small peninsula that juts out to the sea. Steep cliffs drop to the unbelievably blue sea. Quaint streets wind through the colorful town where you can browse in the many smart boutiques, sip a cappuccino at a small café, or simply enjoy the incredible view. The scent of oranges is in the air and brilliantly colored bougainvilleas lace the medieval buildings.

However, it is not just the natural beauty of its spectacular setting that makes Taormina so popular. As in all of Sicily, your leisure pleasure is enhanced with fabulous sights to see. The prime archaeological target for your sightseeing is the **Greek Theater**. From the center of town an easy walk up Via Teatro Greco takes you to a magnificent theater dug into the sloping hillside above the town. Built by the Greeks in the 3rd century B.C., the open-air amphitheater has only a token few of its original columns remaining, making the effect even more romantic. As you gaze beyond the rows of seats to the stage below and out to the vivid blue sea beyond, you will think there is no prettier picture in all of Italy.

After visiting the Greek Theater, most of the remainder of your sightseeing can be done informally while strolling through town. First pick up a map and general information at the tourist office located in the **Palazzo Corvaia,** a 15th-century palace located on the Piazza Vittorio Emanuele. From the Palazzo Corvaia, continue through town and stop at the 17th-century **St. Giuseppe Church** in Piazza Nove Aprile. As you walk on, be sure to step inside the 13th-century **cathedral** in the Piazza del Duomo to enjoy the paintings. Farther on you come to the 12th-century **Torre dell'Orologio,** the portal that leads into the oldest and most colorful part of Taormina, **Borgo Medieval.**

DESTINATION I   AGRIGENTO

When it is time to leave Taormina, follow the A18 south toward Catania. When you reach Catania, take the A19 west in the direction of Palermo, then when the highway splits (not long after passing Enna), instead of continuing north to Palermo, head southwest in the direction of Caltanissetta and Agrigento. After Caltanissetta, the expressway ends and you are on a two-lane road for the final leg of your journey to Agrigento.

Along the route from Palermo to Agrigento, we recommend two side excursions. It would make your day too long to include them both, but if you get an early start, you can squeeze in enough time for one of them.

Suggested Side Excursion: If you are a Greek history buff, take this 128-kilometer detour to see one of the wealthiest, most powerful cities of the ancient Greek Empire (rivaling only Athens in importance). When you reach Catania, don't turn west toward Palermo, but continue south, following signs to **Syracuse,** founded in 734 B.C. by the Corinthians. In the **Archaeological Park** at the edge of town are two theaters—a 6th-century B.C. **Greek Theater** (one of the most magnificently preserved in the world) and the ruins of a 2nd-century A.D. **Roman Amphitheater** (one of the largest arenas the Romans ever built). From the Archaeological Park, skip the sprawling modern city and cross the Ponte

Nuovo that spans Syracuse's harbor to **Ortygia,** the island where the Greeks first founded Syracuse. Visit the two main squares, the beautiful **Piazza del Duomo** where the cathedral (built upon the ancient temple of Minerva) is located and the **Piazza Archimede** enhanced by a baroque fountain. After sightseeing in Syracuse, return to Catania and take A19 west in the direction of Palermo.

Suggested Side Excursion: If you are a Roman history buff, take this 74-kilometer round-trip excursion to visit the **Villa of Casale.** En route from Taormina to Agrigento on the A19, turn south at Enna to Piazza Armerina. Continue southwest beyond Piazza Armerina for 5 kilometers to your sightseeing target, Villa of Casale, rivaling in splendor the home built by Tiberius on the island of Capri. The foundations of this sumptuous Roman villa were hidden under a blanket of mud for 700 years—not discovered by archaeologists until 1950. The fact that this ostentatious villa was built when the Roman Empire was on the verge of financial ruin is all the more fascinating. You cannot help wondering if the obviously vast expense of its construction was indicative of the flamboyant spending style that led to the collapse of the Roman Empire. Built in the 3rd century A.D., this mansion surely must have belonged to someone of great importance—perhaps Emperor Maximilian. What remains is the outline of an enormous, summer home complex, with various buildings cut into the levels of the hillside, joined by passageways and courtyards. In all, the home covers an area almost three times the size of a football field. The outstanding feature is the 3,500 square meters of mosaics that decorated the floors of this sumptuous villa. Following the home's foundations are 40 mosaic floors of extraordinary quality, sheltered by a clear protective cover. These beautifully preserved ancient Roman mosaics are considered the finest in the world. Slip back almost 1,700 years and imagine what life must have been like: the scenes show hunting expeditions, wild animals, mythical sea creatures, chariot races, cupids fishing, slaves working, girls cavorting. Once you have visited this Roman showplace, return north to Enna, then turn west following the route to Agrigento.

Exploring the Wonders of Sicily

Thankfully, your hotel is not in the center of **Agrigento,** which is a congested, not very pretty city. Instead, follow the signs for the **Valle dei Templi**. This is the archaeological zone where both your sightseeing and hotel are located. The name is misleading: the site is actually on a plateau to the west of town—not in a valley at all. Go directly to your hotel, the **Villa Athena,** and get settled. The Villa Athena has a somewhat commercial ambiance and buses will probably be parked outside since (due to its convenient location

in the heart of the archaeological zone) this is a favorite luncheon stop for small tour groups. But although this is not an intimate hotel, the management is friendly and the setting incomparable. In Agrigento, the Villa Athena is definitely THE place to stay. Ask for a room with a view of the archeological zone—these cost a bit more, but are worth it. To wake up in the morning and look across at the sun rising on the Temple of Concordia is certainly the way to begin your day of sightseeing.

Plan to spend two nights in Agrigento so that you can spend one entire day leisurely seeing the ruins. From the gardens of the Villa Athena, walk down a footpath directly to the area where the temples are located. A wide pedestrian road connects the temples—start at one end and see them all. Most of these Doric temples are in ruins, with only enough columns remaining to give you an idea of what they used to be in their glory. The best preserved is the **Temple of Concordia** which dates back to 440 B.C. See them all: the **Temple of Juno,** the **Temple of Hercules,** the **Temple of Dioscuri,** the **Temple of Jupiter,** and the **Temple of Castor and Pollux**. The setting is beautiful with the sea in the distance and wildflowers in the surrounding fields. It is a thrill to stroll from one temple to the other, marveling at their grandeur and trying to envision what these incredible structures dedicated to Greek gods looked like 2,000 years ago.

To complement your sightseeing at the temples, walk to the **Archaeological Museum** (take the same path as to the temples, but go in the opposite direction). The museum has a mock-up of the Temple of Jupiter, plus many vases and artifacts from the site.

DESTINATION II   ERICE

From Agrigento, continue west on 115 toward Castelvetrano. About 10 kilometers before you arrive in Castelvetrano, turn left on the 115 dir toward the coast, signposted to Selinunte. For such major ruins, there is little commercialism. You might well miss the main east entrance on the 115 dir—as you drive toward the coast, look for a parking area to the right of the road (if you go under the railroad tracks, you have gone too far).

Park your car in the designated area, buy your ticket, and walk through the tunnel into the enormous field where the remains of the temples of Selinunte lie scattered amongst the wildflowers. In its prime, **Selinunte** was one of the finest cities in Sicily. It met disaster in 407 B.C. when the Carthaginians (it is thought under the command of Hannibal) razed the city, slaughtered 16,000 people, and took thousands into slavery. The giant temples, however, were probably destroyed by earthquake, not by the sword. Here, spread along a huge plateau overlooking the ocean, are the impressive remains of some of the most gigantic temples built by the Greeks. It is staggering to imagine how more than 2,500 years ago they had the skill and technology to lift and piece together these huge blocks of stone weighing over 100 tons each (slaves undoubtedly helped). Of the original seven temples, only one has been reconstructed, but the massive columns lying on the ground indicate the scope and grandeur of what used to be.

From Selinunte, return to the A 115, taking the coastal route to Erice. Stop for lunch at one of the restaurants along the seafront promenade in **Mazara del Vallo**, an ancient city that was at one time a colony of Selinunte. Browse through the historical center to see the beautiful **Piazza della Repubblica** and the **cathedral**.

The next large town after Mazara del Vallo is **Marsala**, a large city well-known throughout the world for its excellent wine. Ironically, it was not an Italian, but an Englishman named John Woodhouse who experimented by lacing the native wine with a bit of alcohol.

Based on Woodhouse's formula, Marsala quickly became one of the staples of the British Navy and a special favorite of Lord Nelson. Along the road between Selinunte and Marsala are various wineries that are open to the public. One of the most popular is the **Florio Winery**—one of the three original companies to produce Marsala.

From Marsala, the road heads north to Trapani. Bypass Trapani and head northeast to **Erice**. Positioned over 750 meters above the coast (about 10 kilometers from Trapani), Erice is a delightful medieval walled town, cooled by breezes from the sea. Park your car and walk through the **Porta Trapani** and up the cobbled street. A few blocks

on your right is the **Moderno**, a friendly, well run small hotel. The Moderno is simple, but very pleasant, and well located in the heart of town, close to restaurants and shopping. There are no deluxe hotels in Erice.

Erice is best discovered by exploring on foot. Narrow cobbled streets and steep stairways form a maze throughout the town which is so small that you cannot get lost for long. Just wander, discovering tiny churches, picturesque squares, characterful stone houses, arcaded passageways, and shops selling the locally-produced handmade carpets with colorful geometric designs. Walk to the **Castello Normanno,** built upon the ruins of the Temple of Venus. From the tower you have a splendid view over looking the town of Trapani and out to the sea.

Erice, Sicily

If you like to get off the beaten path, from Erice drive down to Trapani and take a hydrofoil to the **Egadi Isles,** all within an hour by boat from Trapani. Just a short distance off shore, **Favignana** the largest of the three islands, was once a great center for tuna. The major cannery was owned by Ignazio Florio (the same Florio who founded the Florio Winery). **Levanzo**, the smallest of the islands, has a very small population due to its lack of fresh water. The island farthest from Trapani, **Maréttimo**, is basically a fisherman's island.

Erice also makes a convenient base for an excursion to visit **Segesta.** Wind down the hill from Erice and turn left on the A29 going east in the direction of Palermo. Thirty kilometers after getting on the freeway, take the Segesta exit and follow signs for the Segesta archaeological site, located close the highway. Although

Exploring the Wonders of Sicily

you have seen many ruins by this stage of your holiday in Sicily, don't miss this one—it is special. First drive to the designated parking area and walk up the hillside to visit what most experts believe to be the world's finest example of a **Doric Greek temple**. The temple with 36 columns looks much as it must have in 400 B.C. There is no roof—there never was because this isolated temple to some unknown God was never completed. One of the most superb aspects of this temple is its setting—there is nothing to jar the senses. The temple stands alone in a field of wildflowers with great natural beauty all around. Leisurely enjoy the romance of this gem, then drive down the hill and park your car by the information center where there is a nice restaurant. Eat lunch here and then walk the marked path to see the **Greek Theater**. It is about a kilometer away, but a lovely walk through untouched fields. There are so few signs, you'll wonder if you are going the right way and be tempted to verify your destination with a fellow tourist you pass en route. Again, the location is what makes this theater so special. What an eye the Greeks had for beauty: the stage is set in such a way that the spectators look out across the mountains to the sea. The theater is mostly in ruins, but sit in one of the ancient benches and enjoy the beautiful surroundings and imagine dramas that took place over 2,000 years ago.

DESTINATION III   PALERMO

Palermo is a large, rather dismal, traffic-congested city. However, there are several places of interest to see in the area. Happily, as a saving grace, Palermo has an excellent place to stay, the deluxe **Villa Igiea Grand Hotel**. Located on the edge of the sea, on the west edge of town, the Villa Igiea is expensive, but a welcome oasis of peace and quiet. It has a swimming pool on the bluffs above the sea and even has its own small ancient temple in the garden. *NOTE:* If you want to skip overnighting in Palermo, the following sightseeing suggestions could also be accomplished from Erice.

The most dramatic sightseeing excursion (just 8 kilometers south of Palermo) is to visit **Monreale**, an awesome cathedral built by William II in 1174. It seems that William II was visited in a dream by an angel who told him of a secret treasure. With his new-found wealth he built Monreale, one of the world's greatest medieval monuments. From the outside, the cathedral doesn't look special, but just wait: the interior is stunning. When you step inside you find are 130 panels of shimmering mosaic, illustrating stories from both the Old and the New Testaments. The bronze doors of the cathedral are spectacular, designed by Bonanno Pisano in the 12th century.

Another sight near Palermo is **Monte Pellegrino**, a 600-meter mountain rising on the west edge of the city. There are several caves in the mountain. The **Grotta di Addaura** is a three-chamber cave with carvings dating to the Palaeolithic Age. Another cave has been transformed into a chapel, the **Sanctuary of Santa Rosalia** commemorating Santa Rosalia, the niece of King William II, who became a hermit—living and dying in this cave. You need to obtain permission from the National Archaeological Museum in Palermo if you want to visit these caves.

Another recommended side trip from Palermo is to visit the ancient fishing village of **Cefalù** built on a rocky peninsula about an hour's drive east from Palermo. Not only is this a very colorful fishing village, complete with brightly hued boats and twisting narrow streets, but there is also a splendid Norman **cathedral** built by King Roger II in the 12th century in fulfillment of a promise he made to God for sparing his life during a storm at sea.

When you are ready to leave Palermo there are several choices. You can take one of the many flights from Palermo to Rome, board a ferry to Naples, or complete your circle of Sicily by driving to Messina for the short ferry ride back to the mainland.

Exploring the Wonders of Sicily

Hotel Descriptions

There is a fascinating area in southeastern Italy with a collection of strange round white buildings with gray-stone conical-shaped roofs. These ancient houses, which seem to be left over from some Moorish tribe that must have inhabited this part of Italy long ago, are called *trulli* and are usually seen in groups of two or three. In the town of Alberobello there is actually a whole village of the conical little houses whose jumble of domed roofs, whitewashed walls, and crooked little chimneys creates a most unusual sight. Fortunately there is a good hotel in the area that is located within walking distance of the trulli village. Not only is its location excellent, but the hotel captures the mood of the area since it is constructed within some of the trulli houses. Small bungalows are scattered around a large parklike area connected by winding pathways under the pine trees. Each bungalow is actually a suite with a living room with fireplace, one or more bedrooms, and a private patio. The recently renovated suites are spacious with attractively tiled bathrooms. The dining rooms and the reception area each occupy their own trulli. Within the grounds are a pool and children's play yard. If you are on your way to Greece, you will find the Hotel dei Trulli a convenient choice: very close to Brindisi and Bari, the two major ferry ports.

HOTEL DEI TRULLI
Manager: Luigi Farace
Via Cadore, 28
70011 Alberobello (BA), Italy
Tel: (080) 93 23 555 Fax: (080) 93 23 560
28 rooms, Double: Lire 340,000*
*Rate includes breakfast and dinner
Open all year
Credit cards: all major
Restaurant open daily
68 km NW of Brindisi, 55 km SW of Bari

If you've ever dreamed of waking up in an Italian villa where you could open your bedroom windows to one of the world's most romantic views, then the Albergo Belvedere will surely capture your heart. This lovely 18th-century villa with its mustard-yellow façade, crisp-white trim, and dove-gray shutters has a superb setting. Only a private terrace separates it from Lake Como. Amazingly, this intimate inn is an incredible value—but do not expect a luxury hotel: the dated furnishings are simple. The guestrooms have direct-dial phones, but do not have satellite TVs, hair dryers, or mini-bars. What you get is much more: an incomparable setting, genuine warmth of hospitality, and old-fashioned comfort enhanced by immaculate housekeeping. An added bonus is the outstanding food. Giorgio Cappelletti oversees the kitchen which produces not fancy gourmet dishes, but just simple home cooking in the best Italian tradition. There is no menu: your selection each evening is based upon what is the catch of the day and what produce is in season. Jane Cappelletti (born in Scotland) met and fell in love with Giorgio when visiting Italy. Her friendliness and Scottish eye for a tidy house are great assets. Steamers and hydrofoils depart from the dock just steps from the hotel, but you might never want to leave the terrace with its view of the ever-so-blue lake backdropped by magical green mountains which shelter clusters of romantic villages. Splurge and ask for a view of the lake. Rooms 7 and 15 are especially inviting.

ALBERGO BELVEDERE
Owners: Jane & Giorgio Cappelletti
Via Milano 8
22010 Argegno, Lake Como (CO), Italy
Tel: (031) 82 11 16 Fax: (031) 82 15 71
18 rooms, Double: Lire 160,000
Open mid-March to mid-November
Credit cards: MC, VS
Restaurant open daily
On E shore of Lake Como
70 km N of Milan

As the road twists and turns ever farther into the wooded hills above Assisi, one can't help wondering what treasure could await at the trail's end, or if anyone could possibly have found it before you. What a surprise then to finally turn off the graveled road and discover the parking lot filled with luxury cars. In this secluded hillside setting with a sweeping panorama of wooded hills, worldly cares quickly slip away. Although the hotel is built into a cluster of ancient stone houses (dating back to the 10th century), all the modern-day luxuries are present including a beautiful swimming pool on the right as you enter and, on a lower terrace, tennis courts. Behind the main building is a separate stone house where you find a most appealing lounge with deep-green sofas and chairs grouped around a giant fireplace. Doors from the lounge lead into an intimate little bar and beyond to a dining room with honey-colored stone walls, beamed ceiling, and terra-cotta floors with tables dressed in the finest of linens. The individually decorated bedrooms sport a rustic, yet elegant, ambiance. The well equipped bathrooms offer enormous towels, fragrant soaps, hair dryers, and bathrobes. *NOTE:* Le Silve di Armenzano is not in the town of Assisi. To find the hotel, follow the signs from Assisi toward Gualdo-Tadino and immediately as you leave the town walls of Assisi, watch for and take the road to the right signposted Armenzano. When you reach Armenzano, the hotel is well marked.

ROMANTIK HOTEL "LE SILVE DI ARMENZANO
Manager: Daniela Taddia
06081 Localita Armenzano, Assisi (PG), Italy
Tel: (075) 80 19 000 Fax: (075) 80 19 005
15 rooms, Double: Lire 270,000
Closed January & February
Credit cards: all major
Restaurant open daily
Located 15 km E of Assisi
USA Rep: Euro-Connection 800-645-3876

Asolo is a beautiful medieval town in the low-lying hills northwest of Venice, dominated by castle ruins on the hillside above and filled with charming streets, Gothic arcades, and frescoed façades. It is here in this magical town where one of our favorite hotels in Italy, the Villa Cipriani, is secreted in a garden just a short stroll from the center of the village. However, since the price tag at the Cipriani does not fit everyone's budget, for those who do not want to splurge on accommodations, a good alternative choice is the Hotel Duse. Although lacking the romantic ambiance of the Villa Cipriani, its location is superb—right in the very heart of Asolo, surrounded by quaint streets lined with elegant shops. The Hotel Duse's management is very personalized yet very professional—friendly, helpful, and eager to please in every way. There is a tiny reception lobby leading up to the guestrooms that have all been renovated since our last visit. We have not seen the new decor, but the owners wrote that the bedrooms (which previously had a modern motif) now exude a cozy provincial charm. Each room has air conditioning, television, direct-dial phone, mini-bar, and a spotlessly clean bathroom.

HOTEL DUSE
Manager: Donatella Dal Monte
Via Browning, 190
31011 Asolo (TV), Italy
Tel: (0423) 55 241 Fax: (0423) 95 04 04
14 rooms, Double: Lire 200,000
Open all year
Credit cards: all major
No restaurant, breakfast only
65 km NW of Venice, 14 km E of Bassano

The Villa Cipriani is just as I had envisioned in every dream of Italy: an old villa snuggled on a hill, her softly faded exterior emphasized by dark-green shutters, masses of roses creeping over trellises, columns adorned with vines, lazy views over rolling green hills, faded ocher-colored walls half-hidden by tall cypress trees dotting nearby hilltops, birds singing in the garden, the sentimental rhythmical peal of church bells, a pianist on the terrace playing old love songs, the fragrance of flowers drifting through the air like the finest perfume, a balmy night under the stars—perfection. My impression of a romantic paradise must not have been a unique experience for in the garden was a wedding party. A beautiful bride, a handsome groom, they had fallen in love at the Cipriani and had returned with family and friends from the United States for their marriage. The Villa Cipriani is located in Asolo, a charming, small, medieval, walled hilltown less than two hours northwest of Venice which has an atmosphere so delightful that Robert Browning chose it as a residence. And the home he chose? The Cipriani. Luckily, his home is now a hotel and you, too, can live for a while in Asolo. Although the Villa Cipriani is a sophisticated, polished hotel, the warmth of reception is as gracious as in a small, family run inn: the manager, Giuseppe Kamenar, personally sees that all of his guests are properly pampered.

VILLA CIPRIANI
Manager: Giuseppe Kamenar
Via Canova, 298
31011 Asolo (TV), Italy
Tel: (0423) 95 21 66 Fax: (0423) 95 20 95
31 rooms, Double: Lire 404,800–536,800
Open all year
Credit cards: all major
Restaurant open daily
65 km NW of Venice, 14 km E of Bassano
U.S.A. Rep: Luxury Collection 800-325-3589
* or Relais & Chateaux 212-856-0115*

The Hotel Subasio is located in Assisi with one wall forming part of the ancient square in front of the Basilica of St. Francis. The hotel is linked to the basilica by an arched colonnade. The setting is marvelous, with the rear of the hotel facing the beautiful Umbrian countryside. On the lower level there are several glorious terraces romantically shaded by vines. Many of the rooms also have splendid vistas over the valley. Request one of the deluxe rooms with a balcony—these are delightful. The Subasio's public rooms are pleasant, but rather stilted and formal, but you will not be inside much anyway. The terraces are magic: to sit and watch the lovely fields mellow in the evening sun with that very special glow that is so characteristic of Umbria is certainly one of life's real pleasures. It is no wonder that many celebrities have chosen the Hotel Subasio for residence when visiting Assisi: such famous names as Charlie Chaplin and James Stewart grace the guest book. Andrea Rossi personally oversees the management of the hotel and there is a friendliness in the air from the gentle maid who turns down your bed in the evening to the charming waiter who helps select your local wine with dinner.

HOTEL SUBASIO
Owner: Sergio Elisei
Manager: Andrea Rossi
Via Frate Elia, 2
06081 Assisi (PG), Italy
Tel: (075) 81 22 06 Fax: (075) 81 66 91
56 rooms, Double: Lire 260,000
10 suites Lire 300,000–320,000
Open all year
Credit cards: VS
Restaurant open daily
177 km N of Rome, 26 km E of Perugia

For a moderately priced place to stay in the heart of Assisi, the Hotel Umbra is an unbeatable choice. The hotel is located just a few steps down a narrow little alley that leads off the Piazza del Commune, one of the central plazas in town. The entrance is through wrought-iron gates that open to a tiny patio where you are treated to an idyllic oasis with tables set under a trellis covered by vines that paint a lacy pattern of shadows. There is a lovely view from this intimate terrace. After passing through the patio, you enter into a lounge/reception area with doors opening into the dining room where very good meals are served. The public rooms have accents of antiques, but have a homey rather than grand ambiance. Steps lead to the simple bedrooms that are individually decorated. Most have been recently refurbished and are very pleasant. Splurge and ask for a room (such as 34) with a panoramic vista of the Umbrian valley. However, do not be disappointed if one is not available—the rooms (such as 35) overlooking the jumble of tiled roofs are also very nice. If you like small, family-run hotels that are not decorator perfect in every detail, but offer great heart and hospitality, the Hotel Umbra is an excellent choice. The delightful Alberto Laudenzi family oversee every detail of their small inn and make guests feel at home. The staff too is extremely gracious and accommodating. Best of all, the location is absolutely perfect.

HOTEL UMBRA
Owners: Alberto Laudenzi Family
Via degli Archi 6-Piazza de Comune
06081 Assisi (PG), Italy
Tel: (075) 81 22 40 Fax: (075) 81 36 53
26 rooms, Double: Lire 150,000–170,000
Closed mid-January to mid-March
Credit cards: all major
Restaurant closed Tuesdays
Central location off main square
177 km N of Rome, 26 km E of Perugia

The Hotel Florence is a moderately priced hotel in the charming ancient port of Bellagio. The location is prime—right on the main square. Across the street, next to the lake is a lovely, wisteria-covered terrace where you can have a snack while watching the boat traffic. If you are lucky enough to snare a front room with a balcony, you can step out through your French doors and be treated to a splendid view of Lake Como. There is a small reception area and, down a few steps to your left, an intimate lounge with a fireplace, beamed ceiling, and chairs set around tiny tables. A staircase leads to the upper floor where the guest dining room is located—it has no view of the lake, but does have a fireplace to warm the room on chilly days. There is also a gourmet restaurant open to the public. All of the guestrooms (which been redecorated with pretty new fabrics and antique furnishings) have satellite TV and hair dryers. Splurge and ask for the corner room with French doors opening onto a large terrace with lounge chairs invitingly set for viewing the lake. If you want to economize, room 19 is a very sweet standard room. The hotel is owned by the Ketzlar family, who are real pros—the inn has been in their family for over 150 years. It is now managed by Freidl Ketzlar, her daughter, Roberta, and son, Ronald—all speak excellent English and welcome guests with genuine hospitality.

HOTEL FLORENCE
Owners: Ketzlar Family
Piazza Mazzimi 42
22021 Bellagio-Lake Como (CO), Italy
Tel: (031) 95 03 42 Fax: (031) 95 17 22
38 rooms, Double: Lire 180,000–195,000
Suite: Lire 200,000
Open mid-April to mid-October
Credit cards: MC, VS
Restaurant open daily
Lakefront location
80 km N of Milan, 31 km NE of Como

The Grand Hotel Villa Serbelloni is certainly appropriately named—it definitely is "grand." In fact, the public rooms are almost overwhelming, with intricately painted ceilings, gold mirrors, fancy columns, Oriental rugs, gilded chairs, massive chandeliers, and a sweeping marble staircase. The bedrooms are quite nice, although I did not think the decor outstanding. However, the quality is superb: lovely percale sheets, soft down pillows, and large towels. The service, too, is excellent. Located in the gardens by the lake there is a large swimming pool. If you prefer sightseeing or shopping to swimming, the colorful old port of Bellagio is just steps from the hotel and if you tire of exploring the town of Bellagio, the ferry is only a few minutes away. If you want to be discreet, the concierge can arrange a special boat to pick you up at the private pier in front of the hotel. For sports enthusiasts, the Villa Serbelloni has added a fitness and beauty center, squash court, and two tennis courts. The original grandeur of the Grand Hotel Villa Serbelloni has faded, but if opulent surroundings and the feeling of living in a masterpiece of a palace appeal to you, I think you will enjoy your stay here. Pretend you are a guest at a weekend house party—given by royalty, of course.

GRAND HOTEL VILLA SERBELLONI
Owners: Bucher Family
Manager: Giuseppe Spinelli
22021 Bellagio-Lake Como (CO), Italy
Tel: (031) 95 02 16 Fax: (031) 95 15 29
85 rooms, Double: from Lire 419,000
13 apartments with cooking facilities*
*from Lire 900,000 (one-week minimum)
Open April 10 to October 20
Credit cards: all major
Restaurant open daily
78 km N of Milan, 31 km NE of Como
USA Rep: JDB Associates 800-346-5358

When visiting the charming medieval village of Bellagio, most travelers make a bee-line for a hotel steps from Lake Como. However, if you are looking for a very reasonably priced place to stay that affords a breathtaking view, then Il Perlo Panorama, located on the hill above Bellagio, certainly meets your requirements. Although the oldest part of the hotel dates back to the early 1900s, the construction of this boxy, three-story building looks new. The interior is modern with rather nondescript furnishings both in the public rooms and in the guestrooms. (Number 16 is one of the best—a pleasant corner room with a balcony.) However, although the decor is bland, there is certainly nothing commonplace about the view and you might never leave the concrete terrace that stretches in front of the hotel. From here a stunning, bird's-eye panorama spreads out before you: wooded hills extending steeply down to Lake Como and on beyond to a backdrop of soaring mountains. This prime piece of real estate has been handed down through the Sancassano family and is today managed by the gracious Piera Sancassano who speaks not only Italian, but a little English, German, and French. She personally sees that all of her guests are well taken care of. Remember, this hotel is inexpensive, so don't expect luxury. But if you are on a budget and yet want the romance of an awesome view of Lake Como, this just might fill the bill.

IL PERLO PANORAMA
Manager: Piera Sancassano
Via Valassina, 180
22021 Bellagio, Lake Como (CO), Italy
Tel: (031) 95 02 29 Fax: (031) 95 15 56
13 rooms, Double: Lire 115,000–130,000
Open Easter to October
Credit cards: all major
Separate restaurant just below the hotel
3 km south of Bellagio
80 km N of Milan, 31 km NE of Como

Although surrounded by a sprawling, uninteresting concrete metropolis, the center of Bologna shelters a fascinating maze of ancient twisting streets, arcaded passageways, marvelous shopping under porticoed walkways, and some of the best food in all of Italy. The Corona d'Oro, located in the heart of the medieval quarter, is a small, well managed hotel whose elegantly designed construction conserves architectural elements of various periods. In the inner courtyard (covered over with a skylight which rolls back to allow the room to return to its original open-air status) you can admire a portico that dates back to the 14th century. The hall and stairwell, exquisitely done in the Liberty style of the early 1900s, lead up to the bedrooms which are individually decorated, mostly with modern furnishings, but with a touch of the traditional in the sedate color schemes and prints nicely displayed on the walls. Some of the rooms have recessed block-panel ceilings with paintings of coats of arms and landscapes dating back to the 15th and 16th centuries. The hotel does not charge a premium for the few rooms that have small balconies or terraces.

HOTEL CORONA D'ORO 1890
Manager: Mauro Orsi
Via Oberdan, 12
40126 Bologna, Italy
Tel: (051) 23 64 56 Fax: (051) 26 26 79
35 rooms, Double: Lire 310,000–420,000
Closed August
Credit cards: all major
No restaurant, breakfast only
Located in heart of Bologna

In 1550, King John of Portugal decided to give a little gift to the Emperor Ferdinand of Austria, so he purchased an elephant in India, shipped it to Genoa, then planned to walk it to Austria. This giant beast grew weary about the time it reached Bressanone and was stabled for two weeks at the Am Hohen Feld Inn. Young and old came from far and wide to see this impromptu circus. The proprietor of the Am Hohen Feld was obviously a master at marketing: to maintain the fame of his establishment, he promptly renamed his hotel—you guessed it—the Elefant. A picture of our friend the elephant was painted on the front of the building commemorating the sensational event. But even without an elephant story this hotel is a winner. Although the bedrooms themselves are a little drab, they are immaculately clean and comfortable. In contrast to the simplicity of the bedrooms, the reception areas and dining rooms are lovely, incorporating antiques, museum-quality paintings, and magnificent paneling. The Elefant is also well-known for its dining—most of the eggs, butter, milk, fruit, and vegetables, and even the wine, come from the hotel's own farms. *NOTE:* Bressanone is called Brixen on some maps.

HOTEL ELEFANT
Manager: Karl Heinz Falk
Via Rio Bianco, 4
39042 Bressanone (Brixen) (BZ), Italy
Tel: (0472) 83 27 50 Fax: (0472) 83 65 79
43 rooms, Double: Lire 266,000–336,000
Open March to November & Christmas
Credit cards: all major
Restaurant closed Mondays
40 km NE of Bolzano, near Brenner pass

The Cenobio dei Dogi was formerly the summer home of the Genoese doges, so it is no wonder that it has such an idyllic location nestled on a small hill that forms one end of Camogli's miniature half-moon bay. From the hotel terrace there is an enchanting view of the tiny cove lined with marvelous narrow old fishermen's cottages painted in all shades of ochres and siennas. The hotel has a very nice swimming pool, as well as a private (though pebbly) beach. Many of the bedrooms have balconies boasting romantic views of this story-book scene. For tennis buffs, there is a tennis court, although I cannot imagine anyone wanting to play tennis with all the beautiful walking trails which make enticing spider-web designs on the peninsula. The Cenobio dei Dogi is a larger, less personalized hotel than most that appear in this guide, but although its decor seems a bit dated, the hotel possesses a solid, comfortable, no-nonsense kind of charm. It is not chic in the jet-set style of hotels frequently found on the Riviera. However, if you relate to lovely flower gardens, exceptional views, and slightly faded old-world comfort, you will like this hotel.

HOTEL CENOBIO DEI DOGI
Manager: Gianluca Bungaro
Via Nicolo Cuneo, 34
16032 Camogli (GE), Italy
Tel: (0185) 77 00 41 Fax: (0185) 77 27 96
110 rooms, Double: Lire 260,000–480,000
Closed January & February
Credit cards: all major
Restaurant open daily
Near Portofino–Italian Riviera
20 km SE of Genoa, 14 km NW of Portofino

As an alternative to staying in Florence, you might want to consider instead the Villa La Massa, a noble Renaissance residence. The hotel is located on the banks of the Arno—only about a 15-minute drive from the heart of Florence yet far removed from its noise and traffic. This beautiful estate originally belonged to the rich and powerful Giraldi family: inscribed tombstones, underground tunnels, and a chapel still remain from this period of the villa's history. Immediately after World War II, its present owners (the Broggini Grillini family) lovingly converted the villa into a hotel, carefully preserving the original features while at the same time offering all the comfort of modern luxury including tennis courts, a swimming pool, air conditioning, and refrigerators in the guestrooms. The restaurant, Il Verrocchio, has a beautiful terrace overlooking the Arno river for outdoor dining and offers the best of Tuscan specialties. If you have a car, then the Villa La Massa might make an appealing alternative to staying in the heart of Florence: especially in summer when you can do your sightseeing during the day and return to a pool and garden setting at night. There is also a courtesy bus service to take you into Florence or to the airport.

HOTEL VILLA LA MASSA
Owner: Carlo Grillini
Manager: Monique Roche
50012 Candeli (FI), Italy
Tel: (055) 65 10 101 Fax: (055) 65 10 109
40 rooms, Double: Lire 440,000–500,000
Open all year
Credit cards: all major
Restaurant open daily
Located on River Arno
7 km E of Florence

The Hotel Flora in the center of Capri is truly a delight. Just beyond the landmark Quisisana Hotel you find this stark white building reflecting the sun's rays and trimmed with lush deep purple bougainvillea vines. Signora Vuotto runs her hotel with great care and attention—striving to make her guests feel the Hotel Flora is their home away from home. She has succeeded. The small 24-room hotel has become known above all for its impeccable yet friendly service. The prim dining room (breakfast is the only meal served), with its smart yellow-and-green-striped armchairs and colorful ceramic plates lining the walls, opens out to a large terrace overflowing with potted Mediterranean flowers and miniature palms. When the weather is pleasant, guests linger on the terrace in comfortable wicker chairs while sipping their morning cappuccino and taking in the view over the San Giacomo ancient monastery and out to the sea. There is a fresh, perfumed air about this elegant jewel of a hotel which is carried out through the lovely bedrooms and suites finely decorated with antiques and colorful Pierre Deux fabrics. Each of the bedrooms has television, a small refrigerator, and, best of all, a terrace with a view of the famous Faraglioni rocks. Spotless bathrooms are tiled in typical Caprese style.

HOTEL FLORA
Owner: Virginia Vuotto
Via Federico Serena, 26
80073 Capri (NA), Italy
Tel: (081) 83 70 211 Fax: (081) 83 78 949
24 rooms, Double: Lire 250,000–350,000
7 suites: from Lire 400,000
Open Easter to October
Credit cards: all major
No restaurant, breakfast only
Island of Capri, ferry from Sorrento or Naples

The Hotel Luna savors one of the most beautiful locations on the Island of Capri. It is just a short walk from the village, yet, in atmosphere, it seems far away from the bustle and noise. The overall mood at the hotel is set by its delightful approach, a covered trellis pathway which in summer is completely shaded by brilliant bougainvillea and grape vines and bordered by flowers: a wonderful introduction to the Hotel Luna and to a restful interlude by the sea. To the left of the path as you approach the hotel, you see the Luna's large swimming pool surrounded by flowers and a view to the sea. The hotel is perched on the cliffs overlooking a spectacular coastline of green hills dropping straight into the sea, from which emerge giant rock formations. On two sides of the hotel there is a terrace with comfortable chairs where guests may enjoy this spectacular view. Just below the terrace is one of the most outstanding features of the hotel—an open-air restaurant set on a balcony that hangs out over the cliffs with an unsurpassed panorama of the sea. The guestrooms and lounges are decorated in pastel colors and the furnishings are reproduction, formal antiques. The ambiance is similar to that found in many commercial hotels. Splurge and ask for one of the best guestrooms that face the sea—although these cost more, the vista is memorable.

HOTEL LUNA
Manager: Luisa Vuotto
Viale Giacomo Matteotti, 3
80073 Capri (NA), Italy
Tel: (081) 83 70 433 Fax: (081) 83 77 459
44 rooms, Double: Lire 240,000–450,000
Open April to October
Credit cards: all major
Restaurant open daily
Island of Capri, ferry from Sorrento or Naples

Hugging a hillside with a ship's prow position overlooking the sea, the Hotel Punta Tragara is definitely one of Capri's landmarks. Whereas most of the island's villas and hotels have white façades that sparkle in the sunlight, the Hotel Punta Tragara is painted a deep sandy beige, accented by wrought-iron grills, dark-green shutters, and, of course, the profusion of flowers and greenery that make Capri so special. The hotel is reached by a pleasant 15-minute walk from the center of town—a path that dead-ends at the point where the hillside drops steeply down to the sea. Here the picturesque Faraglioni islands thrust their jagged peaks just below the hotel, affording fabulous views. Perhaps this spectacular setting is what made Eisenhower and Churchill choose the Punta Tragara for accommodation when they visited Capri. There is a certain formality to this small hotel—the staff seems professionally accommodating, but there is not the warmth often found in a small, family-run establishment. Sea chests, paintings of old sailing vessels, aged-bronze divers' helmets, ships' bells, and antique maps create a pleasing, nautical theme. It is not the decor, but rather the setting that makes Hotel Punta Tragara special. Request a deluxe room with a view. However, even if your room is not one of the deluxe category, you can settle by one of the two swimming pools and soak up the sun and scenery.

HOTEL PUNTA TRAGARA
Owner: Ceglia Goffredo
Via Tragara 57
80073 Capri (NA), Italy
Tel: (081) 83.70.844 Fax: (081) 83.77.790
35 rooms, Double: Lire 380,000–480,000
Open Easter to mid-October
Credit cards: all major
Restaurant open daily
Island of Capri, ferry from Sorrento or Naples

The Grand Hotel Quisisana conjures up the image of a Hollywood setting where the jet set gather. The women, adorned in jewels and the latest swimming ensembles, sit in the sun and gossip about the latest scandal while their husbands (or boyfriends?) sit pool-side drinking Scotch and playing the game of grown boys—discussing their latest business ventures. But it is all great fun and quite in the mood of Capri which has been a playground for the wealthy since the time of the early Romans. The Grand Hotel Quisisana is a deluxe hotel with a gorgeous oval pool overlooking the blue Mediterranean. The air of formal elegance appears as soon as you enter the lobby decorated with marble floors, soft-green velvet chairs, Oriental carpets, ornate statues, crystal chandeliers, and beautiful paintings. All the bedrooms are well appointed and the deluxe rooms even have separate his-and-hers half-baths. Room rates include breakfast and lunch or dinner and you can choose from almost anything on the menu. The Grand Hotel Quisisana most definitely provides a setting and atmosphere to reflect the image of, and cater to, their jet-set clientele.

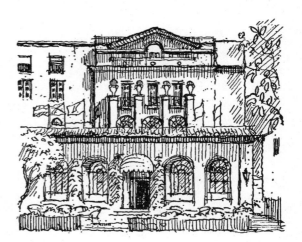

GRAND HOTEL QUISISANA
Ownesr: Morgano Family
Manager: Gianfranco Morgano
Via Camerelle, 2
80073 Capri (NA), Italy
Tel: (081) 83 70 788 Fax: (081) 83 76 080
150 rooms, Double: Lire 380,000–650,000
Open April to October
Credit cards: all major
Restaurant open daily
Island of Capri, ferry from Sorrento or Naples
USA Rep: LHW 800-223-6800

The Villa Brunella is a small jewel located on the most picturesque and peaceful street of Capri, the Tragara, only a ten-minute walk to the center of town. The modern hotel, overlooking the Marina Piccola, squeezes the greatest advantage from its narrow, very deep lot. The hotel is built on levels starting at the street level with the terrace restaurant and stepping down the steep hillside to the blue swimming pool—at this point, only halfway down to the sea level (the beach is only about a five-minute walk down the hill). The hotel is run more like a private home than a commercial hotel. The ever-gracious Vincenzo and his wife Brunella take great pleasure in entertaining guests and making them feel welcome. The 20 bedrooms, each with private bath, telephone, mini-bar, and air conditioning, are tastefully put together with pretty pink or powder-blue floral bedspreads and matching curtains. The cool ceramic-tiled floors, creamy-white walls, and potted plants add to the charm. Decoration in the rooms is really superfluous as the eye can hardly be torn away from the spectacularly dramatic views of the sea and island from one's own terrace. Simply heavenly.

VILLA BRUNELLA
Hosts: Brunella & Vincenzo Ruggiero
Via Tragara 24
80073 Capri (NA), Italy
Tel: (081) 83 70 122 Fax: (081) 83 70 430
20 rooms, Double: Lire 345,000
Suite: Lire 410,000
Open: Easter to October
Credit cards: all major
Restaurant open daily
Island of Capri, ferry from Sorrento or Naples

If you are approaching Florence from the west, perhaps on your way from Milan, we highly recommend stopping just before you reach Florence at the Paggeria Medicea. The hotel's address is Artimino, but the town is so small that I doubt you will find it on any map. Mark Carmignano on your map instead and when you arrive there you will find signs to Artimino, only a few minutes' drive farther on. The hotel is cleverly incorporated into what were once the pages' quarters for the adjoining 16th-century Medicea Villa La Ferdinanda. The long, narrow structure has been cleverly restored, preserving the many original chimneys which adorn the heavy, red-tiled roof. An open corridor whose heavily beamed ceiling is supported by a stately row of columns forms a walkway in front of the rooms. All of the guestrooms are simple, but very inviting, with tiled floors, pretty prints on the white walls, hand-loomed-looking white drapes hanging from wooden rods above the windows, and attractive antiques or copies of antiques as accents in each room. There is a snack bar in the same wing as the hotel, but the main restaurant, Biagio Pignatta (which serves simple but delicious Italian cooking), is located in a nearby building which at one time housed the butler for the villa. If you are a guest at the hotel, you can enjoy the use of the swimming pool, two tennis courts, and a running track, in addition to having access to a delightful small Etruscan museum situated in the vaults of the adjoining Medicea Villa La Ferdinanda.

PAGGERIA MEDICEA
Manager: Alessandro Gualtieri
Viale Papa Giovanni XXIII
50040 Carmignano-Artimino (FI), Italy
Tel: (055) 87 18 081 Fax: (055) 87 18 080
37 rooms, Double: Lire 180,00–270,000
Open all year
Credit cards: all major
Restaurant closed Wednesdays
20 km SW of Florence, 15 km S of Prato

CASTELLINA IN CHIANTI   HOTEL IL COLOMBAIO   Map: 8c/d

We happened upon this inn during our exploration of Italy's glorious Tuscany region, well-known for its rolling, vineyard-covered hills. Just as the road curved into the small town of Castellina in Chianti, we noticed an inn we had never seen before and stopped for an inspection at the Hotel Il Colombaio. The building is very old—probably at one time a farmer's home with its typical heavy-tiled roof, thick walls, and courtyard. This comfortable inn is owned by the Baldini family and Roberta Baldini, the gracious daughter, is the manager. She speaks very good English and gave us a complete tour of the small hotel. The guestrooms are quite inviting, many with wrought-iron beds and antique accents giving an appealing country flavor. There are 15 rooms and 1 suite in the main house, with 6 more rooms in a small annex across the street. All have private bathrooms and are fresh and pretty. The dining room is especially cozy, again decorated with a rustic motif in keeping with the Tuscany countryside. A Continental breakfast is the only meal served here, but Roberta is happy to recommend a good local *ristorante* for dining. On hot summer days, a welcome bonus is the swimming pool, located on a terrace behind the inn. (As a reader pointed out, the pool is nice, but not as dramatic as the one depicted in the hotel brochure.) For a reasonably priced place to stay with an old-world ambiance, the Hotel Il Colombaio is a welcome addition to the Tuscany region.

HOTEL IL COLOMBAIO
Owner: Baldini Family
Manager: Roberta Baldini
Via Chiantigiana, 29
53011 Castellina in Chianti (SI), Italy
Tel & fax: (0577) 74 04 44
22 rooms, Double: Lire 140,000
Closed November
Credit cards: all major
No restaurant, breakfast only
21 km N of Siena on road 222

The Tenuta di Ricavo is unique—not a hotel at all in the usual connotation, but rather a tiny village with peasants' cottages which have been transformed into delightful guestrooms. The stables are now the dining room and the barn is now the office. Unlike many of the over-renovated hotels in Tuscany where much of what you see is almost 100% new construction, Ricavo is **all** real, an authentic Tuscan hamlet of stone cottages (attractively furnished with antiques) which have been lovingly restored to retain their original rustic charm. You enter the large property along a lane that leads through a huge pine forest where small cottages are nestled in amongst the trees. Gardens are everywhere and roses embellish the weathered stone cottages, giving them a fairy-tale appearance. The total effect is absolutely enchanting. Before it became a hotel, the village was the summer-holiday home of a Swiss family, who, after World War II, transformed it into an exquisite resort. The family seeks no publicity, nor do they need it: the hotel is always filled with fortunate guests who have discovered this paradise. However, the Tenuta di Ricavo is not for everyone. It is quiet. It is remote. It is unstructured. But it is a haven for the traveler for whom a good book, a walk through the forest, a swim in the pool, a drink at sunset, and a delicious dinner are fulfillment. Excellent English is spoken—especially by the gracious Christine Lobrano.

ROMANTIK HOTEL TENUTA DI RICAVO
Owners: Lobrano-Scotoni Family
53011 Castellina in Chianti (SI), Italy
Tel: (0577) 74 02 21 Fax: (0577) 74 10 14
23 rooms, Double: Lire 280,000–420,000*
*3-night minimum, 7-night minimum high season
Open mid-March to November
Credit cards: MC, VS
Restaurant closed Mondays and lunch on Tuesdays
21 km N of Siena on road 22, 50 km S of Florence
USA Rep: Euro-Connection 800-645-3876

Castelrotto, a medieval village abounding in old-world character, is located in the heart of the Dolomite mountains in northeastern Italy. In the center of town, the Hotel Cavallino d'Oro faces the market square which highlights an especially quaint, colorfully painted fountain. The entrance to the hotel is signposted with a golden horse, reflecting the name of this 14th-century inn. The façade is a deep-mustard color highlighted by dark-green shutters and flowerboxes overflowing with cheerful geraniums. There is a traditional, old-world atmosphere throughout this small inn. All of the guestrooms are individual in decor, and nicely furnished in a typical Tyrolean style. Three rooms with light-pine, four-poster beds are especially pretty. From the beginning of its history the Cavallino has always provided accommodations. When first documented in 1393, the inn was a coaching station providing food and rooms for the weary traveler and facilities to care for the horses. The original hospitality is certainly ongoing. Susanne and Stefan (both of whom speak excellent English) have now taken over as the third generation of the Urthaler family to run the hotel. Not only do they exude a boundless, youthful enthusiasm and a gracious warmth of welcome, they are also constantly upgrading their small hotel by incorporating more antiques into the decor and renovating guestrooms. The dining room was closed on the day of my visit, but Stefan tells me the kitchen is excellent, with the chef specializing in regional dishes.

HOTEL CAVALLINO D'ORO
Owners: Susanne & Stefan Urthaler
39040 Castelrotto (Kastelruth) (BZ), Italy
Tel: (0471) 70 63 37 Fax: (0471) 70 71.72
24 rooms, Double: Lire 85,000–150,000
Open all year
Credit cards: all major
Restaurant closed Tuesdays
140 km S of Innsbruck, 24 km NE of Bolzano

A book on the most charming hotels in Italy would not be complete without including one of world's premier hotels, the Villa d'Este. Originally the hotel was a private villa built in 1568 by Cardinal Tolomeo Gallio. He obviously had elegant (and expensive) taste, for the Villa d'Este is truly a fantasy come true. From the moment you enter the enormous lobby with the sweeping staircase, marble, crystal, soaring ceilings, statues, and columns surround you. Everything is elaborate and ornate. The bedrooms are all elegantly furnished—no two are alike, but all are beautiful with color-coordinated carpets, wall-coverings and bedspreads. Some of the bedrooms have prime locations overlooking the lake. Although the interior is lovely, it is the outside where the fun really begins. The hotel opens onto a large terrace where guests relax with refreshing drinks. Just a short distance beyond the terrace is the lake where there is a dock for boats and a very large swimming pool which extends out over the water. Tucked away in the park there are eight tennis courts, and in the nearby area, seven golf courses. However, the most stunning feature of the Villa d'Este is the park: it surrounds the hotel with lovely pathways winding between the trees, a jogging course, glorious flower gardens, statues, and even a formal garden with dramatic mosaic colonnade.

VILLA D'ESTE
Manager: Marco Sorbellini
22010 Cernobbio, Lake Como (CO), Italy
Tel: (031) 34 81 Fax: (031) 34 88 44
156 rooms, Double: from Lire 775,000
Open March to November
Credit cards: all major
Restaurant open daily
53 km N of Milan, 5 km N of Como (town)
USA Rep: LHW 800-223-6800

Conveniently located about midway between Rome and Florence, La Frateria di Padre Eligio makes an excellent base for exploring the beauties of Tuscany and Umbria. However, this very special hotel is so utterly bewitching that you will be tempted to forego any idea of sightseeing and not set foot from the property. The guestrooms in this 13th-century convent (founded by St. Francis) are housed in the original guest quarters where the friars lodged passing pilgrims. They are simply, yet tastefully, furnished with antiques. There is nothing to interrupt the enchantment—bathrooms and telephones are the only concessions to the modern era. The silence is sweetened by the song of birds and the air by the fragrance of flowers. A centuries-old forest surrounds the hotel with beckoning paths where you can stroll in perfect stillness. The restoration of this masterpiece of history is superb, but the miracle is how it was accomplished. La Frateria di Padre, in addition to housing a deluxe hotel, is home to a commune of once-troubled young people who toiled for 12 years to bring the Convento San Francesco back to its former beauty. Today these remarkable young men and women awaken at 6 am to begin long days of labor. They meticulously groom the gardens, tend the vegetable garden, run the hotel, bake the fresh breads, prepare the meals (exclusively using produce from the farm), and serve in the restaurant.

LA FRATERIA DI PADRE ELIGIO
Manager: Maria Grazia Daolio
Convento San Francesco
53040 Cetona (SI), Italy
Tel & fax: (0578) 23.80.15 or 23.82.61
7 rooms, Double: Lire 280,000–380,000
Open mid-February to January 6
Credit cards: all major
Restaurant open daily
89 km SE of Siena, 62 km NW of Orvieto

The Villa Anna Maria is located in Champoluc, a small town at the end of the beautiful Ayas valley which stretches north into the Alps almost to the Swiss border. The glaciers of the Monte Rosa (one of the 4,000-meter peaks of the Alps) provide a glorious backdrop as you drive up the valley. Champoluc is a well-known ski center in winter as well as a favorite mountain summer resort. As you drive through Champoluc you see a small sign for the Villa Anna Maria on the right side of the road just before you leave town. Turn right on this little lane which winds up the hill and look for the Anna Maria on your right, set in a serene pine grove. The Villa Anna Maria is not a luxury hotel, but rather an old mountain chalet that is now a simple, but very charming, inn. A large deck for sunning stretches across the entrance. Inside there is a lovely dining room—my favorite room—which exudes warmth and coziness with its wooden Alpine-style country chairs, wooden tables, and gay red-checked curtains at the windows. Upstairs, the bedrooms are not luxurious but most agreeable, with wooden paneling on the walls and a rustic ambiance, each one with a private bathroom. The atmosphere is homey— wonderful for those seeking a friendly country inn in a mountain village.

VILLA ANNA MARIA
Owner: Miki Origone
Via Croues, 5
11020 Champoluc, Monte Rosa (AO), Italy
Tel: (0125) 30 71 28 Fax: (0125) 30 79 84
20 rooms, Double: Lire 184,000
Open all year
Restaurant open June 20 to mid-September,
  December 10 to mid-April
Mountain location–NW Italy
175 km NW of Milan, 100 km N of Turin

The Ca'Peo, a well-known restaurant serving some of the finest food in Italy, is located high in the coastal hills south of Genoa. You might think you will never arrive as the road winds ever upward through groves of olive and chestnut trees. But the way is well signposted, and just about the time you might be ready to despair, you will find a wonderful old farmhouse, owned by Franco Solari, who is host and in charge of the wines, and his wife, Melly, who is the chef. As we checked in, the entire family was in the kitchen busily chopping vegetables, rolling out pastry, and preparing the fish for the evening meal. The dining room, enclosed on three sides by large arched windows, takes advantage of a sweeping view to the sea. Be aware that the meals are **very** expensive, but if you appreciate fine food and wines, superb. Dining is definitely the main feature; however, in a modern annex there are five suites available for guests who want to spend the night. The decor here is not antique, but each of the large suites is pleasant, and after lingering over a wonderful meal accompanied by delicious wines, how nice to walk just a few steps to your bed. A final note: The Ca'Peo is only about half-an-hour's drive from the popular resort of Portofino, so you might want to stay here instead or at least treat yourself to a memorable meal—but call ahead as reservations are necessary.

CA'PEO
Owners: Melly & Franco Solari
Via dei Caduti, 80
16040 Chiavari a Leivi (GE), Italy
Tel: (0185) 31 96 96 Fax: (0185) 31 96 71
5 suites: Lire 190,000
Closed November
Credit cards: AX, VS
Restaurant closed Mondays
6 km N of Chiavari toward Leivi
44 km SE of Genoa, 22 km NE of Portofino

The 16th-century Locanda del Sant'Uffizio, originally a Benedictine monastery, then a farm, has been converted over the years by Signor Giuseppe Firato (Beppe), a native of this tiny village, into a delightful resort offering 35 guestrooms and an exquisite restaurant serving the finest of Piedmontese cuisine. All furnishings are antique and every detail of the decor has been rigorously overseen personally by Signor Beppe and his wife, Carla, with the result being a very tasteful, elegant, yet relaxed hotel cozily nestled amongst vineyards in the hills of Monferrato with its own swimming pool and tennis court. There are many features that make the Locanda del Sant'Uffizio very special, but, without a doubt, the Firato family is responsible for the ambiance of warmth and hospitality that radiates throughout the hotel. Signor Beppe speaks no English, but he does not need to—his charismatic charm transcends all language barriers. It is no wonder his one-Michelin-star restaurant—isolated in the countryside—is filled each night with chicly dressed Italian clientele: Beppe greets each of them with an exuberant warmth, and the food is outstanding, truly a gourmet delight. Since we originally visited the Locanda del Sant'Uffizio, Beppe and his wife have been joined in its operation by their two sons, Fabio and Massimo, who both speak English and French. Be aware that the meals and wine are **very** expensive.

LOCANDA DEL SANT'UFFIZIO
RISTORANTE DA BEPPE
Owner: Giuseppe Firato
Near Moncalvo
14030 Cioccaro di Penango (AT), Italy
Tel: (0141) 91 62 92 Fax: (0141) 91 60 68
*35 rooms, Double: Lire 480,000 **
**Rate includes breakfast and dinner*
Closed January & August 10–20
Credit cards: MC, VS
Restaurant open daily
5 km SE of Moncalvo, 60 km E of Turin
21 km N of Asti toward Moncalvo

The Hotel Menardi dates back over 200 years. Originally it was a peasant's farmhouse, but as Cortina's popularity as a fabulous ski center has spread, so has the town, and now the farm is located right on the outskirts of town on the main road heading north. Nevertheless, the Menardi family, who have owned the home for a century and a half, have managed to maintain the country flavor through the use of many antiques, nostalgic prints on the walls, old clocks, giant dowry chests, Oriental carpets, and beautiful hanging cupboards—all set off by the warmth and gaiety of flowers everywhere. The dining room is appealingly cozy and the delicious food is impeccably served. The individually decorated bedrooms are all attractive. In addition to the original inn which has 40 bedrooms, there is a new house in the back garden with an additional 15 rooms. It seems that, due to its location on the main road, the Menardi farm just naturally evolved into a hotel. At first it gave shelter to the men carting loads over the Cimabanche Pass who needed a place to sleep—more often than not in the hay loft. Today the inn is a simple, but wonderful, small hotel whose special ingredient is the old-fashioned warmth and hospitality of the gracious Menardi family who personally see that every guest is made to feel welcome.

HOTEL MENARDI
Owners: Menardi Family
112 Via Majon
32043 Cortina d'Ampezzo (BL), Italy
Tel: (0436) 24 00 Fax: (0436) 86 21 83
55 rooms, Double: Lire 150,000–230,000
Open July to September & Christmas to March
Credit cards: VS
Restaurant open daily
133 km E of Bolzano
71 km N of Belluno

Corvara, a mountain village in northeastern Italy, is popular with guests who enjoy walking through high Alpine meadows in summer and skiing down snow-covered slopes in winter. Although the Dolomite region is one of the most beautiful in Italy and offers many hotels, there is not a rich choice for visitors who prefer small inns with an old-world, antique ambiance. Luckily, La Perla, located in the center of Corvara, offers not only a convenient place to stay, but also a cozy ambiance. This small inn is owned and managed by the Costa family who lovingly oversee every detail. The day I visited, Signora Costa was busily engaged in supervising the table arrangements to be sure everything was perfect. You enter into a large reception lobby where heavy wooden beams, Oriental carpets on tiled floors, fresh plants, and country-patterned drapes set the mood. But the real winners are the dining rooms with a selection of lovely places to eat, each with its own personality—all absolutely oozing with cozy charm. Antique clocks, tiled ovens, low-beamed ceilings, painted chests, warm antique-wood paneling, abundant accents of copper, plus handsome linens, fresh flowers, and candlelight make each room a dream. The guestrooms have all the modern amenities, but do not display the old-world ambiance of the public rooms.

ROMANTIK HOTEL LA PERLA
Owners: Costa Family
39033 Corvara (BZ), Italy
Tel: (0471) 83 61 32 Fax: (0471) 83 65 68
50 rooms, Double: Lire 220,000–520,000
Open July to September
  and mid-December to Easter
Credit cards: VS
Restaurant open daily
65 km E of Bolzano, 47 km W of Cortina
USA Rep: Euro-Connection 800-645-3876

The Punta Est is a lovely old villa perched on a hilltop overlooking the sea. When the home was converted to a villa, an annex was added to provide more bedrooms, but it still gives the friendly feeling of a private home. This warmth of reception and attention to detail are the result of the management of the Podestà family who own and manage the inn. They seem dedicated to making your stay as enjoyable as possible—even their German Shepherd seems to want to welcome you. There are little terraces with lovely views snuggled at various levels among the trees and on one of these terraces is a swimming pool. There is also access to the public beach of Finale Ligure which can easily be reached by walking down the path to the main highway and following the tunnel beneath the highway to the beach. The rooms in the main villa are smaller and more old-fashioned than those in the newer annex which are more reminiscent of an American motel. There is a small dining room for breakfast which is especially inviting with its blue-and-white English bone-china service. This is just one example of a very nice touch offered by owners who really want to please.

HOTEL PUNTA EST
Owners: Podestà Family
Manager: Attilio Podestà
Via Aurelia N.1
17024 Finale Ligure (SV), Italy
Tel & fax: (019) 60 06 11
37 rooms, Double: Lire 340,000–440,000*
*Rate includes breakfast and lunch or dinner
Open May to October
Credit cards: AX, VS
Restaurant open daily
72 km SW of Genoa, 75 km E of San Remo

The Grand Hotel Villa Cora is a mansion, originally built during the 19th century by the Baron Oppenheim as a gift for his beautiful young bride. Among the many romantic tales of the Villa Cora is the one about Oppenheim's wife who, so the story goes, became enamored of one of her many admirers. The jealous baron was so enraged that he threatened to burn the entire mansion, but, luckily for you and me, he was stopped in time from this mad endeavor by his friends, and today this magnificent villa is a stunning hotel. Although only about a 5-minute taxi ride from the center of Florence (or a 15-minute walk), the Grand Hotel Villa Cora is eons away in atmosphere—you feel more like a guest on a country estate rather than in a city hotel. The interior of the hotel is rather ornate and sumptuous. The villa is set in intricate gardens and even has a pool. You can almost hear the sounds of laughter and music drifting through the gardens, and indeed the mansion has always been famous for its dramatic parties: at one time the villa was the residence of Napoleon's wife, Empress Eugenia, whose gay entertaining was the talk of Florence. Now this grand palace-like home can be yours for days of dreams and romance. There is free limousine service for guests to and from Florence.

GRAND HOTEL VILLA CORA
Manager: Luigi Zaccardi
Viale Machiavelli, 18/20
50125 Florence, Italy
Tel: (055) 22 98 451 Fax: (055) 22 90 86
48 rooms, Double: Lire 650,000–750,000
Open all year
Credit cards: all major
Restaurant open daily
15-minute walk from the heart of Florence
USA Rep: JDB Associates 800-346-5358

After being closed for two years for complete renovation, the Hotel Helvetia and Bristol reopened in late 1989 and instantly became, in my estimation, the finest luxury hotel in the center of Florence. Nothing has been spared to make this showplace a true beauty—the decor is outstanding. The lounges, exquisitely decorated with an elegant, yet extremely comfortable, home-like ambiance, exude quality without flamboyance. Each of the guestrooms is also superbly decorated, and, as in a private home, no two are alike. Abundant use of exquisite padded-fabric wall coverings, with color-coordinated draperies, upholstered chairs, and bedspreads along with lovely antiques make each one special. I fell in love with each of the rooms, but my very favorites were the mini-suites: room 257 in gorgeous shades of muted green and room 363 in lovely golds, creams, and dusty pinks, with a sumptuous marble bathroom with Jacuzzi tub, heated towel racks, plus the added bonus of a tiny terrace. The dining room, cozy yet elegant with dark walls and soft lighting, features Tuscan cuisine. For light refreshments, a cool drink, or just relaxing, the *Giardino d'Inverno* (Winter Garden) is a marvelous retreat—light and airy with a domed, old-fashioned skylight, potted plants, and nostalgic wicker furniture. The Helvetia and Bristol is expensive, but no more so than the other luxury hotels in Florence, and for those who appreciate quality and refinement, it is unsurpassed.

HOTEL HELVETIA AND BRISTOL
Manager: Franco Ensoli
Via dei Pescioni, 2
50123 Florence, Italy
Tel: (055) 28 78 14 Fax: (055) 28 83 53
52 rooms, Double: Lire 489,000–599,000
Open all year
Credit cards: all major
Restaurant open daily
In the heart of Florence
USA Rep: Relais & Chateaux 212-856-0115

Each time we visit the Loggiato dei Serviti, we are again impressed with what a pleasant small hotel this is for the money. Many of the hotels in Florence are lovely, but fabulously expensive: others are reasonably priced, but shabby and dark. So it is an exceedingly happy surprise to find a light, airy, antique-filled small hotel—at a reasonable rate. This is not a deluxe hotel, but we think you will be well pleased. The building dates back to the 16th century when it was built for the order of the Serviti fathers. The character of the original building has been meticulously maintained, adding greatly to the charm of the hotel. The location is superb: right in the heart of Florence on the historical Piazza SS Annunziata. There is a small reception area as you enter, beyond which is an intimate little bar where snacks are served (there is no restaurant at the hotel). A miniature elevator—just large enough for two people to squeeze into—takes you upstairs to the spacious bedrooms, each with private bath and each individually decorated in excellent taste with liberal use of antiques. There are four suites, one of which even has two bedrooms and two bathrooms. Although of course more expensive than the standard double room, these suites are most attractive and good value for a family.

LOGGIATO DEI SERVITI
Owner: Rodolfo Budini Gattai
Piazza SS. Annunziata, 3
50122 Florence, Italy
Tel: (055) 21 91 65 Fax: (055) 28 95 95
29 rooms, Double: from Lire 240,000
Open all year
Credit cards: all major
No restaurant, breakfast only
In the heart of Florence

The Lungarno Hotel is superbly located directly on the River Arno and only a few minutes' walk from the Ponte Vecchio. Although most of the hotel is of new construction, the architect cleverly incorporated an ancient stone tower into the hotel so it is easy to rationalize including this hotel—one of my favorites in Florence—into this travel guide. The interior of the hotel is traditional rather than antique in decor, but the decorating is done with excellent taste and the effect is most pleasing. Lovely soft colors are used throughout, with beautiful prints on the wall and many fresh flowers. The bedrooms are very comfortable and those who book well in advance can request one of the rooms overlooking the Arno. Those who really plan ahead might even be lucky enough to secure one of the few rooms with a large terrace overlooking the river—these rooms are very special and well worth the extra cost. What a treat to sit on your own terrace in the evening and watch the Arno fade into gold and the Ponte Vecchio glow in the setting sun. There are several rooms in the tower itself, one of which is especially romantic with its old stone wall and its staircase leading up to a little balcony and a third bed. Several of the other rooms in the new portion of the hotel also have lofts which can be used as sleeping alcoves.

LUNGARNO HOTEL
Manager: Nedo Naldini
Borgo San Jacopo, 14
50125 Florence, Italy
Tel: (055) 26 42 11 Fax: (055) 26 84 37
66 rooms, Double: from Lire 410,000
Open all year
Credit cards: all major
No restaurant, breakfast only
Short walk to Ponte Vecchio
Directly on the Arno River

Mario's came highly recommended to us by several readers, and after seeing the hotel for ourselves, we agree that it is a delightful small hotel, moderately priced for Florence. It is conveniently located two blocks from the train station, and within easy walking distance to the city's major sightseeing. From the street, the appeal of the hotel is not readily evident as it is housed in a rather nondescript building. But after ascending the stairs to the second floor and stepping into the cozy, beamed-ceilinged lobby, you know you've arrived at a well tended small hotel with an old Florentine ambiance. Facing the reception desk is an inviting sitting area with sofas arranged under a wall of pictures, Oriental carpets enhancing the dark tile floors, and artfully arranged pictures and plants setting off the cream-colored walls. All of the guestrooms have a country-fresh feeling with antique armoires, wrought-iron headboards, rustic wooden desks and chairs and pretty bedspreads. The rooms are not large, but are very pleasing and immaculately tidy. A copious breakfast is served family-style at long dining tables in a charming room whose walls are hung with many pictures. Guests choose from a wonderful selection of breads, cheese, yogurt, boiled eggs, coffee, tea, and chocolate. The nicest aspect of this hotel is the fact that it is small enough to be very personalized. Mario sees that every guest feels special, and will even (upon prior arrangement) give driving tours to Tuscany.

MARIO'S
Owner: Mario Noce
Via Faenza, 89
50123 Florence, Italy
Tel: (055) 21 68 01 Fax: (055) 21 20 39
16 rooms, Double: Lire 190,000
Open all year
Credit cards: all major
No restaurant, breakfast only
2 blocks from the Florence train station

The Regency is located on a small parklike square only a ten-minute walk from the heart of Florence. It is, however, a world away in atmosphere—instead of the noise of motorcycles and the bustle of tourist-filled streets, you have a peaceful, quiet, elegant setting. The mood of being away from it all is enhanced as you enter the hotel. Again you are protected: the front door is usually kept locked and only guests of the hotel are allowed inside. You ring the front door bell just as you would in a private home. Although small, the Regency is a deluxe hotel and, in fact, it is quite amazing that with only 38 rooms the Regency can offer so many of the luxuries that are usually found only in larger hotels, such as a concierge to assist you with any of your personal needs and an intimate restaurant in a gorgeous wood-paneled dining room. The bedrooms are spacious and luxurious, with lavish antique mirrors, excellent lighting and elegant marble bathrooms. I would prefer a few more antiques, but these are found mostly in the lounges and the dining room. At the present time, the Regency spreads into several adjacent homes with a garden connecting the wings.

HOTEL REGENCY
Owner: Amedeo Ottaviani
Manager: Pietro Panelli
Piazza Massimo d'Azeglio, 3
50121 Florence, Italy
Tel: (055) 24 52 47 Fax: (055) 23 46 735
38 rooms, Double: Lire 350,000–550,000
Open all year
Credit cards: all major
Restaurant open daily
10-minute walk to the heart of Florence
USA Rep: LHW 800-223-6800
 or Relais & Chateaux 212-856-0115

The Torre di Bellosguardo is a romantic villa nestled on the shelf of a hill with an unsurpassed view of Florence. Below the hotel, the tiled rooftops, steeples, towers, and domes of the city seem like a fairyland at your fingertips. It is not surprising that the setting of the Torre di Bellosguardo is so fabulous: it was chosen by a nobleman, Guido Cavalcanti (a friend of Dante's), as the most beautiful site in Florence on which to build his home. The villa is owned today by Amerigo Franchetti who inherited the fabulous property from his grandmother, a baroness. All of the guestrooms are decorated in antiques and vary in size as they would in a private home. The most splendid feature of the hotel is its gorgeous setting and meticulously groomed garden which highlights a swimming pool set on a terrace overlooking Florence. What a delight to relax after a day of sightseeing and watch the beautiful buildings below you melt in the twilight, to reappear as a panorama of twinkling lights. In summer lunch is served by the swimming pool, but otherwise breakfast is the only meal served, so guests must wind back down a narrow twisting road to go to a restaurant. However, many guests feel this is a small price to pay for the opportunity to live in a secluded villa, away from the hustle and bustle of the city.

TORRE DI BELLOSGUARDO
Owner: Amerigo Franchetti
Via Roti Michelozzi, 2
50124 Florence, Italy
Tel: (055) 22 98 145 Fax: (082) 22 90 08
16 rooms, Double: from Lire 440,000
Suite: Lire 590,000
Open all year
Credit cards: all major
No restaurant, breakfast only
Lunch served by the pool during summer
5-minute drive to the heart of Florence

The Bencista is a real find for the traveler looking for a congenial, appealing, family-run hotel near Florence that has charm and yet is reasonably priced. This delightful old villa, romantically nestled in the foothills overlooking Florence, is owned and managed by the Simoni family who are always about, personally seeing to every need of their guests. Simone Simoni speaks excellent English, and on the day of my arrival he was patiently engrossed in conversation with one of the guests, giving him tips for sightseeing. Downstairs there is a jumble of rooms, each nicely decorated with rather dark Victorian furniture. Upstairs are the bedrooms which vary in size, location, and furnishings. Some are far superior to others; however, they are all divided into only two price categories: with or without private bathroom. Many people return year after year to their own favorite room. During the season, reservations are usually given only to guests who plan to spend several days at the hotel—this is an easy requirement because the hotel is beautifully located for sightseeing in both Florence and Tuscany. (If you do not have a car, you can take the bus that runs regularly into Florence from the top of the road.) Two meals (breakfast and a choice of lunch or dinner of family-style Italian cooking) are included in the price. One of the outstanding features of the pensione is its splendid terrace where guests can enjoy a sweeping panorama of Florence.

PENSIONE BENCISTA
Owner: Simone Simoni
50014 Fiesole (FI), Italy
Tel & fax: (055) 59 163
44 rooms, Double: Lire 250,000*
Double without private bath: Lire 210,000*
*Rate include breakfast, and dinner or lunch
Open all year
Credit cards: none accepted
Restaurant open daily, for guests only
8 km NE of Florence

It would be difficult to find another hotel with as many attributes as the Villa San Michele—in fact, almost impossible. How could you surpass a wooded hillside setting overlooking Florence, a stunning view, gorgeous antiques, impeccable management, gourmet dining, and, as if this were not enough, a building designed by Michelangelo. The Villa San Michele was originally a monastery whose inner courtyard dates back to the 15th century. No expense has been spared in the reconstruction of this fabulous building to maintain the ancient ambiance. There are only 26 guestrooms, and, although not large, they are decorated with elegant taste. In addition, there are ten suites, two located in the Villa San Michele, six in the Italian garden, and two in the *Limonaia*. All have stunning views of Florence and the Arno valley. The lounges, dining rooms, terraces, and gardens are also exquisite. Meals can be enjoyed either in a beautiful dining room or on a lovely veranda that stretches along the entire length of the building. A swimming pool has been built on a secluded little terrace above the hotel and, as with every feature of the Villa San Michele, it is beautiful, perfectly situated to capture the view and surrounded by fragrant gardens.

VILLA SAN MICHELE
Manager: Maurizio Saccani
Via Doccia, 4
50014 Fiesole (FI), Italy
Tel: (055) 59 451 or 59 452 Fax: (055) 59 87 34
36 rooms, Double: Lire 990,000–1,240,000*
*Rate includes breakfast, and dinner or lunch
Open March to November
Credit cards: all major
Restaurant open daily
7 km NE of Florence
USA Rep: LHW 800-223-6800
* or Relais & Chateaux 212-856-0115*

Nestled in the foothills of the Alps, in the small town of Follina, you'll find a jewel of a hotel, the Romantik Hotel Abbazia. Situated across from the picturesque 12th-century abbey from which it draws its name, the Hotel Abbazia reflects the tranquillity of the abbey's famed cloister. As you enter the 17th-century palazzo graced by fine antiques, Oriental carpets, and lovely flowers, you feel as if you are being received at the Zanon family home. Each of the palazzo's 17 rooms is superbly decorated by the Zanons in an English country-manor style, with every room given its own individual character. You'll also find six suites in the recently restored 19th-century Liberty-style villa across the garden from the main palazzo. Although there is no restaurant, the Abbazia is surrounded by excellent places to dine, one example being the superb Ristorante da Gigetto, located in a delightful villa brimming with country antiques. In the cellar is an outstanding wine collection with an incredible selection of priceless wines beautifully displayed in a museum-like setting. Just ask the owner, Gigetto, to give you a tour. For lovers of art and architecture, the area is rich in medieval villages and Palladian villas. Just 20 kilometers from Follina is the charming town of Asolo in one direction and in the other, the historic town of Vittorio Veneto

ROMANTIK HOTEL ABBAZIA
Owner: Zanon Family
Via Martiri della Liberta
31051 Follina (TV), Italy
Tel: (0438) 97 12 77 Fax: (0438) 97 00 01
17 rooms, Double: Lire 195,000–240,000
6 suites: Lire 280,000–360,000
Open all year
Credit cards: all major
No restaurant, breakfast only
90 km S. of Cortina, 60 km NW of Venice
USA Rep: Euro-Connection 800-645-3876

I was enchanted with the Villa Fiordaliso (a fetching pink and white villa superbly located on the shore of Lake Garda) when I spent the night in one of its antique-filled bedrooms overlooking the lake several years ago. At that time, I wrote a glowing description of this beautiful little hotel, only to learn from the manager that I was one of the last guests—the villa was closing to the public. Nevertheless, when researching for a later edition, I went by the Villa Fiordaliso for old times' sake and, to my delight, found it open again as a small hotel. Although the emphasis now is definitely on dining (the meals are expensive, but excellent), there are seven bedrooms—each unique in decor, yet each with every modern comfort. The rooms facing the lake have a lovely view and are quieter since they are away from the noise of the street. Throughout the interior there is a blend of antique and stylish modern furniture, nicely set off by ornate parquetry floors, cool marble pillars, and magnificent gilded and painted ceilings. For history buffs, the villa offers a bit of romance—the Villa Fiordaliso was a gift from Mussolini to his mistress, Claretta Petacci. In fact, Claretta's bedroom is one of the rooms available and is a real winner, with an enormous marble bathroom. The Villa Fiordaliso is owned and managed by the Tossetti family whose warmth of welcome mellows the sophisticated ambiance of this small hotel.

VILLA FIORDALISO
Owner: Giuseppe Tossetti
Via Zanardelli, 132
Lake Garda, 25083 Gardone Riviera (BS), Italy
Tel: (0365) 20 15 8 Fax: (0365) 29 00 11
7 rooms, Double: from Lire 300,000
Suites: to Lire 700,000 (Claretta's suite)
Closed Nov 1 to Dec 20 & Jan 7 to Feb 12
Credit cards: all major
Restaurant closed Mondays
130 km E of Milan, 66 km W of Verona

La Foresteria Serègo Alighieri is in a working farm producing wine and olive oil. Only a discreet brass sign on the gate hints at any commercialism, yet it is indeed a fabulous place to stay. Each reasonably priced guestroom is a one- or two-bedroom apartment with a well equipped kitchen, charming living room, and a large bathroom tiled in local marble. The decor throughout reflects tasteful, elegant simplicity—whitewashed walls set off country antiques, and comfortable sofas are upholstered in Venetian pure-cotton fabrics in green and cream stripes. Soft-green is repeated in the pretty cotton drapes and bedspreads. It is not surprising that La Foresteria has been developed with such love and meticulous care to maintain the estate's authentic charm—the present owner, the gracious Count di Serègo Alighieri, is the 20th generation to own the property! Family records indicate the first ancestor to own the land was the poet Dante's son, who purchased the estate in 1353. This vast farm was almost doomed at the end of World War II when the receding armies had orders to destroy it. As a forestalling tactic, the present count's father invited the commanding officers to a magnificent party. Perhaps it was the abundance of the excellent wines served, but happily the officers forgot their orders. To celebrate this miracle of the saving of the town, every April the local town people make a pilgrimage to the estate to celebrate mass—followed, of course, by a little wine.

LA FORESTERIA SERÈGO ALIGHIERI
Owner: Count Pieralvise di Serègo Alighieri
Via Stazione 2
37020 Gargagnago di Valpolicella (VR), Italy
Tel: (045) 77 03 622 Fax: (045) 77 03 523
8 apartments Double: Lire 140,000–260,000
Open February to December
Credit cards: all major
No restaurant, breakfast* on request
 *Lire 12,000 per person
18 km NW of Verona, 20 km E of Lake Garda

When we first saw the Hotel Villa Giulia it was rated by the government as a third-class pensione, but the hotel is no longer a simple pensione. On our last visit we were pleased to note that all the rooms now have a private bathroom and even a swimming pool has been built in the garden. The inn is a Victorian-style villa in a large park that extends down to Lake Garda. A dramatic staircase at the end of the hallway leads to the simple bedrooms. In addition to the rooms in the main villa, guestrooms are available in a modern annex. Although not fancy, all of the rooms offer satellite television, mini-bar, and safe. On the same level as the entrance hall is a dining room which is quite appealing, with enormous chandeliers and antique-style chairs. On a lower level, opening out onto the garden, is another dining room which is quite modern and lacking in charm. When the weather is warm, the favorite place to dine is on the terrace where tables are set to enjoy the sun and a view of the lake. Wherever you choose to dine, you will enjoy good home-style Italian cooking—it is not surprising that the food is well prepared since Signora Bombardelli, the owner, is usually bustling about in the kitchen personally overseeing the preparation of the next meal. She does not speak much English, but is extremely gracious and is always about seeing that her guests are happy. The Hotel Villa Giulia offers a pleasant stay at reasonable prices and a superb lakefront location.

HOTEL VILLA GIULIA
Owner: Rina Bombardelli
Via Rimembranza, 20
25084 Gargnano, Lake Garda (BS), Italy
Tel: (0365) 71 289 Fax: (0365) 72 774
30 rooms, Double: Lire 280,000
Open April to October
Credit cards: none accepted
Restaurant open daily
140 km E of Milan, 78 km W of Verona

The entrance to Baia d'Oro is off the narrow cobbled street that runs through the quaint lakeside town of Gargnano-Villa. Once inside, there is a small lounge, intimate bar, and a dining room. To truly appreciate the attributes that make this small inn so very special, you must step outside to the terrace which stretches out over the water. In the daytime this sun-drenched oasis is a favorite with the luncheon crowd, then in the evening as the sun sets, fresh flowers and candles are placed on small tables dressed with fresh linens: a romantic scene that will beckon you again and again to the Baia d'Oro. The food lives up to all expectations: the pasta is homemade in the kitchen, the fish is fresh from the lake. As you dine there is a constant parade of beautiful yachts pulling up to the dock, unloading their cargo of laughing, chicly dressed, obviously well-to-do Italians who have come to dine. After dinner, you go up a narrow staircase to the basic bedrooms which are perfect for the young of heart who are not expecting decorator-perfect furnishings. The Baia d'Oro is owned by the Terzi family (Gianbattista Terzi is a well-known artist). Their son, Gabriele, has taken over the management and does a superb job personally orchestrating the dinner each evening and seeing that all overnight guests are happy.

BAIA D'ORO
Owner: Terzi Family
Manager: Gabriele Terzi
Via Gamberera, 13, 25084 Gargnano-Villa
Lake Garda (BS), Italy
Tel: (0365) 71 17 1 Fax: (0365) 72 56 8
13 rooms, Double: Lire 300,000*
*Rate includes breakfast and dinner
Open April to October
Credit cards: all major
Restaurant open daily
140 km E of Milan, 78 km W of Verona

Romantically surrounded by a vast estate of olive trees, vineyards, and long avenues of towering cypress trees, the Castello di Uzzano is ideally located in the heart of Tuscany. Without disturbing the authentic charm of the 12th-century castle, six apartments (facing the fortified courtyard) have been incorporated into the walls of the castle. Each apartment has a complete kitchen so breakfast is not included in the price of the room (although, upon prior notice, breakfast can be ordered, also lunch or dinner for small groups). However, most guests seem to prefer buying fresh produce in the local markets and fixing simple meals at home. Each of the one- or two-bedroom apartments is decorated using color-coordinated fabrics and handsome antiques. One of my favorite apartments (the least expensive) is *Il Madonninio* with a country-cozy living room and sweetly decorated bedroom. My other favorite (the most expensive) is *Nidcolò da Uzzano* whose spacious rooms are decorator-perfect in every detail. There is a two-night minimum, but for guests who can stretch their stay, the rates go down. I have left the very best for last: terraced below the 15th-century villa wing of the castle (the birthplace of Leonardo da Vinci's Mona Lisa) is an incredibly gorgeous, perfectly tended, formal garden—it must be the most beautiful in Tuscany. This garden is so outstanding, it would be worth a stay at Castello di Uzzano on its merits alone.

CASTELLO DI UZZANO
Owner: Marion de Jacobert
Via Uzzano 5
50022 Greve in Chianti (FI), Italy
Tel: (055) 85 40 32 Fax: (055) 85 43 75
6 apartments Double: Lire 260,000–425,000*
*Breakfast not included, 2-night minimum
Open all year
Credit cards: all major
No restaurant
27 km SE of Florence, 40 km N of Siena

Finally there is a very special place to stay near the Rome airport. However, to merely say that a void has been filled is totally inadequate, for La Posta Vecchia without a doubt offers some of the most sensational accommodations in all of Italy—in all the world. Not that everyone will be able to afford to stay here, for this is an expensive small inn—very expensive, but if you have the money, it is a real bargain. This is the opportunity of a lifetime for those who want to taste the lifestyle of the rich and famous. La Posta Vecchia was the late John Paul Getty's home—his Italian villa nestled on the edge of the ocean just north of Rome's airport. Just imagine: there are only 17 rooms, mostly suites, tucked into an enormous mansion, secluded by manicured gardens artfully created to emphasize the ruins of a Pompeii-like Roman villa whose beautiful mosaic floor peeks from between surrounding flowers and hedges. Within the villa, priceless antique furniture, statues, and fabulous fabrics adorn the rooms, artfully blended by Getty's interior designer to create an opulent, tasteful splendor. For Getty nothing was too special, nothing too expensive. All has been retained as it was in Getty's day, the only changes being some cosmetic spiffing such as painting and new drapes (this was taking a while because the factory in Paris where the original fabric had been woven had to be tracked down—but replacements were on the way at the time of our visit). The new owner has accomplished a remarkable feat of returning the villa to its original magnificence. The primary use of the villa is for individual guests, but from time to time the hotel can be entirely rented for private conferences, think-tanks, seminars, or family reunions. If you want the entire villa for an exclusive holiday, you need have no worry about security since columns, discreetly positioned on each corner of the property, send out detector rays to keep anyone from the premises, while there is bullet-proof glass in the Getty bedroom and steel reinforcement in the walls. The East and West wings of the second floor in the villa have been artfully renovated and now host five guestrooms.

When Getty was renovating the villa for his personal use and installing the magnificent pool in the northern wing of the house, he found the villa dated back much earlier than he originally speculated. Beneath the house were the foundations of a Roman villa thought perhaps to be the weekend retreat of Julius Caesar. Getty, who was profoundly interested in archaeology, spared no expense to preserve this antiquity. The Roman ruins now encompass the lower level of the home and guests can wonder at the gorgeous mosaic floors, walls ,and pottery displayed as if in a living museum. Parts of the museum can be viewed from the upper level where a panel of glass has been installed in the floor so that the mosaic under-flooring can be viewed. Since La Posta Vecchia is sometimes rented to small groups there will be times when it isn't available for individual bookings. But if you are lucky and can snare a room, this is truly an experience of a lifetime.

LA POSTA VECCHIA
Manager: Harry Charles Mills Sciò
00055 Palo Laziale
Ladispoli (Roma), Italy
Tel: (06) 99 49 500 Fax: (06) 99 49 507
17 rooms, Double: Lire 640,000–840,000
Suite: Lire 1,340,000–2,140,000
Lunch or dinner: Lire 120,000 per person
Credit cards: all major
Restaurant open daily
2 km S of Ladispoli at Palo
25 km N of Rome Airport, 40 km NW of Rome
USA Rep: Relais & Chateaux 212-856-0115

Cinqueterre is the name given to five villages (Monterosso, Riomaggiore, Vernazza, Manarola, and Cornigllia) that are built into the mountainous coast of Liguria. Several of these picturesque villages are accessible only by foot or train. A favorite base for exploring these tiny fishing hamlets is the modest resort of Levanto. The Hotel Stella Maris is a simple, two-star hotel, but it exudes such warmth and caring that it is highly recommended to the traveler who values true hospitality rather than decorator-perfect accommodation. Not that the hotel is lacking in character: it is located on the second floor of a 17th-century palazzo and remnants of its past grandeur remain. Many of the bedrooms feature high, elaborately frescoed ceilings and handsome antique beds. I think my favorite is number 4, an especially inviting room with a romantic wooden French-style headboard. The dining room also has a frescoed ceiling and a fancy mural depicting a maharajah and his elephant train. Breakfast and dinner are included in the room rate. Several readers have written to us that they were disappointed in the food, though they enjoyed the hospitality of the owners. Although only a little English is spoken, Renza and Sandro exude a rare, merry warmth that is sure to touch your heart.

HOTEL STELLA MARIS
Owners: Renza & Alexandro Italiani
Via Marconi 4
19015 Levanto (SP), Italy
Tel: (0187) 80 82 58 Fax: (0187) 80 73 51
14 rooms, Double: Lire 260,000*
*Rate includes breakfast and dinner
Closed November
Credit cards: MC, VS
Restaurant open daily
83 km SE of Genoa, 36 km NW of La Spezia

Limone sul Garda is a small town tucked into a pocket of a hillside at the edge of Lake Garda. This very old town of pastel-colored houses adorned with bougainvillea and twisting cobbled streets attracts so many visitors that in high season it is wall-to-wall tourists. Nevertheless, the town is very quaint, and especially appealing off season when you can avoid some of the crowds. There are several large modern hotels on the hillside, but the Hotel Le Palme (in a building dating back to the 17th century) is in the heart of town, directly on the lake. Whereas many of our suggestions in the Lake Garda area are intimate, family-operated inns, Le Palme is a hotel with a more commercial ambiance. You enter into the lobby and go down a few steps to a small bar and an especially attractive dining room with handsome wooden, antique-style, high-back chairs and beautifully set tables. From the dining room, French doors open onto an appealing outside dining room on a balcony overlooking the lake. Along the side of the hotel is another, more casual, place to eat in a garden terrace overlooking the lake where white wrought-iron tables and chairs are set under the centuries-old palm trees among many plants and colorful flowers. The price is the same for all the guestrooms, but the ones overlooking the lake are prime. The rooms, all with satellite TV, are pleasant and a few have some antique pieces of furniture. The Risatti brothers who own Le Palme own several hotels in town and guests can use the pool at another of their hotels, La Pergola.

HOTEL LE PALME
Owner: Risatti Family
Via Porto, 36
25010 Limone sul Garda (BS), Italy
Tel: (0365) 95 46 81 Fax: (0365) 95 41 20
28 rooms, Double: Lire 190,000
Open Easter to October
Credit cards: all major
Restaurant open daily
160 km NE of Milan, 97 km NW of Verona

The Albergo del Sole, located about an hour's drive south of Milan, came highly recommended to us as one of Italy's finest restaurants with rooms so we arrived eagerly for our first visit. Happily, this little inn surpassed our highest expectations, offering an elegantly rustic setting and delicious meals. This 600-year-old farmhouse is now a food connoisseur's dream come true. From the moment you enter this old stone home you are enveloped in a country ambiance enhanced by fine antiques, heavy beams, copper pots hanging on the walls, and extravagant bouquets of flowers. The heart of the inn is its kitchen, long famous as one of Italy's finest, and well deserving of its Michelin star. The food, featuring regional specialties prepared from the freshest of locally produced ingredients, is **very** expensive, but outstanding. If you cannot overnight here, the inn is well worth a visit simply for its atmosphere and cuisine. However, if possible, plan to spend the night so you can linger over your dinner and savor the fine food and wines. Some of the guestrooms are in the main building, others are in rooms tucked around the back garden. Each of the bedrooms is nicely decorated, but with a much more modern mood than the dining rooms. Although the food and country-style furnishings are outstanding, it is the traditional Italian welcome and caring warmth of the owners, Franco Colombani and his sons Francesca and Mario, that make the Albergo del Sole so special.

ALBERGO DEL SOLE
Owners: Franco Colombani and Sons
Via Trabattoni 22
20076 Maleo (MI), Italy
Tel: (0377) 58 142 Fax: (0377) 45 80 58
8 rooms, Double: Lire 290,000–320,000
Closed January & August
Credit cards: all major
Restaurant closed Sunday evenings & Mondays
60 km S of Milan, 23 km W of Cremona

Clinging to the steep hillside above the beautiful coast of Basilicata, Maratea is a charming village of very old colorful houses and narrow cobbled streets. As the road loops ever-upward through the town, you soon come to the Locanda delle Donne Monache, carved into the rocky slope next to the tiny parish church of St. Maria. Originally a nunnery dating back to the early 1700s, the convent has been meticulously transformed into a deluxe small hotel. Obviously no expense was spared in the reconstruction—every detail exudes quality and refinement. The exterior—salmon-colored stuccoed walls with white trim and rustic heavy-tiled roof—blends well with other houses in the village. Inside, the color scheme continues with sky-blue added for accent. The dramatically decorated bedrooms are tucked throughout the hotel, each taking advantage of its special vista. The largest guestrooms are designated as suites. Number 9 is especially enchanting, with a stunning bathtub carved into the rocks and a pretty view out over the tiled rooftops. On the upper terrace next to the small church, a swimming pool seems to float in the air, suspended above the jumble of village rooftops. On balmy summer evenings guests enjoy superb meals outside under the stars. The quiet serenity that must have appealed to the nuns so long ago greets guests each morning as the sweet fresh air, the fragrance of flowers, the song of birds, and the church bells cast their spell.

LA LOCANDA DELLE DONNE MONACHE
Owner: Raffaele Bruno
Via Carlo Mazzei, 4
85046 Maratea (PZ), Italy
Tel: (0973) 87 74 87 Fax: (0973) 87 76 87
30 rooms, Double: Lire 300,000–450,000
Open April to October
Credit cards: all major
Restaurant open daily
220 km S of Naples, 5 km W of Maratea

The sienna-and-cream-colored, Liberty-style Villa Cheta Elite is located on the main coastal road just south of Acquafredda. A steep path winds up through the garden to the hotel, which has a series of tall French doors opening onto a shaded terrace where glimpses of the sea can be seen through the flowers and the trees. The hotel retains the genuine warmth and charm of a private home, without any hint of the formal commercialism of a hotel. Throughout there is a comfortable lived-in, old-fashioned elegance. The exceptionally gracious owner personally supervises every detail in the operation of his small hotel and welcome one and all as guests in a private home. Some of the staff speak English, but Lamberto does not need to—his smile and infectious laughter transcend any language barrier. Each bedroom is individually decorated using homey, family antiques. When the weather is balmy guests eat dinner on the terrace whose white wrought-iron tables are prettily set with fresh linens and bouquets of flowers from the garden. The home-cooked meals are outstanding. If you prefer small, family-owned hotels to the sophisticated glamour of expensive resort-style hotels along this magical coast of southern Italy, the Villa Cheta Elite will definitely win your heart.

ROMANTIK HOTEL VILLA CHETA ELITE
Owner: Lamberto Aquadro
Via Timpone, 46
85041 Acquafredda di Maratea (PZ), Italy
Tel: (0973) 87 81 34 Fax: (0973) 87 81 35
20 rooms, Double: Lire 160,000–190,000
Open March 26 to October 23
Credit cards: all major
Restaurant open daily, for guests only
1 km S of Acquafredda, 210 km S of Naples
USA Rep: Euro-Connection 800-645-3876

The Hotel Santavenere was a wonderful surprise. I had seen pictures of the hotel before I arrived and it looked rather like a motel—a long, narrow building with each floor a row of guestrooms. The photographs did not do it justice—the hotel is absolutely a knockout. From the moment you walk into the lobby, the gracious ambiance of an exquisite country home surrounds you. The living room is elegant, but not stuffy—soft, comfortable sofas and lounge chairs, slipcovered in an attractive country print, form cozy conversation nooks. Excellent antiques lend further charm and the many nautical accents, such as models of sailboats, give even more interest to the room. The dining room follows in excellent taste—a large, airy room with high-backed wooden chairs, fresh flowers on the tables, and white linen tablecloths. The bedrooms are beautifully decorated with excellent copies of antiques and have modern bathrooms. Each bedroom opens onto its own terrace or balcony with lovely sea views. The location too is exceptional: there is a lush lawn adorned with a swimming pool stretching to the side of the hotel. Beyond the lawn the cliffs drop down a steep wooded hillside to the crystal-clear deep-blue sea and a footpath winds down through the trees to a small pier.

HOTEL SANTAVENERE
Owner: I.T.G.P. S.p.A
Località Fiumicello di Santa Venere
85040 Maratea Porto (PZ), Italy
Tel: (0973) 87 69 10 Fax: (0973) 87 76 54
44 rooms, Double: Lire 420,000
Open June to September
Credit cards: AX, VS
Restaurant open daily, for guests only
220 km S of Naples, 5 km W of Maratea

The Castel Freiberg is a fantasy castle cresting a hilltop in the mountains near Merano. The location is truly superb. You wind up the mountains to the lovely old castle whose setting affords a sweeping view of the valley far below. Although the address is given as Merano, the hotel is actually in the mountains south of town. All of the public rooms are a decorator's dream where priceless antiques abound. The bedrooms are each individual in decor, and some have balconies overlooking the mountains. The dining room (with an antique green-and-white ceramic stove against one wall) is especially enchanting: its walls and ceiling are richly paneled in antique wood which has achieved a mellow patina with age. There is a beautiful pool in a garden setting with the mountains as a dramatic backdrop, as well as an inside pool, clay tennis courts, and an exercise room. For further exercise, a maze of splendid walking paths surround the hotel (the concierge can direct you to them). The Castel Freiberg has always been one of our favorites, but we have had some readers say that they thought the hotel staff not overly friendly and the decor in the guestrooms not especially tasteful. We will be eager for more feedback.

HOTEL CASTEL FREIBERG
Owners: Bortolotti Family
Via Labers
39012 Merano (BZ), Italy
Tel: (0473) 24 41 96 Fax: (0473) 24 44 88
30 rooms, Double: Lire 340,000–370,000
Open mid-April to November
Credit cards: all major
Restaurant open daily (dinner only)
In the countryside 7 km S of Merano
28 km NW of Bolzano

Castel Labers (also called Schloss Labers) is a lovely old castle that dates back to the 11th century. It has a picturesque setting on a hillside surrounded by vineyards and overlooking the beautiful Merano Valley which is framed by dramatic mountains. Although not luxurious, this castle has character and charm. Probably its major attribute is excellent management by the Stapf-Neubert family who oversee every detail of the operation and take personal responsibility to ensure that everyone is properly pampered. I spoke to Signor Neubert who told me that his great-grandfather came from Copenhagen in 1885 and bought the castle which became so popular with his visiting friends that it soon became a prosperous hotel. The lounges and dining rooms are not fancy, but have a lived-in, comfortable atmosphere. Many fresh foods are included in the menu and both red and white wines, produced from the inn's own vineyards, are served with meals. The central staircase leads dramatically upstairs where many of the bedrooms have lovely mountain views. The setting of this old castle is peaceful and quiet, and if you enjoy being in the countryside, you will delight in the marvelous network of walking paths that abound in this area.

HOTEL CASTEL LABERS
Owner: Stapf-Neubert Family
Via Labers, 25
39012 Merano (BZ), Italy
Tel: (0473) 23 44 84 Fax: (0473) 23 41 46
32 rooms, Double: Lire 240,000–290,000
Open April to November
Credit cards: all major
Restaurant open daily, for guests only
In the countryside 3 km NE above Merano
28 km NW of Bolzano

If you love picturesque chalet-style hotels in quiet, isolated surroundings, then the Hotel Vigiljoch will definitely be your cup of tea. There is absolutely no highway noise—there are no cars. The only way to reach the hotel is by cable car which you take from the town of Lana near Merano in the mountains of northeastern Italy. The cable car rises quickly from the floor of the valley and presents breathtaking views of the vineyards and apple orchards. When the cable car reaches the top and slowly joggles into the terminal, you will see the Hotel Vigiljoch just to the left of the station. In summer, flowers cascade from every windowbox and umbrellas gaily decorate the front terrace. Inside, you find quite simple bedrooms, many of which have balconies with a sweeping view of valley and mountains. The bedrooms are small but pleasantly furnished, with furniture painted in an Alpine motif. A sprinkling of antiques highlights the lounges. My very favorite room is an intimate, wood-paneled dining room whose wonderful country prints of blue and red are complemented by attractive light-pine furniture. The gracious owner, Karl Gapp, is extremely knowledgeable about what to see and do in the area. He is very active with the tourist office and can assist guests with their various travel plans.

HOTEL VIGILJOCH
Owner: Karl Gapp
39011 Vigiljoch
Lana bei Merano (BZ), Italy
Tel: (0473) 56 12 36 Fax: (0473) 56 14 10
35 rooms, Double: from Lire 130,000
Open mid-March to mid-November
Credit cards: none accepted
Restaurant open daily
Accessible only by cable car
9 km S of Merano on route 238
24 km NW of Bolzano

Hotel Carrobbio is located on a narrow side street, just a few steps off the Via Torino, a major street leading to the Duomo. From the outside the hotel appears nondescript—a not-too interesting, modern, four-story building. However, I was glad I stopped to take a look because this small hotel has a lot to offer. Not that it can compare with its neighbor, the elegant Hotel Pierre Milan, but the prices are much lower. The reception area is small and guests are greeted warmly. According to the friendly reception manager, Franco Grassi, the hotel is small enough to know guests by name: they are never just a number. Beyond the reception area is a bar which leads into a lounge with chairs and sofas upholstered in black leather. One end of the room is mirrored, reflecting puffy Austrian drapes and potted palms. A skylight, illuminating the core of the building, imparts a cheerful ambiance. Well-lit hallways lead to the bedrooms which are all similar in decor, with built-in headboards, good reading lights, color-coordinated bedspreads and chair coverings, mini-bars, and television. Ask for one of the bedrooms on the top floor—three of these have spacious terraces with tables and chairs for sitting outside when the weather is nice. A large buffet breakfast (served in a rather plain, white-walled room) is included in the room rate. One of the nicest aspects of the Hotel Carrobbio is that it is so well kept. Everything looks fresh and new—not surprising as the hotel only opened in 1990.

HOTEL CARROBBIO
Manager: Antonio Vivaldo
Via Medici
20123 Milan, Italy
Tel: (02) 89 01 07 40 Fax: (02) 80 53 334
35 rooms, Double: Lire 352,000
Open all year
Credit cards: all major
No restaurant, breakfast only
Located about a 10-minute walk from the Duomo

Milan has very few deluxe small hotels with character, but since the Hotel Pierre Milan came on the scene a few years ago, that need has been superbly fulfilled. The Pierre Milan is expensive, but no more so than other hotels in the same category. You walk under the canopy, through a large glass entry flanked by two handsome statues of prancing horses, and into the spacious reception lounge decorated in tones of beige accentuated by cream-colored marbles. Even when the hotel is fully booked, there is an air of quiet refinement. An inner courtyard provides a garden effect for the chic dining room with just a handful of tables, exquisitely set with fine linens. A hallway leads to the American bar, which opens onto a sophisticated, intimate lounge with black-leather sofas and a grand piano. The guestrooms are not large (except for the suites), but each is individually decorated in impeccable taste: walls covered with fine fabrics, color-coordinating with the carpets, drapes, and bedspreads. On the bedside table a control panel allows you to call housekeeping, turn off the lights, turn on the television, put a "do not disturb" sign outside the door, and even electronically lower the window shades without getting out of bed. Many rooms have an antique desk or writing table. One of my favorites, room 210 (with French-blue walls and drapes) has an antique wooden king-sized sleigh bed. The Hotel Pierre is located in the historically interesting Sant'Ambrogio district.

HOTEL PIERRE MILAN
Manager: Lorenzo de Lodi
Via De Amicis, 32
20123 Milan, Italy
Tel: (02) 72 00 05 81 Fax (02) 80 52 157
47 rooms, Double: Lire 370,000–500,000*
*Weekend specials (on request): Double: Lire 320,000
Closed August 1–21 & December 23–January 8
Credit cards: all major
Restaurant open daily
15-minute walk to the Duomo

We were delighted to find a hotel of character less than a ten-minute drive from the popular Milan Malpensa airport. And although the Hotel Villa Malpensa is not inexpensive, you can stay here for a fraction of the cost of staying in a fancy hotel in Milan, with the added bonus of knowing you don't have to rush to catch your early-morning flight. You can even squeeze in a quick swim in the pool before you leave for the airport. This stately, four-story formal mansion was once the home of the counts of Caproni (one of the wealthiest families of northern Italy). You enter into a formal hallway painted a soft-cream color, with a soaring ceiling, walls enhanced by ornate plaster sculpturing, marble floors, and Oriental carpets. Throughout the original core of the hotel, the past magnificence of this 1931 villa lives on through ornate architectural features. However, throughout the rest of the hotel there is no great flair to the decor—the contemporary furnishings are typical of a commercial hotel, but you cannot fault the amenities. All of the spacious guestrooms have built-in headboards with proper reading lights, comfortable mattresses, satellite televisions, mini-bars, direct-dial telephones, hair dryers, and air conditioning. Some of the bedrooms have balconies where you can watch the planes taking off and landing.

HOTEL VILLA MALPENSA
Owner: Fausto Bonini
Via Don Andrea Sacconago, 1
21010 Vizzola Ticino (VA), Italy
Tel: (0331) 23 09 44 Fax: (0331) 23 09 50
59 rooms, Double: Lire 280,000
6 suites being added in 1996
Open all year
Credit cards: all major
Restaurant open daily
4 km SW of Milan-Malpensa Airport

During the 17th and 18th centuries it was fashionable for wealthy Venetian nobles to build palatial retreats along the cool banks of the River Brenta, and so the waterway became lined with sensational villas all the way from Venice to Padua. Today villages and commerce have built up in the area, but many of the mansions still survive, filled with statues, frescos, and Murano glasswork, attesting to the opulent lifestyle of days gone by. Some mansions are now open as museums, but for those who really want to experience living the noble life there is the lovely 17th-century Villa Margherita, an elegant small hotel. It is situated across the highway from the canal, just a short stroll from one of the villa museums and a short drive from the others. Many converted villas in Italy are beautiful but faded, reflecting genteel neglect: not so with the Villa Margherita where all is beautifully maintained and every detail is perfect. From the lounges with their elegant antiques to the guestrooms with color-coordinated fabrics, each detail shows the care and involvement of the owners, Valeria and Remigio dal Corso. Far from the hubbub of Venice, yet only a 20-minute drive away, the Villa Margherita is an excellent hotel choice for those who prefer to avoid the hustle and bustle of the city. If you go into Venice, it's easiest to take the bus, thus avoiding the congestion of traffic and high cost of parking.

ROMANTIK HOTEL VILLA MARGHERITA
Owners: Valeria & Remigio dal Corso
Via Nazionale 416
30030 Mira (VE), Italy
Tel: (041) 42 65 800 Fax: (041) 42 65 838
19 rooms, Double: Lire 220,000–300,000
Open all year
Credit cards: all major
Restaurant open daily
On canal 2 km W of Mira
20 km W of Venice
USA Rep: Euro-Connection 800-645-3876

Il Melograno is a rarity: a small, luxury hotel that is truly managed by the family—creating a warmth and cordiality seldom found in a hotel of this sophistication. Camillo Guerra oversees every detail of his hotel, ably assisted by his children. One daughter cordially manages the front desk, another oversees the health spa, while his son works behind the scene in the business office. White walls enclose a parcel of land whose core is a 16th-century fortified farmhouse which for many years was the holiday retreat of the Guerra family. In 1985, Signor Guerra (an antique and fine-art dealer from Bari) decided to expand his home-away-from-home into a hotel. Taking meticulous care to preserve the ancient olive trees (one 2,000 years old), he built a series of superbly furnished guestrooms clustered in white Moorish-style buildings facing intimate patios. The original farmhouse now houses the reception, romantic bar, beautiful dining room, and lounges which are exquisitely decorated in antiques. Cheerful floral-slip-covered chairs and Oriental carpets accent stark white walls and floors. One of the inner patios is a fragrant small orange grove, watered by an ancient stone irrigation system. The dining room opens onto a pool-side terrace where meals are served overlooking the pomegranate and fig trees. Il Melograno makes an excellent, luxurious base for exploring the fascinating Apulia region of southern Italy.

IL MELOGRANO
Owners: Guerra Family
Contrada Torricella 345
70043 Monopoli (BA) Italy
Tel: (080) 69 09 030 Fax: (080) 74 79 08
37 rooms, Double: Lire 290,000–750,000
Closed January to March 22
Credit cards: all major
Restaurant open daily
On the heel of Italy, 70 km NW of Brindisi
USA Rep: Relais & Chateaux 212-856-0115

For those who wish for accommodations with all the trimmings, yet still want to feel like a pampered guest in a private home, Villa Pambuffetti is an ideal choice. Situated in Umbria, the green heart of Italy, in the well preserved hilltop town of Montefalco with its 13th-century Francescano frescoes, this splendid villa was once a private home. Although the hotel is managed with professional skill, the gracious Pambuffetti family has a magic touch that makes each guest feel very special. The decision to transform their country house into a 15-room inn seemed a natural choice when gracious Signora Pambuffetti's daughter, Alessandra, and her husband, Mauro, returned from the United States with a wealth of experience in the hotel and restaurant business. Alessandra demonstrates her culinary skills preparing Umbrian specialties for guests. Her delicious cakes, tarts, and homemade jams are part of the full breakfast served in the elegant cream-and-dusty-rose-colored dining room. Here guests are treated to the same spectacular panoramic view taking in Assisi, Perugia, Spoleto, and Spello as described by the Nobel-prize-winning author Herman Hesse in 1907. The villa itself, with its manicured gardens (which now have a swimming pool) and centuries-old cypress trees, is also mentioned. Every small detail is tended to in the individually decorated rooms with their travertine marble bathrooms. The room in the tower, the *Torre dell'Amore*, with its 360-degree vistas, is always a favorite.

VILLA PAMBUFFETTI
Owners: Pambuffetti Family
Via della Vittoria 20
06036 Montefalco (PG), Italy
Tel: (0742) 37 88 23 Fax: (0742) 37 92 45
15 rooms, Double: Lire 240,000–320,000
Open all year
Credit cards: all major
Restaurant open daily for dinner
30 km S of Assisi, 80 km NE of Orvieto

La Chiusa, nestled in the hills of Tuscany southeast of Siena, is an old stone farmhouse whose restaurant is so well-known that guests come from far and wide to enjoy the meals where everything is fresh, homemade, and delicious. Dania and Umberto Lucherini are the gracious owners and Dania is the talented chef. Almost all the vegetables, olive oil, meats, wines, and cheeses come either from the inn's own farm or from those nearby. The original wood-burning oven still stands in the courtyard in front of the inn, emitting delicious aromas of freshly baking bread. The dining room is large and airy, with an uncluttered simple elegance enhanced by windows overlooking rolling hills. When the weather is balmy, meals are also served on the back terrace which is ideally positioned with a sweeping view. The emphasis here is definitely on the exquisite meals, but happily there are also bedrooms for guests who want to spend the night. Like the dining room, the guestrooms are perfectly in keeping with the ambiance of the old farmhouse, lovely in their rustic simplicity yet with every modern convenience. If you appreciate and are willing to pay for gourmet meals, this is a perfect base for exploring Tuscany.

LA CHIUSA
Owners: Lucherini Family
Manager:Franco Sodi
Via della Madonnina 88
53040 Montefollonico (SI), Italy
Tel: (0577) 66 96 68 Fax: (0577) 66 95 93
12 rooms, Double: from Lire 280,000
2 suites: from Lire 450,000
Open mid-March to November 5
  & December 26 to January 7
Credit cards: all major
Restaurant closed Tuesdays
60 km S of Siena, 10 km NW of Montepulciano

The Gasthof Obereggen, located in the Val d'Ega (Ega Valley) is very simple, but quite wonderful. The inn is situated on the side of a hill overlooking a gorgeous mountain valley in one of the most beautiful mountain regions of northeastern Italy. The town of Obereggen is a ski resort and the lift is just a few minutes' walk away. From the sun-drenched deck which extends generously out from the hotel, there is an absolutely glorious vista across the green meadows to the mountains. Behind the hotel even more majestic mountains poke their jagged peaks into the sky. Inside, there is a cozy dining room. Signor Pichler must be a hunter, for trophies line the walls and there is a typical tiled stove against one wall to keep the room toasty on cold days. The inn has 12 bedrooms—those on the second floor open out onto lovely view-balconies. The greatest asset of this inn, and the real reason for its inclusion, is Signora Pichler: she is very special, running her little inn with such a warmth and gaiety that just being in the same room with her is fun. Signora Pichler speaks no English, but her hospitality crosses all language barriers and her bountiful, delicious home-style cooking speaks to all who love to eat. *NOTE:* Obereggen is not on most maps. If coming from Bolzano, head southeast through the Val d'Ega for approximately 16 kilometers and turn to right for Obereggen. The closest town on the Hallwag map is Ega (Ega is also called San Floriano).

GASTHOF OBEREGGEN
Owners: Pichler Family
39050 Obereggen (San Floriano)
Val d'Ega (BZ), Italy
Tel: (0471) 61 57 22 Fax: (0471) 61.58.89
12 rooms, Double: Lire 112,000–120,000*
*Rate includes breakfast and dinner
Closed May & November
Credit cards: none accepted
Restaurant open daily
25 km SE of Bolzano, 3 km S of Nova Levante

The town of Orvieto, just off the main expressway between Rome and Florence, is one of the most picturesque of all the Umbrian hilltowns. The small city crowns the top of a hill—an intriguing sight that can be viewed from many kilometers away. Less than a ten-minute drive south of Orvieto is a 12th-century Gothic abbey that has been converted into a hotel where you can stay surrounded by the romantic ruins of yesteryear. In our last edition of this guide we mentioned that the staff of La Badia was rather impersonal, but we have received several letters saying that this is no longer true—that the reception is very friendly and the staff most helpful. (We will be glad of more feedback.) At any rate, you are bound to enjoy the setting, the pool, and the old-world ambiance. The location of La Badia, near the stunning town of Orvieto, is excellent. The hotel itself is nice: the dining room is especially attractive with an enormous, high vaulted stone ceiling, wrought-iron fixtures, heavy wooden beams, eye-catching copper accents, and, at one end, a cavernous fireplace complete with a roasting spit. The bedrooms are not large, but are comfortable and many have a stunning view of the town of Orvieto. In the meadows behind the monastery there is a pool which makes a welcome respite from a day on the road.

LA BADIA
Manager: Contessa Luisa Fiumi
05019 Orvieto Scalo (TR), Italy
Tel: (0763) 90 359 Fax: (0763) 92 796
24 rooms, Double: Lire 266,000–296,000
Suites: Lire 406,000–486,000
Open March to December
Credit cards: all major
Restaurant closed Wednesdays
4 km S of Orvieto
115 km N of Rome

The Villa le Barone was once the home of the famous Tuscan family, Della Robbia, whose delightful terra cottas are still seen throughout Italy. Most of the estate now has been beautifully converted into a deluxe small hotel, but the present owner, Duchessa Franca Viviani Della Robbia, still maintains a charming vine-covered cottage for her own use. Although she is now in her 80s, the Duchessa comes frequently to the villa to ensure that her impeccable standards and exquisite taste prevail. Staying at the Villa le Barone is very much like being the fortunate guest in a private, elegant home set in the gorgeous Tuscany hills. There are only 25 guestrooms, all of which vary in size and decor, but each with an individual charm. In addition, there is a lovely pool on a terrace overlooking the vineyards and out to the mellow hills beyond. Wonderful little terraces are found secluded in the parklike setting where guests can find a quiet nook to read or just to sit and soak in the beauty. The food is divine and in balmy weather lunch can be taken in the garden and dinner inside in a charming dining room which formerly housed the stables. Reservations are accepted for a minimum of three nights, but that should be no problem—three nights will be too short an interlude to spend in this romantic paradise. *NOTE:* The closest town on the Hallwag map is Greve.

VILLA LE BARONE
Owner: Duchessa Franca Viviani Della Robbia
Manager: Caterina Buonamici
Via San Leolino, 19
50020 Panzano in Chianti (FI), Italy
Tel: (055) 85 26 21 Fax: (055) 85 22 77
25 rooms, Double: Lire 390,000–450,000*
*Rate includes breakfast and dinner, 3-night minimum
Open Easter to October
Credit cards: AX
Restaurant open daily, for guests only
31 km S of Florence, 6 km S of Greve

Relax in the countryside just 5 kilometers from the bustling city of Verona at the exquisite Villa del Quar where you can enjoy excellent accommodations, gourmet dining, and the warmth and charm of a family-managed hotel. The gracious owner, Leopoldo Montresor, is a talented architect who spared no expense to assure that his personally supervised renovations resulted in an estate exuding charm and taste. The Montresors live in one wing of the villa, conveniently close for Evelina Acampora-Montresor who manages the hotel. The property has been in the Montresor family for many generations—ever since Leopoldo's great, great, great-grandfather won the land in a game of cards at the casino in Venice in the early 1800s. Your heart will be captivated from the moment you pass the family chapel and enter the reception lounge (formerly the storage barn), elegantly decorated with finely upholstered sofas in warm shades of pinks and mellow yellows. Sunlight floods the room through a wall of windows which open onto an inviting side terrace where guests dine in warm weather. There is also a most attractive beamed-ceilinged dining room where meals are served elegantly on tables set with fine linens. The guestrooms are equally appealing and furnished in antiques. As an added bonus, a large swimming pool is set enchantingly in a meadow with vineyards stretching almost to the edge of the pool.

HOTEL VILLA DEL QUAR
Owners: Evelina Acampora-Montresor
& Leopoldo Montresor
Via Quar N 12
37020 Pedemonte (VR), Italy
Tel: (045) 68 00 681 Fax: (045) 68 00 604
22 rooms, Double: Lire 350,000–510,000
Open all year
Credit cards: all major
Restaurant open daily
10 km N of Verona, 15 km E of Lake Garda

How smug I felt at discovering the Castel Pergine, for here is a picture-book castle perfect for the budget-minded tourist. No need to forfeit romance and glamour, for even though the Castel Pergine is inexpensive, it has a fabulous location dominating a hilltop above the town of Pergine. Luckily, this castle has been delightfully transformed into a small hotel with incredible views out over the valleys and wooded hills. From the tower you can even see in the distance two small lakes which invite a picnic. The Castel Pergine is more famous as a restaurant than a hotel: in fact the Michelin guide gives the kitchen a two-fork rating. The dining room has an engaging medieval decor, gorgeous views, and delicious food. In another wing of the castle the guestrooms offer accommodation ranging from rather basic to comfortably charming. About half of the 21 rooms have private baths—these are more expensive, but also more appealingly decorated with handsome wooden paneling and rustic, country-style furnishings. All the guestrooms are pleasant, most offering lovely views, but room 27, a corner room, is especially large and pretty. The Castel Pergine is a real bargain for the price-conscious traveler and its secluded hilltop setting is definitely a winner—especially if you are traveling with children who will love their own Disneyland-like castle.

CASTEL PERGINE
Managers: Verena & Theo Schneider
38057 Pergine (TN), Italy
Tel: (0461) 53 11 58 Fax: (0461) 53.11.58
21 rooms, Double: Lire 190,000*
*Rate includes breakfast and dinner
Open May to mid-October
Credit cards: VS
Restaurant open daily in high season
71 km S of Bolzano, 10 km E of Trento
2.5 km E of Pergine

I am such a romantic that, as the boat chugged across the lake from Stresa to the medieval fishing village of Isola dei Pescatori (Fisherman's Island) and I saw the Hotel Verbano with its reddish-brown walls, dark-green shutters, and tables set on the terrace overlooking the lake, my heart was won—completely. To accommodate the many people who clamor off the excursion boats each day to visit this picturesque island, the hotel has a large dining room with arched windows overlooking Lake Maggiore. However, when the weather is warm, the favorite place to dine is outside on the idyllic terrace overlooking nearby Isola Bella (Beautiful Island). In the evening, when most of the tourists have departed, the terrace becomes even more romantic—particularly with a full moon reflecting on the rippling water. The food is excellent, featuring freshly-caught fish from the lake. There are 12 bedrooms, each with a view of the lake. When we first visited, many years ago, their interior was a bit drab, but we are happy to report that they have been redecorated with a simple, old-fashioned charm. My favorite is Camelia (number 11), a pretty corner room on the third floor with blue floral wallpaper, writing desk, armoire, antique iron king-sized bed, and shuttered doors leading out to a small balcony. *NOTE:* Take the public scheduled ferry from Stresa, since the private water taxis are exorbitantly expensive.

HOTEL VERBANO
Owner: Alberto Zacchera
Via Ugo Ara, 2
28049 Isola dei Pescatori, Stresa
Borromee Isole, Lake Maggiore (NO), Italy
Tel: (0323) 30 408 Fax: (0323) 33 129
12 rooms, Double: Lire 210,000
Open March to January
Credit cards: all major
Restaurant open daily
80 km NW of Milan, ferry from Stresa

Taking a small road that winds up the hill from the nondescript hamlet of Pievescola, you soon see on your left a big gate leading into a large courtyard faced by a lovely old castle (in former days the villa of Pope Julius II). The castle, parts of which date from the 14th century, others from the 16th, exhibits a combination of styles, incorporating Renaissance arcades with older, more fortress-like architecture. The noble Ricci family live in one part of the castle, while the other section is an elegant hotel. The public rooms and bedrooms are furnished with dramatic family antiques and an astounding museum-quality art collection. There is no feeling of this being a slickly run, sophisticated operation: instead, guests have the sensation of actually living the noble life of a bygone era. In addition to the guestrooms in the castle, there are simpler rooms in the former horse stables across the road. Although very pleasant, these rooms are less stately than those in the main house. Also across the road, the restaurant, Oliviera, located in the former olive-pressing building, serves Tuscan cuisine (as well as other specialties), taking advantage of the produce from La Suvera's farm. The wine cellar is extensive, featuring wines produced in vineyards that date back to the 12th century.

LA SUVERA
Owner: Marchese Giuseppe Ricci
Manager: Massimo Mariotti
53030 Pievescola di Casole d'Elsa
Val d'Elsa (SI), Italy
24 rooms, Double: Lire 330,000–600,000
Suite: to Lire 500,000
Tel: (0577) 96 03 00 Fax: (0577) 96 02 20
Open April 4 to November
Credit cards: all major
Restaurant open daily
25 km W of Siena, 16 km S of Colle Val d'Elsa

It is difficult to find a hotel in Rome with windows thick enough to keep out the ever-present buzz of traffic. Less than an hour's drive from the city, the Borgo Paraelios (a prestigious Relais & Chateaux hotel) offers the perfect solution: a luxurious country villa immersed in the lovely Tuscan-like hills of Sabinia. In this splendid villa, filled to the brim with elegant antiques, rich, warm-colored tapestries, and period paintings, it is impossible to find a detail overlooked. It is a masterpiece of harmonizing old and new, with antique terra-cotta tile floors, stone fireplaces, beamed ceilings, and antique doors from castles and villas brought here and cleverly incorporated into the building. The very inviting bedrooms, each with its own character and color scheme, look out over the lush garden where guests can breakfast among flower-laden terra-cotta pots. Meandering through the gracious living room, two libraries, billiard and bridge rooms, one has the sense of having been invited to the country home of nobility for a weekend of absolute peace and tranquillity. A golf course and a spectacular indoor swimming pool add to the ambiance. For an additional charge, transportation is available to and from Rome. When you return from the bustle of the city, exquisite meals are served in the frescoed formal dining room. *NOTE:* Ask for driving instructions: the Borgo Paraelios is tricky to find, but you will discover a true jewel at your journey's end.

HOTEL BORGO PARAELIOS
Owner: Adolfo Salabé
Localita Valle Collicchia
02040 Poggio Mirteto Scalo (RI), Italy
Tel: (0765) 26 267 Fax: (0765) 26 268
15 rooms, Double: from Lire 500,000
Open all year
Credit cards: AX, VS
Restaurant open daily
45 km NE of Rome, 2 km N of Poggio Mirteto
USA Rep: Relais & Chateaux 212-856-0115

Not so far away from the world-famous island of Capri, but definitely out of the limelight, sits the delightful island fishing village of Ponza. For reasons unknown—or possibly due to its very short season—this island remains a stranger to foreigners. The hydrofoil (or ferry) makes its one-hour journey from Anzio (one hour south of Rome) to the horseshoe-shaped harbor with its whitewashed and pastel box-like houses covering the hill like building blocks. The pink-walled port, resembling a ship, holds simple shops and sidewalk cafés on the upper deck and a fresh-fish market on the lower deck. Casa Giulia sits high above the sea on a point opposite Ponza town, offering unique accommodation for travelers who want to literally get away from it all. Although a road does exit, the inn is accessed primarily by boat, which picks guests up at the launch and shuttles to and from town at specific times during the day and evening. The whitewashed complex includes 12 guestrooms, each with balcony or patio, a large terrace overlooking the sea where breakfast is served, and a lovely saltwater pool, all personally overseen by gracious hostesses (and sisters), Daniela and Stefania. The cool, colorfully tiled rooms with simple bamboo and wicker furniture reflect the true spirit of the island. A nearby beach is reached by foot. The crystal-clear turquoise waters can best be enjoyed by renting a *gozzo*, a colorful outboard motorboat used by fishermen, for the day to tour the group of islands. A small piece of paradise.

CASA GIULIA MARINE HOTEL
Owners: Daniela & Stefania Vecchiarelli
Localita Frontone
04027 Isola di Ponza (LT), Italy
Tel: (0771) 80 407 Fax: (0771) 80 407
12 rooms, Double: Lire 220,000
Open May to September
Credit cards: none accepted
No restaurant, breakfast only
Island of Ponza, ferry from Anzio

Over its 30-year history the Grand Hotel Chiaia di Luna has always been considered the best hotel on the island of Ponza. This is due primarily to its enviable position atop a hill, dominating the port of Ponza to one side and overlooking the sea and dramatic crescent-shaped beach to the other. Cool green-and-yellow-floral handpainted tiles cover the floors of the entrance, leading to a series of sitting rooms where an occasional antique is displayed. A door opens out to a seawater swimming pool, edged by a glassed-in restaurant on two sides and a rather spartan bar/outdoor eating area on the other. Only a few of the recently renovated rooms (type A) have sea views and a terrace—a must in Ponza—and are tastefully decorated with matching floral spreads and curtains, framed botanical prints, and stenciled borders on walls. The hotel is a five-minute ride from the port and hydrofoil launch where guests are met by the hotel's private mini-van. You can dine poolside or choose from plenty of very good (mostly seafood) restaurants nearby. The Chiaia di Luna certainly stands out among the other rather mediocre accommodations on the island.

GRAND HOTEL CHIAIA DI LUNA
Directors: Flora Visocchi Family
Via Chiaia di Luna
04027 Isola di Ponza (LT), Italy
Tel: (0771) 80 113 Fax: (0771) 80 98 21
42 rooms, Double: Lire 150,000–200,000
Credit cards: all major
Restaurant
Island of Ponza, ferry from Anzio

The Relais El Toulà is a small, super-deluxe inn quietly located in the countryside, less than an hour's drive north of Venice. A lane lined by vineyards leads to tall wrought-iron gates which swing open to a courtyard faced by the Relais El Toulà, an elegant two-story villa with red-tiled roof and green shutters. This 18th-century mansion is flanked by two arcaded wings which stretch to the sides, giving the building an elegant long, low image. Inside there is an abundance of fresh flowers in the superbly furnished lounges. The ambiance in the public rooms and also in the individually decorated bedrooms reflects the skill of a professional decorator. In addition to the secluded, parklike setting and the mood of sophisticated elegance, there is another bonus—the food and wines are outstanding. It is not surprising that the hotel is so exceptional, for its standards were set by former owner Alfredo Beltrame, a real pro in the inn-keeping profession—he was the founder of the very successful Toulà hotel chain. Today the Relais El Toulà caters to the discriminating traveler who is seeking luxurious accommodation and doesn't mind the cost. The hotel is a member of the prestigious Relais & Chateaux group of hotels and is rated as one of their most deluxe Italian properties.

RELAIS EL TOULÀ
Manager: Giorgio Zamuner
Via Postumia, 63
31050 Ponzano (TV), Italy
Tel: (0422) 44 07 51 Fax: (0422) 44 07 54
10 rooms, Double: from Lire 410,000
Open all year
Credit cards: all major
Restaurant open daily
2 km N of Ponzano Veneto toward Paderno
35 km N of Venice, 5 km NW of Treviso
USA Rep: Relais & Chateaux 212-856-0115

The Al Vecchio Convento is a real gem, offering quality accommodation for a moderate price. Its several dining rooms are brimming with rustic country charm and serve delicious meals prepared from local produce. There are nine guestrooms, each with a private bathroom and each tastefully decorated with antiques. The town of Portico di Romagna is, like the inn, inviting yet unpretentious—a very old village surrounded by wooded hills and clear mountain streams. A stroll through medieval pathways that twist down between the weathered stone houses leads you to an ancient stone bridge gracefully arching over a rushing stream. The inn too is very old. At first I thought its origin must have been an old convent because of its name, but the wonderfully gracious owner, Marisa Raggi, told me that the name came from a restaurant, located in a convent, that she and her husband, Giovanni (who is the chef), used to operate. Later, when they moved the restaurant to its present location and added a few guestrooms, they kept the original name, Al Vecchio Convento. The restaurant is still their main focus, featuring fine meals beautifully prepared from local produce. Due to the winding, two-lane mountain highway that leads to the village, it takes about two hours to drive from Florence, but if you enjoy the adventure of exploring Italy's back-roads, this small hotel will certainly be one of your favorites, as it is mine.

ALBERGO AL VECCHIO CONVENTO
Owners: Marisa Raggi & Giovanni Cameli
Via Roma, 7
47010 Portico di Romagna (FO), Italy
Tel: (0543) 96 70 53 Fax: (0543) 96 71 57
9 rooms, Double: from Lire 140,000
Open all year
Credit cards: all major
Restaurant closed Wednesdays
75 km NE of Florence, 34 km SW of Forli

The Il Pellicano has been beautifully designed in the traditional villa style and, although not old, looks as though it has snuggled on its prime hillside position overlooking the Mediterranean for many years. The façade is of stucco, painted a typical Italian russet and set off by a heavily tiled roof. Vines enwrap the building, further enhancing its inviting look. One enters into a spacious, attractive lobby where the sun streams through the windows enhancing the white walls, terra-cotta floors, and wood-beamed ceilings. The cheerful ambiance continues with pretty sofas, antique accents, and enormous displays of fresh flowers enlivening every conceivable nook and cranny. The overall impression is one of light and color—and great taste. Beyond the reception area is an outdoor dining terrace, a favorite place to eat when the weather is balmy: the chef frequently serves elaborate buffets outside (the food at Il Pellicano is expensive, but excellent). From the terrace, a lawn dotted with trees extends down the hillside to where there is a beautiful pool romantically perched at the cliff's edge. From the pool a staircase leads to a pier at the water's edge. Along this path, small individual terraces with lounge chairs and mats for sunning have been built into the rocks. In front of the hotel is a tennis court, again surrounded by flowers. The Il Pellicano is truly an idyllic retreat.

IL PELLICANO
Manager: Signora Cinzia Fanciulli
58018 Porto Ercole (GR), Italy
Tel: (0564) 83 38 01 Fax: (0564) 83 34 18
30 rooms, Double: Lire 275,000–840,000
4 suites in cottages: Lire 680,000–1,700,000
Open April to November
Credit cards: all major
Restaurant open daily
South end of peninsula, Hwy 1 exit Orbetello
160 km N of Rome, 4.5 km S of Porto Ercole
USA Rep: Relais & Chateaux 212-856-0115

If money doesn't matter, when in Portofino settle in for a long stay at the incomparable Hotel Splendido. But since not everyone's travel budget can stretch to such luxury, the Hotel Eden is a welcome alternative. Although the price at the Eden might seem high for the accommodation offered, just remember that Portofino is the target of the wealthy from around the world, and rates in restaurants and places to stay reflect this popularity. If you are prepared for simplicity (tempered with the warmth of hospitality offered at family-run hotels), you will be happy to discover the Eden, tucked right in the heart of Portofino, not facing the harbor, but down a little lane, just two minutes' walk away. Wrought-iron gates open to steps leading to the front garden, a peaceful oasis of flowers and green lawn. Facing the garden is a side terrace where meals are served outside when the weather is warm. The hotel is a soft mustard-colored villa with green shutters. As you enter, to the right is a porch-like dining room with rather ordinary tables and chairs. Farther on you find the registration desk where the personable Signor Osta will probably be waiting to check you in. Don't expect too much in the guestrooms—they are all extremely simple in decor. The best (and the favorite of guests who return each year) is number 7 which has its own small patio. Room 6 (with an antique white iron bed) is another of the better rooms.

HOTEL EDEN
Owner: Ferruccio Osta
Via Dritto 18
16034 Portofino (GE), Italy
Tel: (0185) 26 90 91 Fax: (0185) 26 90 47
12 rooms, Double: Lire 200,000–280,000
Open all year
Credit cards: all major
Restaurant open daily
5 km S of Santa Margherita Ligure
35 km E of Genoa

Located up a winding, wooded road high above the town of Portofino, the super-deluxe Hotel Splendido sits majestically above the beautiful blue Mediterranean, overlooking the boats moored in Portofino's lovely harbor. Stretching across the front of the hotel is a magnificent terrace—a favorite choice of guests who enjoy dining outside with an incredible vista of the sea. As would be expected in such a world-class hotel, the food is outstanding and beautifully served. Leading from the hotel are romantic little pathways where you can stroll through the wooded grounds and stop along the way at strategically placed benches to enjoy incomparable views. For those who would like more serious exercise, on a terrace below the hotel is an enormous swimming pool, while located in the gardens to the left of the hotel are tennis courts. The public rooms are charming, with comfortable chairs covered with floral prints and fresh flowers galore. Every detail is perfect and in excellent taste. The bedrooms too are lovely and decorator-perfect, many with balconies that afford a splendid view of Portofino. The Splendido is expensive, but without a doubt one of the most special resorts in Italy.

HOTEL SPLENDIDO
Manager: Maurizio Saccani
16034 Portofino (GE), Italy
Tel: (0185) 26 95 51 Fax: (0185) 26 96 14
64 rooms, Double: from Lire 990,000*
*Rate includes breakfast and dinner or lunch
Closed January 3 to March 21
Credit cards: all major
Restaurant open daily
5 km S of Santa Margherita Ligure
35 km E of Genoa
USA Rep: LHW 800-223-6800
* or Relais & Chateaux 212-856-0115*

The Albergo Casa Albertina is a prime example of what a difference management can make. There is a wide choice of hotels in the picturesque little fishing village of Positano—many, like the Casa Albertina, with spectacular views, pleasant decor, and good meals. However, they don't have Michele Cinque who is an outstanding hôtelier: gracious and warmhearted—willing to do whatever is required to make each guest feel very special. It is not surprising that Michele is such a pro—he has been in the hotel business for many years, having been the manager of one of Positano's most deluxe hotels (Le Sirenuse) before deciding to help his wife and mother-in-law manage the Casa Albertina full-time. The hotel is really a family operation: Michele is usually at the front desk ready to care for the guests, his mother-in-law is in charge of the kitchen, while his wife helps out wherever needed. Two sons are also working at the hotel and Lorenzo Cinque has taken over its official management—and quite ably, I might add. The hotel (which is built into a 12th-century house) clings to the hillside above Positano, a position that affords superlative views, but also means a strenuous walk into town.

ALBERGO CASA ALBERTINA
Owners: Cinque Family
Via della Tavolozza, 4
84017 Positano (SA), Italy
Tel: (089) 8 75 143 Fax: (089) 81 15 40
20 rooms, Double: from Lire 300,000*
*Rate includes breakfast and dinner
Open all year
Credit cards: all major
Restaurant open daily, for guests only
55 km S of Naples, 17 km S of Sorrento

For those who want to be smack in the middle of the colorful fishing village of Positano, the Palazzo Murat might be just your cup of tea. It is superbly located—surrounded by shops and only steps down to the beach. The hotel consists of two parts: the original building (a 200-year-old palace) plus a new wing to the side. The new section is a standard hotel—pleasant but not unusual. However, the palace is quite special, with a faded-pink patina whose charm is accented by wonderful arched alcoves, intricately designed windows, and magenta bougainvillea clinging to the walls and cascading from the wrought-iron balconies. The entrance to the hotel is through a sun-drenched patio, a favorite gathering spot for guests. Within, the old world feeling is maintained with tiled floors, white walls, and formal settings of antique sofas and chairs. My favorite bedrooms are the five located upstairs in the characterful palace section: especially appealing are those with shuttered French doors opening onto small balconies that capture a view of the bay. All the rooms are comfortable and have television, radio, mini-bar, and air conditioning. In summer a large buffet-style breakfast is served outside on the patio. Breakfast is the only meal served, but this is no problem as there are many enticing restaurants nearby. The hotel has its own boat that takes guests for excursions along the coast three times a week.

HOTEL PALAZZO MURAT
Owners: Attanasio Family
Manager: Carlo Attansio
Via dei Mulini, 23
84017 Positano (SA), Italy
Tel: (089) 87 51 77 Fax: (089) 87 51 77
28 rooms, Double: Lire 245,000–295,000
Open Easter to mid-October
No restaurant, breakfast only
Near the beach—heart of Positano
55 km S of Naples, 17 km S of Sorrento

The Il San Pietro di Positano is touted as one of the most delightful deluxe hotels in the world. It is—there is no question about it. From the moment you approach the hotel class is evident: no large signs; no gaudy advertising; just an ancient chapel along the road indicates to the knowledgeable that an oasis is below the hill. After parking in the designated area near the road, you take an elevator which whisks you down to the lounge and lobby. You walk out of the elevator to a dream world—an open spacious world of sparkling white walls, tiled floors, colorful lounge chairs, Oriental rugs, antique chests, flowers absolutely everywhere, and arches of glass through which vistas of greenery and sea appear. To the right is a bar and to the left is a marvelous dining room—again with windows of glass opening to the view, but with the outdoors appearing to come in, with the walls and ceilings covered with plants and vines. The bedrooms too seem to be almost a Hollywood creation—more walls of glass, bathrooms with views to the sea, and balconies on which to sit and dream. If you can tear yourself away from your oasis of a bedroom, an elevator will whisk you down the remainder of the cliff to the small terrace at the water's edge. If all this sounds gaudy, it isn't. It is perfect.

IL SAN PIETRO DI POSITANO
Owners: Virginia & Salvatore Attanasio
84017 Positano (SA), Italy
Tel: (089) 87 54 55 Fax: (089) 81 14 49
55 rooms, Double: Lire 520,000–680,000
Suite: Lire 750,000–1,000
Closed December to mid-March
Credit cards: all major
Restaurant open daily, for guests only
2 km south of Positano on Amalfi Drive
55 km S of Naples, 17 km S of Sorrento
USA Rep: Relais & Chateaux 212-856-0115

Le Sirenuse is a superb luxury hotel tucked smack in the middle of the picturesque ancient fishing village of Positano. It is no wonder that so many writers and artists have been attracted to this colorful town of brightly hued houses clinging to the precipitous hillside as it drops down to its own small bay. And it is also no wonder that so many of these famous people have found their way to the oasis of Le Sirenuse. From the moment you enter the hotel lobby the mood is set with fresh white walls, tiled floors, oil paintings on the walls, and accents of antiques. The hotel cascades down the hill and so almost all the rooms capture a wonderful view out over the quaint rooftops and the tiled domed cathedral to the shimmering blue waters of the bay. It is only a short walk through the perpendicular streets until you are on the beach. The dining room has walls of glass which allow the maximum enjoyment of the vista below, but most diners prefer the splendor of eating outdoors on the deck. On another level of the hotel there is a small pool for sunning and dipping. *NOTE*: The hotel hosts a cooking school in April and October, and has recently opened a new fitness center.

LE SIRENUSE HOTEL
Manager: Antonio Sersale
Via C. Colombo, 30
84017 Positano (SA), Italy
Tel: (089) 87 50 66 Fax: (089) 81 17 98
60 rooms, Double: Lire 400,000–610,000
Open all year
Credit cards: all major
Restaurant open daily
Old fishing village on Amalfi Drive
55 km S of Naples, 17 km S of Sorrento
USA Rep: LHW 800-223-6800

The Villa Franca, with a commanding position overlooking the sea, is one of Positano's newly renovated classic hotels, perfectly priced for the quality it offers. There is an immediate warmth and charm as soon as you walk in to the redesigned and redecorated villa. The Russo family wanted to create an attractive full-service hotel combined with the friendliness and service of a small inn, and it is just that. The fresh Mediterranean decor is most appealing, with royal-blue slip-covered armchairs, a profusion of plants, lacquered terra-cotta vases, white-tiled floors and walls, and arched windows everywhere, so that you don't miss a second of the mesmerizing views of the sea. The elegant glassed-in restaurant with floral-tapestry chairs and blue tablecloths specializes in fresh local seafood. The food is exceptional: Mario Russo is himself a talented chef and personally oversees both the food and impeccable service. In the winter, the hotel sponsors a cooking school where Diana Folonari teaches her pupils the art of Italian-Mediterranean specialties. The bedrooms follow the same cheerful theme with colorful ceramic tiled floors, cream bedspreads with green-and-yellow-striped trim and exquisite views. The cherry on top of the cake is the rooftop swimming pool surrounded by yellow chaise lounges and palms with a 360-degree panoramic view over the world's most beautiful coastline.

HOTEL VILLA FRANCA
Owner: Mario Russo
Viale Pasitea, 318
Positano 84017 (SA), Italy
Tel: (089) 87 56 55 Fax: (089) 87 57 35
28 rooms, Double: Lire 300,000–320,000
Open: Easter to October
Credit cards: all major
Restaurant open daily
55 km S of Naples, 18 km S of Sorrento
USA Rep: E&M 800-223-9832

The Relais Fattoria Vignale is a very polished, sophisticated small hotel located in the heart of the Chianti wine region in the small town of Radda. The hotel was the manor house of one of the large wine estates where the family's wines are still produced and are readily available in a winery shop across the street. Although located right on the main street near the center of town, a country atmosphere prevails because the back of the hotel opens up to lovely views of rolling hills laced with vineyards and dotted with olive trees. The rooms in the annex across the street also have a pretty view looking over the valley. Also capturing an idyllic vista is the hotel's large swimming pool. Inside, the rooms are all beautifully decorated with a combination of authentic antiques and excellent reproductions. Care has been taken in the restoration to preserve many of the nice architectural features of the manor such as heavy beams, arched hallways, decorative fireplaces, and painted ceilings. Only 300 meters from the hotel is the Ristorante Vignale, which is under the same ownership as the hotel.

RELAIS FATTORIA VIGNALE
Manager: Silvia Kummer
Via Pianigiani, 15
53017 Radda in Chianti (SI), Italy
Tel: (0577) 73 83 00 Fax: (0577) 73 85 92
26 rooms, Double: Lire 270,000–330,000
Open mid-March to mid-November
Credit cards: AX, VS
Restaurant closed Thursdays
In the heart of Chianti wine region
52 km S of Florence, 31 km N of Siena

Vescine, a medieval hamlet in the heart of Chianti, has been restored into a four-star hotel comprised of individual stone cottages accented by red-tiled roofs. One of the larger of the old stone buildings is now the reception area, bar, breakfast room, and lounge. Nearby, the guestrooms are in clusters of old houses, romantically connected by stone stairways. The decor is simple, yet extremely appealing and sympathetic to the rustic nature of the village. Tiled floors, beamed ceilings, whitewashed walls, wrought-iron or wooden headboards, and wooden-shuttered windows lend an authentic country look. All of the bedrooms are similar and from most of them there is a lovely view. Many of the rooms have attractive wrought-iron beds, some have terraces. Sixty hectares surround the village, offering vistas of densely wooded hills interspersed by fields of grapes. One of the most magnificent of the views is captured from the swimming pool terrace, which offers a sweeping panorama of the Tuscan hills. Breakfast is the only meal served, but within walking distance is La Cantoniera di Vescine, a restaurant in an ancient farmhouse featuring Tuscan cuisine and Chianti wines. *NOTE:* Although the address is Radda, the hotel is not in town, but well signposted—about midway on the road that runs between Radda and Castellina.

VESCINE–IL RELAIS DEL CHIANTI
Manager: Birgit Fleig
Localita Vescine
53017 Radda in Chianti (SI), Italy
Tel: (0577) 74 11 44 Fax: (0577) 74 02 63
25 rooms, Double: Lire 250,000–350,000
Open March to November
Credit cards: all major
Restaurant open daily
25 km N of Siena, 55 km S of Florence

The Ansitz Heufler Hotel, built in 1578 by Count Heufler, is actually a castle, but not one of the large foreboding castles sometimes found high on mountain peaks. This is a friendly, almost chalet-like castle, located in a sunny mountain valley in northeastern Italy. Although within a short drive of some of the most dramatic vistas in the Dolomites, the Ansitz Heufler's setting is pretty, but does not include dramatic jagged mountain peaks. However, in winter there is skiing nearby and in summer walking trails beckon in every direction. The Ansitz Heufler does not seem geared to English-speaking guests although we did find one of the staff with whom we could communicate. But even though language might be a problem, the reception is very friendly and everyone seems eager to please. The inn is popular as a restaurant. There is an especially cozy dining room with very old paneled walls and ceiling, planked wooden floors, leaded-glass windows, tables set with pretty linens, and appealing chalet-style chairs with carved-heart backs. In the summer, guests sit out on the terrace where refreshing drinks and snacks are served. The staircase leads up to a wide hallway off which are the bedrooms. These are all different from one another, but are all attractively furnished in a simple, uncluttered style with a liberal use of dark antiques attractively setting off whitewashed walls and freshly scrubbed wooden floors.

ANSITZ HEUFLER HOTEL
Owner: Valentin Pallhuber
Valle di Anterselva
39030 Rasun di Sopra (BZ), Italy
Tel: (0474) 49 62 88 Fax: (0474) 49 81 99
9 rooms, Double: Lire 140,000–210,000
Closed May and November
Credit cards: VS
Restaurant closed Wednesdays
90 km NE of Bolzano, 12 km E of Brunico

It is no wonder that the Hotel Caruso Belvedere has such an especially spectacular site in Ravello—it was built as a palace in the 11th century by a noble family who probably had their pick of real estate. The views of the rugged Amalfi coast from the dining terrace perched high in the clouds is gorgeous. Many of the bedrooms too have vistas. Although the decor is rather drab, the views just can't be surpassed. If you choose the Caruso Belvedere, splurge and ask for one of their most deluxe rooms—these are simply decorated without much style **but** they have enormous balconies that stretch the width of the room to capture again the incredibly romantic coast below. You will wake in the morning to the sound of birds and the scent of flowers intermixed with the fragrance of the vineyards that drifts up from the terraces beneath your balcony. The Hotel Caruso has more to offer than just its marvelous views: the dining room offers excellent food including a divine specialty of the house, a delicious chocolate soufflé that will linger in your memory perhaps as long as the views. The meals are accompanied by wines from the Caruso family vineyards.

HOTEL CARUSO BELVEDERE
Owners: Caruso Family
Manager: Gino Caruso
Via S. Giovanni del Toro, 52
84010 Ravello (SA), Italy
Tel: (089) 85 71 11 Fax: (089) 85 73 72
24 rooms, Double: Lire 200,000–320,000
Open all year
Credit cards: all major
Restaurant open daily
Hilltown above Amalfi coast
66 km S of Naples, 6 km N of Amalfi

The Marmorata Hotel was cleverly converted from the shell of an old paper mill. Only a few of the old paper mills are still in operation, but at one time the Amalfi area was famous for its production of fine paper. The official address of the Marmorata is Ravello; however, it is not located in the cliff town of Ravello, but rather on the coastal highway. As you are driving north from Salerno to Ravello you will see the sign to the hotel which is snuggled in the rocky cliffs between the road and the sea. As you enter the hotel you notice the nautical theme carried throughout the decor from the chairs in the dining room to the mirrors on the walls. The interior is charming, with comfortable leather lounge chairs and small Oriental rugs. There is a lovely terrace and, on a lower level, snuggled into the rocks, a small swimming pool. The bedrooms are small, but nicely decorated, again with the seafaring motif: the beds seem to be built into captains' sea chests and nautical prints hang on the walls. The bathrooms are also small, but modern and attractive. All of the bedrooms have radios, color televisions, telephones, air conditioning, and small refrigerators. Many of the rooms have an excellent view of the water and rugged coast.

MARMORATA HOTEL
Owners: Camera d'Afflitto Family
Strada Statale, 163
84010 Ravello (SA), Italy
Tel: (089) 87 77 77 Fax: (089) 85 11 89
40 rooms, Double: Lire 230,000–330,000
Open all year
Credit cards: all major
Restaurant open daily
On the coast below Ravello
62 km S of Naples, 23 km N of Salerno

There is something magical about the Hotel Palumbo, a 12th-century palace, owned since 1875 by the Vuilleumier family. The location is perfect—high in the clouds overlooking terraced vineyards and beyond to the brilliant blue Mediterranean which dances in and out of the jagged rocky coast. The romance begins when you enter the ceramic-tiled lobby with its ancient atrium of arched colonnades, green plants flowing from every nook, masses of fresh flowers, and beautiful antiques. Each small corner is an oasis of tranquillity, from the intimate bar to the cozy antique-filled tiny lounges. There is a lovely dining room with a crystal chandelier, bentwood chairs, and a fireplace, but usually meals are served on the terrace which perches like a bird's nest in the sky. Wherever you dine, the food is expensive, but excellent. There is a delightful garden in the rear featuring a vine-covered terrace overlooking the Amalfi coast. Another tiny patio which captures both the sun and the view is tucked onto the roof of the villa. There are only 21 bedrooms, each individually decorated and appealing with its own personality. A few guestrooms are located in an annex. The Hotel Palumbo is the most deluxe hotel with charm in Ravello, exuding a romantic ambiance and a wealth of old-world character. Although expensive, it has great style.

HOTEL PALUMBO
Owners: Vuilleumier Family
Manager: Marco Vuilleumier
Via S. Giovanni del Toro 28
84010 Ravello (SA), Italy
Tel: (089) 85 72 44 Fax: (089) 85 81 33
21 rooms, Double: Lire 650,000–840,000
Open all year
Credit cards: all major
Restaurant open daily
66 km S of Naples, 6 km N of Amalfi

The Villa Cimbrone is not only a hotel: its gardens are one of Ravello's most famous attractions. The tourist office proclaims, "The Villa Cimbrone, essence of all the enchantment of Ravello, hangs like a swallow's nest on the cliffs." The villa is reached by a delightful ten-minute walk from the main square of Ravello (the signs are well marked to this favorite sightseeing prize), then, once you pass through the gates, the villa and its magnificent gardens open up like magic. The gardens are truly superb—if you have ever received a postcard from Ravello, chances are it showed the view from the terrace of the Cimbrone. Most dramatic of all is the belvedere with its stately Roman statues accenting the dazzling view. Luckily, this outstanding villa is also a small hotel. The rooms are of museum quality with furniture fit for a king. We toured through the marvelous old building which is not open to the public—only to the guests. This fabulous villa was once the prized possession of an English lord. Later it was sold to the present owner, Marco Vuilleumier, who told us the following romantic tale: toward the end of World War II, the English nobleman (who owned Villa Cimbrone) landed with the Allied troops in Salerno. Somehow he was able to find a jeep, and—you guessed it—wound up the twisting road to see his beloved villa once again.

VILLA CIMBRONE
Owner: Marco Vuilleumier
Manager: Giorgio Vuilleumier
84010 Ravello (SA), Italy
Tel: (089) 85 74 59 Fax: (089) 85 77 77
20 rooms, Double: Lire 270,000–380,000
Open April to October
Credit cards: all major
No restaurant, breakfast only
10-minute walk to parking in town center
66 km S of Naples, 6 km N of Amalfi

The Villa Maria is perhaps best known for its absolutely delightful terrace restaurant which has a bird's eye view of the magnificent coast. Whereas most of the hotels in Ravello capture the southern view, the Villa Maria features the equally lovely vista to the north. The Villa Maria is easy to find because it is on the same path which winds its way from the main square to the Villa Cimbrone. Park your car in the main square of Ravello (or at the Hotel Giordano which is under the same ownership) and look for the signposts for Villa Maria. After about a two-minute walk, you find the hotel perched on the cliffs to your right. The building is a romantic old villa with a garden stretching to the side where tables and chairs are set—a favorite place to dine while enjoying the superb view. Inside, there is a cozy dining room overlooking the garden. The bedrooms have old-fashioned brass beds and antique furniture. The bathrooms have been freshly remodeled and some even have Jacuzzi tubs. The hotel is owned by Vincenzo Palumbo whose staff speaks excellent English, which very helpful if you call for a reservation. Vincenzo Palumbo also owns the nearby Hotel Giordano with its heated pool which can be used free by guests at the Villa Maria. Many readers have written to us saying how gracious and warm a welcome they receive at the Villa Maria. How lucky to be able to have the best of all worlds should you be on a budget—a wonderful view and location plus a charming villa.

VILLA MARIA
Owner: Vincenzo Palumbo
Via S. Chiara, 2
84010 Ravello (SA), Italy
Tel: (089) 85 72 55 Fax: (089) 85 70 71
17 rooms, Double: Lire 200,000–225,000
Open all year
Credit cards: all major
Restaurant open daily
66 km S of Naples, 6 km N of Amalfi

The Villa Rigacci, once a private residence, now an inviting small inn, is only about a half-hour's drive from Florence, easily accessible from the A1 to Rome. This 15th-century building is a picture-perfect example of a Tuscan villa with its creamy-white stucco façade, thick walls, heavy weathered red-tile roof, green-shuttered windows, and parklike gardens. Federico Pierazzi and his sister, Fiorenza, take great care to see that all guests receive personal attention and are made to feel "at home." In summer, after a day of sightseeing, guests relax in the back garden where a large pool, surrounded by lounge chairs and umbrellas, stretches out on a terraced lawn. Inside, handsome antiques adorn the sitting rooms and library. The dining room is especially appealing and, according to the guests staying at the inn, the chef is excellent. In summer guests usually choose to take their meals outside on the terrace. All of the bedrooms have air conditioning, direct-dial telephone, color television, small bar, and bathroom. Each is individually decorated with very attractive country-style antiques and lovely fabrics creating rooms that blend beautifully with the old-world ambiance of the villa. Although I personally prefer the area of Tuscany that stretches directly south of Florence where the villages seem more secluded, the conveniently located Villa Rigacci offers easy access to the expressway and accommodation with charm, hospitality, and warmth. *NOTE:* Vaggio is a small town southwest of Reggello.

HOTEL VILLA RIGACCI
Owners: Fiorenza & Federico Pierazzi
50066 Vaggio-Reggello (FI), Italy
Tel: (055) 86 56 718 Fax: (055) 86 56 537
20 rooms, Double: Lire 190,000–290,000
Open all year
Credit cards: all major
Restaurant closed January
30 km SE of Florence, 5 km S of Reggello

How could one possibly write about hotels in Rome and leave out one of the most historical places to stay in the city—the Albergo del Sole! Dating back to 1467, this is the oldest hotel in Rome—possibly one of the oldest still-operating hotels in the world. In addition to being of great historical interest, the hotel has the blessing of holding a prime location: looking across the ancient Piazza della Rotonda to one of Rome's masterpieces, the Pantheon, which was standing before the birth of Christ. The Albergo del Sole has been meticulously restored, faithfully reflecting its 15th-century heritage. You enter into an attractive long narrow lobby with arched ceiling, red-tiled floor, whitewashed walls, and a very large, ornately framed antique oil painting over the reception desk. From the lobby, doors lead into the various lounges which maintain the same elegantly simple, uncluttered look with white walls, white upholstered chairs and sofas, and antique accent pieces. One floor up is a lovely interior garden-patio which opens onto an intimate breakfast room where the tables are invitingly set with pretty floral-print tablecloths. The bedrooms are each individual in decor, but similar in mood, with color-coordinating bedspreads and draperies. The suite is especially attractive, with a beautiful antique wooden headboard.

ALBERGO DEL SOLE
Manager: Giancarlo Piraino
Piazza della Rotonda, 63
00186 Rome, Italy
Tel: (06) 67 80 441 Fax: (06) 69 94 06 89
26 rooms, Double: Lire 470,000
Open all year
Credit cards: all major
No restaurant, breakfast only
Located in the center of Old Rome

Hotel rates in the center of Rome are usually very expensive, but the Hotel Carriage, tucked into a tiny side street, is both moderately priced and conveniently situated just a short stroll from the bottom of the Spanish Steps. From the outside it is a nondescript, sienna-colored building with green-shuttered windows opening directly onto the street. The small entry lobby is flanked by a little breakfast room and a formal parlor with ornate furnishings including brocade chairs, an enormous gilt mirror, a fancy chandelier, and elaborately carved tables. The pretty soft-blue walls of this room set the color theme for the hotel: the bedrooms I saw that had been redecorated were also done in varying shades of blue. Some of the guestrooms are very small, so it is best to pay a bit more and request one of the best twin-bedded rooms. However, no matter what the size, all the rooms have air conditioning, telephone, radio, small refrigerator, and an old-world flavor. One of the nicest features of the hotel is a rooftop terrace where on summer evenings guests may sit at tables and enjoy the view over a jumble of tiled roofs to the twin spires of the 16th-century church, Trinita dei Monti. The Hotel Carriage is not luxurious, but offers a less expensive alternative for lodging in Rome.

HOTEL CARRIAGE
Manager: Giampiero Cau
Via delle Carrozze, 36
00187 Rome, Italy
Tel: (06) 69 90 124 Fax: (06) 67 88 279
24 rooms, Double: from Lire 290,000
Suite: Lire 400,000–440,000
Open all year
Credit cards: all major
No restaurant, breakfast only
Located near the bottom of the Spanish Steps

For location, the Gregoriana is superb: it is situated on Gregoriana Street which runs into the Piazza Trinita dei Monti at the top of the Spanish Steps. In spite of the perfect location, when I first saw the Gregoriana I just did not see how I could include it in our book because it has no antique ambiance: in fact, the decor motif might be classified as Chinese with a mish-mash of art deco. If you are looking for a hotel with a refined taste, this is not it. However, after staying at this hotel, I just did not see how I could **not** include it—it is such a well run small hotel and has such a sparkle of personality that it brightens the otherwise often impersonal city of Rome. As a guest here, you will not be just one of the thousands of tourists in Rome—upon arrival, the concierge will probably already know you by name and will continue to greet you personally as you come and go. Instead of feeling like a face that goes with a key hanging on the wall, you will experience a warmth and intimacy—as if you were a guest in a private home. The bedrooms are simple and spotlessly clean. Those at the rear are especially quiet and some enjoy a balcony with a view over the rooftops of Rome. Only breakfast is served. However, there is a concierge on duty 24 hours a day to cater to your special needs.

HOTEL GREGORIANA
Owner: Ernesto Panier-Bagat
Manager: Aldo Basso Bondini
Via Gregoriana, 18
00187 Rome, Italy
Tel: (06) 67 94 26 9 Fax: (06) 67 84 25 8
19 rooms, Double: Lire 260,000–300,000
Open all year
Credit cards: none accepted
No restaurant, breakfast only
Located near the top of the Spanish Steps

The Hotel Hassler, located in the heart of the city at the top of the Spanish Steps, is a landmark in Rome. Guests have no need of taxis since the most important monuments and the most elegant shopping center are within walking distance. Free bikes are available to guests who would like to have a ride in the park of Villa Borghese. This small, elite hotel was once a palatial private home and its entrance is sedate and elegant. The reception rooms are a little somber, but this mood is quickly relieved by an inner courtyard—a superb oasis with stone walls covered with vines, statues, flowers, cozy little tables, and a bar. You can linger in the garden, take refreshment in the afternoon, or perhaps meet a friend for an aperitif in the evening. The dining room at the Hassler is also spectacular, boasting one of the finest views in Rome: the entire panorama of the city surrounds you as you dine. As the evening deepens and the city lights begin to flicker, the scene will become one of romance. If money is no object, the Hotel Hassler offers some magnificent suites, some with enormous terraces and a view so beautiful that you will be sorely tempted never to set foot from this gorgeous hotel.

HOTEL HASSLER
Owners: Oscar Wirth Family
Manager: Roberto E. Wirth
Trinita Dei Monti, 6
00187 Rome, Italy
Tel: (06) 67 82 65 1 Fax: (06) 67 89 991
85 rooms,, 15 suites: Double: from Lire 760,000
Open all year
Credit cards: all major
Restaurant open daily
Located at the top of the Spanish Steps
USA Rep: LHW 800-223-6800

The deluxe Hotel d'Inghilterra, definitely one of the finest small hotels in Rome, exudes an ambiance of warmth and dignified charm. The interior is enhanced by strategically placed antiques, lovely paintings, pretty Oriental carpets, antique mirrors, and fresh flowers. Down the hallway from the reception lounge is a charming bar that seems to be the rendezvous spot for everyone staying at the hotel. This appealing bar has beautiful dark-wood paneling adorned with colorful prints, intimate little tables, fine antique carpets, and comfortable leather sofas. There is also a very popular English-style restaurant where the chef specializes in light, innovative preparation of food. The bedrooms are well decorated in traditional decor. A few deluxe rooms have small terraces—a romantic spot for breakfast overlooking the rooftops of Rome. The location of the d'Inghilterra is excellent: a short walk in one direction will lead you through lovely shopping avenues to the bottom of the Spanish Steps, while a short walk in the other direction will lead you to the Trevi Fountain with its hubbub of activity. Originally, the Hotel d'Inghilterra was built as a guesthouse for the famous Torlonia Palace and you will certainly see and appreciate traces of grandeur that are still apparent throughout this once-regal residence.

HOTEL D'INGHILTERRA
Manager: Luigi Richard
Via Bocca di Leone, 14
00187 Rome, Italy
Tel: (06) 69 981 Fax: (06) 69 92 22 43
100 rooms, Double: Lire 420,000–495,000*
*Rate does not include breakfast
Open all year
Credit cards: all major
Restaurant open daily
Located near the bottom of the Spanish Steps
USA Rep: Utell International 800-448-8355

The Hotel Lord Byron is owned by a fascinating man and superb hôtelier, Amedeo Ottaviani, who believes "Hospitality is like an exquisite flower, it must be surrounded by a thousand delicate attentions"—a concept which transforms each of his hotels into far more than just a place to spend the night. Each is designed to be a home away from home—a quiet sanctuary, well run and full of character. Ottaviani's chain of small, unique hotels includes the Lord Byron—tucked on a tiny lane surrounded by glamorous homes, it is much more like a private townhouse than a commercial establishment. The reception desk is discreetly located in the foyer which opens onto an elegant lounge. An elevator takes guests to the bedrooms, each individually decorated: fabrics, carpets, and the materials used on the custom-built pieces of furniture are carefully chosen to suit the personality and exposure of the room. Most of the furniture is new—modern yet traditional in feel. The colors used in fabrics, wall coverings, and carpets are mostly strong, bold colors—frequently with large, bright floral prints, but consistently of excellent quality. On the lower level is an intimate drawing room-bar where guests can relax before or after dining—next door is an elegant restaurant, the Relais Le Jardin, serving without a doubt some of the finest cuisine in Rome.

HOTEL LORD BYRON
Owner: Amedeo Ottaviani
Manager: Orianna Savona
Via G. de Notaris, 5
00197 Rome, Italy
Tel: (06) 32 20 404 Fax: (06) 32 20 405
37 rooms, Double: Lire 360,000–550,000
Open all year
Credit cards: all major
Restaurant closed Sundays
Located on the edge of Villa Borghese Park
USA Rep: LHW 800-223-6800
* or Relais & Chateaux 212-856-0115*

The Hotel Majestic Roma, located on the famous Via Veneto, has emerged from her recent renovation as one of Rome's newest jewels. As with other luxury hotels in Italy, the rates are very high, but so is the quality. From the moment you enter through the circular revolving doorway into the spacious, high-ceilinged lobby with a few well chosen antiques and bouquets of fresh flowers, the mood of quiet elegance is established. Instead of one large lounge, there is a series of intimate parlors where guests can gather. In each room there are beautifully upholstered chairs, and opulent fabrics on the walls and richly draped windows. Be sure to peek in and see the fabulous frescoed ceiling of the 19th-century *Salone Verdi* which is used for special banquets. A wonderful old-fashioned wrought-iron elevator with polished brass trim takes guest to the bedrooms. As in a private home, each has its own personality, all are elegant in decor and traditionally furnished in an old-world, opulent style. On warm days, an outdoor terrace with a view of the city is a perfect place to pause for a cool drink. There is also a beautifully decorated, formal dining room specializing in typical Mediterranean dishes, as well as Continental cuisine.

HOTEL MAJESTIC ROMA
Manager: Carla Milos
Via Veneto, 50
00187 Rome, Italy
Tel: (06) 48 68 41 Fax: (06) 48 80 984
98 rooms, Double: Lire 580,000–660,000
Open all year
Credit cards: all major
Restaurant open daily
In the heart of Rome on Via Veneto

La Residenza was recommended to us by several readers who claimed it to be their favorite place to stay in Rome, and, after a personal visit, we are happy to be able to include it in our guide. This former villa really is quite different from most of the large, commercial places to stay in the center of Rome, appearing to be more like a private residence. Its façade looks very Italian, with typical brown-shuttered windows, greenery, and flowers behind a small paved courtyard where guests may park their cars. The front hall has been converted into a reception area flanked by several guest lounges. The decor of these public rooms is not outstanding: some have contemporary, grass-cloth wallpaper, but others are more traditional in feeling and have a smattering of antique furniture. The breakfast room is spacious, although a bit dark, but the red bentwood chairs add a bit a sparkle. Because the hotel was fully occupied at the time of my visit, I was able to see only a few guestrooms, but those I did see were modern and seemed to be quite adequate. The location just off the Via Veneto is glamorous, so even though the interior of La Residenza does not abound with charm, it is a good choice for travelers who want a small hotel in a good location without paying a fortune.

LA RESIDENZA
Manager: Oliveti Francesco
Via Emilia, 22
00187 Rome, Italy
Tel: (06) 48 80 789 Fax: (06) 48 57 21 ·
27 rooms, Double: Lire 270,000
Suite: Lire 310,000
Open all year
Credit cards: all major
No restaurant, breakfast only
Located between Via Veneto and the Spanish Steps

Finding the appealing Romantik Golf Hotel brought us an unexpected bonus: we discovered a niche of Italy that hugs the border north of Trieste, an absolutely gorgeous region of wooded hills, rolling fields, and vineyards. The Castello Formentini, superbly positioned on a hillock overlooking the countryside, has belonged to the Counts of Formentini since the 16th century. For many years there has been a restaurant within the castle which still serves excellent meals and a medieval banquet on Saturdays. Just outside the castle walls, one of the historic buildings of the castle complex has been converted into a small, charming luxury inn. The attractive, gracious owner, Isabella Formentini, says that all of the magnificent antique furnishings in the hotel are family heirlooms: in fact, she says the furniture is more valuable than the castle. Everything is authentic, even the wonderful prints and paintings. From the intimate lobby to each of the spacious guestrooms, everything is decorator-perfect and exudes a delightful country-manor ambiance. Only four of the rooms are within the castle, but all guests can stroll through the gate and into the castle grounds where the swimming pool lies invitingly in the shaded lawn. There are also a tennis court and a nine-hole pitch-and-putt golf course. *NOTE:* The closest town on the Hallwag map is Gorizia.

ROMANTIK GOLF HOTEL
Owner: Isabella Formentini
San Floriano del Collio
34070 Gorizia (GO), Italy
Tel: (0481) 88 40 51 Fax: (0481) 88 40 52
16 rooms, Double: Lire 290,000
Open March to December
Credit cards: AX, VS
Restaurant closed Mondays
30 km N of Trieste, 7 km N of Gorizia
USA Rep: Euro-Connection 800-645-3876

Without a doubt, San Gimignano is one of the most picturesque places in Tuscany: a postcard-perfect hilltop village punctuated by 14 tall towers. During the day, the town bustles with activity, but after the busloads of tourists depart, the romantic ambiance of yester-year fills the cobbled streets. For the lucky few who spend the night, there is a jewel of small inn, the Hotel L'Antico Pozzo. What a pleasure to see a renovation done with such excellent taste and meticulous attention to maintaining the authentic character of the original building. The name of the hotel derives from an antique stone well (pozzo) which is softly illuminated just off the lobby. The fact that only the most affluent families could afford the luxury of a private well indicates that this 15th-century townhouse was at one time a wealthy residence. A time-worn stone staircase leads up to the air-conditioned bedrooms, tucked at various levels along a maze of hallways. Each one of the quietly elegant rooms has its own personality: frescoed walls, thick stone walls, terra-cotta floors, and beautifully framed antique prints, plus satellite television. One of my favorites, number 20, is a large room with the palest of pastel-peach-colored walls, windows opening onto the terrace, and a fabulous domed ceiling painted with ancient Roman designs. Another that won my heart was 34—a small, romantic room with a large arched window capturing a fabulous view. Breakfast is the only meal served, but restaurants abound, including the superb La Mangiataoia.

HOTEL L'ANTICO POZZO
Manager: Emanuele Marro
Via San Matteo, 87
53037 San Gimignano (SI), Italy
Tel: (0577) 94 20 14 Fax: (0577) 94 21 17
18 rooms, Double: Lire 180,000–230,000
Open all year
Credit cards: all major
No restaurant, breakfast only
55 km SW of Florence, 38 km N of Siena

San Gimignano is one of the most fascinating of the medieval Tuscany hilltowns. As you approach, this looks like a city of skyscrapers: come even closer and the skyscrapers emerge as 14 soaring towers—dramatic reminders of what San Gimignano must have looked like in all her glory when this wealthy town sported 72 giant towers. Most tourists come just for the day to visit this small town, but if you are lucky enough to be able to spend the night, San Gimignano has a simple but very charming hotel, La Cisterna. The hotel is located on the town's main square and fits right into the ancient character of the surrounding buildings with its somber stone walls softened by ivy, arched shuttered doors, and red-tile roof. Inside La Cisterna, the medieval feeling continues with lots of stone, vaulted ceilings, leather chairs, and dark woods. The bedrooms are not fancy, but pleasant, and some have balconies with lovely views of the valley. Renovations in 1991 added air conditioning in the restaurant and satellite TV (for European channels). La Cisterna is probably more famous as a restaurant than as a hotel and people come from far and wide because not only is the food delicious, but the dining rooms are delightful. Especially charming is the dining room with the brick wall, sloping ceiling supported by giant beams, and picture windows framing the gorgeous Tuscany hills.

LA CISTERNA
Owner: S. Salvestrimi
Piazza della Cisterna, 24
53037 San Gimignano (SI), Italy
Tel: (0577) 94 03 28 Fax: (0577) 94 20 80
50 rooms, Double: Lire 156,000–191,000
Suite: to Lire 221,000
Open March 9 to January 10
Credit cards: all major
Restaurant closed Tuesdays and lunch on Wednesdays
54 km SW of Florence, 38 km NW of Siena

The Castel San Gregorio is a sensational small 12th-century stone castle just a short drive from Assisi, reached after following a winding road through a forest that emerges at the top of a hill to a truly romantic secluded hideaway. There is a terrace to the side where tables and chairs are strategically placed to capture a splendid view of the valley far below. The castle, dating from 1140, has been meticulously reconstructed preserving its original appearance outside, and maintaining a castle-like ambiance inside. The interior of the hotel is quite dark due both to the character of the building and the wall coverings. The old-world ambiance is further enhanced by the bountiful use of excellent antiques. The reception desk is in the front lobby: to the left as you enter is an ornate living room; to the right is a dining room where one large table is set each night for the guests to eat together family style. A restaurant is located on a lower level, open to the general public, where elegant dining is offered in a beautifully decorated room. The bedrooms I saw, although somewhat dark, were all quite outstandingly decorated with a collection of fine antiques. Surrounding the hotel are many walking paths leading through the quiet wooded hills. The Castel San Gregorio is a terrific value for a hotel with so much character. *NOTE:* The closest town on the Hallwag map is Pianello: the Castel San Gregorio is on a small road that goes south from town.

CASTEL SAN GREGORIO
Owner: Claudio Bianchi
Via San Gregorio, 16 (Near Pianello)
06081 San Gregorio, Assisi (PG), Italy
Tel: (075) 80 38 009 Fax: (075) 80 38 904
12 rooms, Double: Lire 210,000*
*Rate includes breakfast and dinner
Closed January
Credit cards: all major
Restaurant open daily
16 km NW of Assisi, 2 km S of Pianello

Staying at the Villa Arceno is truly like staying with friends in a sumptuous Italian villa. If you enjoy luxury, exquisite decor, breathtaking vistas, impeccable service, and warmth of welcome, this will definitely be your cup of tea. The mood of grandeur is set as you approach by a seemingly endless private road that winds through lovingly tended vineyards to a classic, three-story, ochre-colored villa. At one time the summer home of royalty, this 17th-century Palladian villa has been masterfully restored, both outside and within. The public rooms are more like lounges in a private home with a sophisticated, yet comfortable, elegance. The 16 individually decorated guestrooms in the main villa are gorgeous—even the standard rooms are enormous and splendidly decorated. All the rooms are so outstanding it is difficult to choose, but I think my favorites are 104 and 204, both with sweeping vistas of vine-covered fields. By the time you arrive, 16 more guestrooms should be available in the characterful winery overlooking the garden. In addition to just reveling in the utter peace and quiet, sightseeing in nearby Siena, or exploring the wonders of Tuscany, you can enjoy bicycles, a swimming pool, a tennis court, and, best of all, a park. Here you can stroll for hours along romantic lanes shaded by imposing rows of centuries-old cypress trees or meander on paths through the forest, passing almost-hidden statues and small temples, down to an idyllic, secluded lake.

HOTEL VILLA ARCENO
Manager: Gualtiero Mancini
53010 San Gusmè (SI), Italy
Tel:(0577) 35 92 92 Fax: (0577) 35 92 76
16 rooms, Double: Lire 400,000
Open March to October
Credit cards: all major
Restaurant open daily
22 km NE of Siena, 9 km NW of Castelnuovo

If you are looking for a place to stay in the heart of Tuscany that is moderately priced, yet does not sacrifice one ounce of charm or quality of accommodation, the family-run Hotel Belvedere di San Leonino is unsurpassable. Ceramic pots of geraniums, trellised grape vines, and climbing roses soften and add color to the weathered stone buildings which were originally a cluster of 15th-century farmers' cottages. Off the central patio area is a small reception area, a living room which is blandly decorated with contemporary furniture, and an attractive dining room with tiled floors, rustic beamed ceiling, and appropriately simple wooden tables and chairs. When the weather is warm, meals are served outside in the garden. Because the rooms are tucked into various parts of the old farmhouses, they vary in size and shape. They also differ in decor, but all have an antique ambiance with wrought-iron headboards, beautiful old armoires, and pretty white curtains. Number 46, a large room overlooking the swimming pool, is especially attractive. What adds the icing to the cake is the setting of the Belvedere, nestled in the very heart of the Chianti wine region, surrounded by stunning scenery—in every direction you look there are idyllic, sweeping vistas of rolling hills dotted with vineyards, olive groves, and pine forests. Another plus: Hotel Belvedere is conveniently located only a short drive from the freeway.

HOTEL BELVEDERE DI SAN LEONINO
Manager: Signora C. Orlandi
Localita San Leonino
53011 Castellina in Chianti (SI), Italy
Tel: (0577) 74.08.87 Fax: (0577) 74.09.24
28 rooms, Double: Lire 140,000
Open mid-March to mid-November
Credit cards: all major
Restaurant open daily
16 km N of Siena, 65 km S of Florence

The Residence San Sano is a small hotel in San Sano—a hamlet in the center of the Chianti wine-growing region. We were charmed by the hotel that is incorporated into a 16th-century stone building. The gracious owners, Giancarlo Matarazzo and his German wife, Heidi, were both schoolteachers in Germany prior to returning to Italy to open a small hotel. They have done a beautiful job in the renovation and in the decor. A cozy dining room serves guests excellent meals featuring typically Tuscan-style cooking. Each of the bedrooms is delightfully furnished in antiques and each has a name incorporating some unique feature of the hotel—the name evolving from the time during reconstruction when Heidi and Giancarlo remembered each room by its special feature. My favorite room was the Bird Room: here birds had claimed the room for many years and had nested in holes that went completely through the wall. With great imagination, the holes were left open to the outside, but on the inside were covered with glass. Now the birds can still nest and guests have the fun of watching the babies. One room is named for a beautiful, long-hidden Romanesque window that was discovered and incorporated into the decor, another room for its very special view, and another for an antique urn uncovered during renovation. On our latest visit, the inn looked even lovelier than ever and a new pool now nestles in the vineyards. *NOTE:* The closest town on the Hallwag map is Radda.

HOTEL RESIDENCE SAN SANO
Owners: Heidi & Giancarlo Matarazzo
Localita San Sano
53010 Lecchi in Chianti (SI), Italy
Tel: (0577) 74 61 30 Fax: (0577) 74 61 56
14 rooms, Double: Lire 170,000–190,000
Closed November to mid-March
Credit cards: all major
Restaurant closed Sunday, for guests only
60 km S of Florence, 9 km S of Radda

The 16th-century Locanda San Vigilio is truly special: our favorite among the tiny luxury inns in the beautiful lake district of northern Italy. And, although it is expensive, it costs less to stay here than at some of the famous well-known queens along the lake. Not only is it a superb small hotel, but the location is unsurpassed: the Locanda San Vigilio is romantically positioned fronting the water on an exquisite, parklike peninsula that juts out into Lake Garda. There is not much action here. If you want to see and be seen by the rich and famous, the glamorous Villa d'Este should be your hub, but if you desire tranquillity accompanied by lovely accommodations, then try the San Vigilio. Here you will find understated luxury, nothing commercial at all—in fact, hardly a sign marks the tree-lined entrance just a few kilometers north of the town of Garda. After parking your car in the designated area, you walk past a gorgeous Italian villa and then down a path to the hotel, a sturdy stone building so close to the water that waves gently lap the walls. The dining room is lovely and if you are lucky, you can eat at one of the cozy tables overlooking the lake. The food is sensational and the decor is faultless. Upstairs, the prize guestrooms overlook the lake. If you long for tranquillity, this is it. Winston Churchill came here to paint—after visiting the San Vigilio you may also be inspired to take up painting.

LOCANDA SAN VIGILIO
Owner: Conte Agostino Guarienti di Brenzone
Manager: Christine Kössler
37016 San Vigilio, Lake Garda (VR), Italy
Tel: (045) 72 56 688 Fax: (045) 72 56 551
7 rooms, Double: Lire 290,000–470,000
Open March to November
Credit cards: all major
Restaurant open daily, for guests only
154 km W of Venice, 3 km N of Garda

Hotel Descriptions

The Pitrizza is a tiny jewel of a hotel located on the Emerald Coast of the island of Sardinia—the playground of the Aga Khan and the jet set of the world. From the moment you enter through the front gate, marked only with a discreet sign, you are in a world of tranquillity and beauty. There is a central clubhouse which has a beautiful lounge, a delightful dining room with hand-hewn wooden chairs, a card room, and a bar. A small protected patio extends from the dining room where meals are served when the weather is warm. French doors from the lounge open onto the terrace which leads down to a most unusual swimming pool, cleverly designed into the natural rock. Once in this wonderful pool, you have the impression that you are swimming in the sea, not a pool, because the water level matches that of the bay. The bedrooms, not especially large, but beautiful, with every detail of the finest quality, are tucked away in small cottages which blend into the landscape. If your idea of a vacation is a frenzy of activity and things to do then the Pitrizza is definitely not for you. There are no planned activities, no sports director, no loud music—only lovely quiet, gourmet food, a beautiful pool, and a delightful small white-sand beach.

HOTEL PITRIZZA
Manager: Pier Angelo Tondina
07020 Porto Cervo, Sardinia, Italy
Tel: (0789) 91 500 Fax: (0789) 91 629
51 rooms, Double: Lire 1,287,000–1,496.000*
*Rate includes breakfast and dinner
Open mid-May to September
Credit cards: all major
Restaurant open daily
Island of Sardinia
NE tip of Sardinia, airport Olbia

Having heard about a lovely little chalet tucked amidst the pines high in the Italian Alps near the French border, I was beginning to wonder what awaited me as the road wound through the ski town of Sauze d'Oulx with its unattractive jumble of modern concrete ski hotels. However, the road soon left the resort town and continued up, twisting higher and higher into the mountains until suddenly Il Capricorno came into view, nestled in the forest to the left of the road. Just as you enter there is a tiny bar and, beyond, a cozy dining room enhanced by dark wooden chalet-style chairs, rustic wooden tables, and a stone fireplace with logs stacked neatly by its side. There is not a hint of elaborate elegance—just a simple, cozy country charm: the perfect kind of inn to come home to after a day of skiing or walking along the beautiful mountain trails. The bedrooms, too, are simple but most pleasant, with dark-pine handmade furniture, neat little bathrooms, and, for a lucky few, balconies with splendid mountain views. However, the greatest assets of this tiny inn are the owners, Mariarosa and Carlo Sacchi. Carlo personally made most of the furniture and will frequently join the guests for skiing. Mariarosa is the chef, a fabulous gourmet cook. This is a very special little hideaway for very special people.

IL CAPRICORNO
Owners: Mariarosa & Carlo Sacchi
Les Clotes
10050 Sauze d'Oulx (TO), Italy
Tel: (0122) 85 02 73 Fax: (0122) 85.02.73
7 rooms, Double: Lire 240,000
Open July to mid-September
  and Christmas to May
Credit cards: VS
Restaurant open daily, for guests only
2 km E of Sauze d'Oulx via small lane
60 km W of Turin, 28 km W of Susa
9 km from autostrada

The Maremma, a beautiful area in the coastal foothills of southern Tuscany, quite undiscovered by tourists, offers a wealth of sightseeing possibilities: walled villages, Etruscan ruins, archaeological sites, and lovely landscapes. Until recently there were few places to stay with charm, but happily this problem was solved when the Pellegrini family recently converted a 200-year-old stone farmhouse into a small hotel. Here you will find true Tuscany hospitality from the moment you enter. Although the Pellegrinis do not speak English, they have made sure to employ front-desk personnel who do. The dining room is the heart of the inn and has tables set in a beamed-ceilinged room which is filled with sunlight from large French doors opening onto a terrace where meals are served on warm days. The guestrooms are small, but comfortable, immaculately clean and each with a private bathroom. The warmth and gracious country-style hospitality of this simple small hotel make a stay here special. Another real bonus is the food: it is wonderful—everything is homemade, including marvelous pastas prepared by the talented chef, Tullio Sassi, and the hotel even produces its own wines which are served with the meals. A specialty of the inn is trekking (or, as we say, horseback riding). In the corral below the hotel, horses are groomed each day for guests' use: in fact, special room rates are offered which include riding in the Maremma countryside.

ANTICO CASALE DI SCANSANO
Owners: Massimo Pellegrini & Family
58054 Castagneta-Scansano (GR), Italy
Tel: (0564) 50 72 19 Fax: (0564) 50 78 05
16 rooms, Double: Lire 155,000–195,000
Closed mid-January to March
Credit cards: all major
Restaurant open daily
30 km S of Grosseto, 2 km E of Scansano

Although the Berghotel Tirol is a new hotel, it happily copies the typical chalet style of the Dolomites. Inside, too, the tasteful decor follows the delightful Alpine motif with light-pine furniture, baskets of flowers, and a few antiques for accent pieces. However, what is so very special about the Berghotel Tirol is its marvelous location on a hillside looking over the lovely village of Sexten and to the fabulous mountains beyond. Many of the rooms have large balconies which capture the view and the warmth of the mountain sun. The Berghotel Tirol is not actually in the town of Sexten (Sesto), but in a suburb called Moos (Moso). This is one of the most scenic areas of the Dolomites and the town of Sexten is one of the most attractive of the mountain towns. In addition to the natural beauty, there is a wonderful network of trails leading in every direction to tempt all into the crisp mountain air. When you return at night to the hotel it is rather like a house party: most of the guests come for at least a week and table-hopping is prevalent as the knicker-clad guests share their day's adventures. Acting as hosts to the house party are the extremely gracious, cordial owners, the Holzer family, who seem to be dedicated to seeing that everyone has a good time.

Berghotel Tirol
Owners: Kurt Holzer & Family
39030 Sexten (Sesto) (BZ), Italy
Tel: (0474) 71.03.86 Fax: (0474) 71.04.55
46 rooms, Double: Lire 170,000–300,000*
*Rate includes breakfast and dinner
Open Christmas to Easter
  and mid-May to October
Credit cards: none accepted
Restaurant open daily
Dolomites–near Austria
2 km SE of Sexton toward Moos
44 km E of Cortina, 116 km W of Bolzano

Agrigento is home to Valle dei Templi, justifiably the most visited archeological site in Sicily. To savor these Greek temples to their fullest, be sure to plan ahead so that you can secure a room at the Villa Athena whose location is absolute perfection. Behind the hotel, the gardens (where a large swimming pool is nestled) extend to the very edge of the archeological site. If you enjoy walking, there is no need for a car—just steps from the hotel, a path leads in one direction to the temples and in the other to the museum where many of the fabulous artifacts from the site are beautifully displayed. In front of the hotel, in a separate building opposite the parking area, is the hotel's restaurant—a popular luncheon stop for tour groups. In the summer, guests of the hotel enjoy dinner served outside on a pretty terrace. As you enter the hotel, there is a reception area which opens onto a contemporary-style bar and lounge with black leather sofas and chairs. The modern bedrooms are all similar in style with comfortable, simple furnishings. What is special about the Villa Athena is not the decor, but the ambiance of the 18th-century villa, and, above all, the awesome views. This is one place you should splurge: request one of the rooms overlooking the ruins. And, if you really want to go all out, ask for a balcony! To wake up in the morning and watch the first rays of the sun cast their glow on the marvelous temple of Concordia is magical.

VILLA ATHENA
Owner: Francesco d'Alessandro
Via dei Templi, 33
92100 Agrigento, Sicily, Italy
Tel: (0922) 59 62 88 Fax: (0922) 40 21 80
40 rooms, Double: from Lire 250,000
Open all year
Credit cards: all major
Restaurant open daily
128 km SE of Palermo, 212 km SW of Taormina

Hugging the crest of a rocky coastal mountain rising 750 meters above Trapani, Erice's authentic testimony to yesteryear is broken only by several tall communication towers just outside the ancient walls. This appealing town of twisting cobbled streets makes a convenient overnight stop when visiting the Greek temple and theater at Segesta. As you wind up the hill toward Erice, watch for the parking area near Porta Trapani: park here and walk through the arched stone entrance and up the Via Vittorio Emanuele to the Hotel Moderno. The intimate reception area is fresh and inviting, with fresh flowers and attractive prints on the walls. A hallway leads to a lounge accented by chairs grouped around small round tables where guests can just relax or enjoy a cold drink from the adjacent bar. A stone staircase leads up to the guestrooms, all of which are immaculately clean and fresh with whitewashed walls and white-tiled floors. Some bedrooms are decorated with light knotty-pine furniture; others have an antique motif. One of my favorites, room 35, has a handsome king-sized iron bed with brass trim and an antique armoire. About half of the rooms are located just across the street in another very old building which has been renovated—these rooms are similar and equally pleasant. My favorite in the annex is number 71, an especially spacious room with a king-sized bed with a handsome French-style headboard.

HOTEL MODERNO
Owner: Giuseppe Catalano
Via Vittorio Emanuele, 63
91016 Erice, Sicily, Italy
Tel: (0923) 86 93 00 Fax: (0923) 86 91 39
41 rooms, Double: Lire 190,000
Open all year
Credit cards: all major
Restaurant open daily
15 km NE of Trapani, 96 km SW of Palermo

Tenuta Gangivecchio is far off the beaten path, but oh-so-worth a detour. Not only will you discover a jewel of a small inn, but the adventure of finding Gangivecchio leads you through Sicily's beautiful Madonie region. The Tornabene family began by converting a room in their home (a characterful 13th-century Benedictine monastery) into a restaurant serving a set-menu lunch based upon fresh produce from the farm. Although a two-hour-drive, the excellence of the simple, yet delicious meals soon brought guests from as far away as Palermo. Happily for the traveler who loves to stay in the countryside, the enterprising Tornabene family have now renovated the stables of the monastery into nine tastefully decorated guestrooms, appealing in their simplicity, with rustic red-tile floors, fresh whitewashed walls, hand-loomed scatter rugs, dark-wood accents, rough-hewn beamed ceilings, attractively framed old prints on the walls, and pretty cotton floral bedspreads. Delicious home-cooked meals are served to guests in a pretty dining room on the ground floor of the inn. Plan to arrive on a weekend for a lunch prepared by Signora Wanda and her daughter Giovanna, served in the dining room of the monastery. *NOTE:* Drive east through Gangi on SS120. Just outside town, turn right at a small signpost for Gangivecchio. Go for about a kilometer and turn left at a tiny yellow sign. Continue up the hill for about 5 kilometers: Tenuta Gangivecchio is on your right

TENUTA GANGIVECCHIO
Owners: Paolo Tornabene & C. da Gangivecchio
90024 Gangi, Sicily, Italy
Tel: (0921) 89 191 Fax: (0921) 89 191
9 rooms, Double: Lire 180,000*
*Rate includes breakfast and lunch or dinner
Closed 1 or 2 weeks end of June
Credit cards: none accepted
Restaurant open daily
125 km SE of Palermo, 130 km NW of Catania

The Villa Igiea Grand Hotel is an oasis of blissful tranquillity in the midst of the large and rather unattractive city of Palermo. With all the fabulous archaeological sites and marvelous cathedrals in the area, it is wonderful to have such a splendid hotel to come home to at night. The approach to the Villa is not scenic, but from the moment you enter the gates you are in another world: a world of spacious lobbies, sweeping verandas, formal dining rooms, and generously sized, well furnished bedrooms with large modern bathrooms. Many of the bedrooms have private balconies overlooking the gardens to the sea. The hotel is called a villa, but it is much more like a small deluxe castle built right at the edge of the sea. A lovely free-form swimming pool fits itself onto a ledge that overhangs the water. Next to the pool the hotel has its very own ancient Greek temple— now how many hotels can top that? The most outstanding attributes of the hotel are the gardens that envelop the building in a nest of beautiful pines and masses of gorgeous flowerbeds intertwined with twisting pathways. Altogether, a most delightful spot.

VILLA IGIEA GRAND HOTEL
Manager: Francesco Arabia
Via Belmonte, 43 (Acquasanta)
90142 Palermo, Sicily, Italy
Tel: (091) 54 37 44 Fax: (091) 54 76 54
117 rooms, Double: Lire 350,000
Open all year
Credit cards: all major
Restaurant open daily
On the northern coast of Sicily
USA Rep: Utell International 800-223-9868

With a glorious, unobstructed view to the sea, the Hotel Belvedere can definitely lay claim to one of the prime positions in the picturesque town of Taormina. Of course this location is not just luck because, undoubtedly, the site was carefully chosen when the Belvedere (one of the first hotels in town) was constructed at the turn of the century. The gentleman who originally built the hotel is the grandfather of the present owners—a continuity that adds greatly to the care and warmth of welcome given to the guests. From first glance, the hotel is immediately appealing—a pale ochre-colored villa laced with ivy and accented by wrought-iron balconies. Flowers abound on the walkways and a romantic garden terraces down below the hotel, providing quiet shady nooks for guests to enjoy the view. On one of the lower terraces, a large swimming pool is practically hidden by a lush blanket of shrubs, shade trees, and towering palms. This cool oasis is a favorite gathering spot for guests, and although there is no formal restaurant, light refreshments including pasta, sandwiches, and cold drinks are available by the pool. The lounges of the hotel are pleasantly decorated with contemporary furniture accented by some family antiques. The guestrooms are modern, with built-in beds. However, it is not the decor that captures the hearts of guests who return each year, but rather the friendliness of the staff and the superb setting.

HOTEL BELVEDERE
Owners: Pecaut-Castorina Family
79 Via Bagnoli Croci
98039 Taormina, Sicily, Italy
Tel: (0942) 23 791 Fax: (0942) 62 58 30
47 rooms, Double: Lire 150,000–226,000
Closed October to mid-March
Credit cards: MC, VS
Snack bar open daily for lunch
On the eastern coast of Sicily

The San Domenico Palace is a super deluxe hotel cleverly incorporated into what was formerly a Dominican monastery. Don't let the monastery bit deter you: absolutely no trace of a life of denial remains. In fact, this is one of the most luxurious hotels in Italy, catering to your every whim. As you enter the building the lobby opens onto the core of the hotel, the beautiful arcaded Renaissance cloister. Around this inner courtyard the vaulted walkway is now glassed in, but filled with light. Leading off the courtyard are various lounges, writing rooms, and game rooms. The dining room is a masterpiece: it has high-backed wooden chairs, enormous arched windows, and a paneled ceiling. The chapel has been converted into a bar. Throughout the hotel there are priceless antiques of a quality that would make a museum blush with pride. Many of the bedrooms look out to the beautiful bay of Taormina. In the rear of the hotel there is a lovely garden filled with gorgeous flowers and laced by pathways with small nooks where you can stop to soak in the splendid sea view. A swimming pool is squeezed into the property just as it drops down to the road below. There is no doubt that this is a **most** dramatic hotel.

SAN DOMENICO PALACE
Manager: Piero D'Anna
Piazza San Domenico, 5
98039 Taormina, Sicily, Italy
Tel: (0942) 23 701 Fax: (0942) 62 55 06
100 rooms, Double: Lire 620,000
Open all year
Credit cards: all major
Restaurant open daily
On the eastern coast of Sicily
USA Rep: E&M 800-223-9832

For those who want to visit the beautiful, yet expensive, resort town of Taormina and yet do not want to pay to pay deluxe hotel rates, the well managed, friendly, home-like Villa Fiorita is an excellent choice. It is easy to find since the hotel is located on the main access into town, just across from the funicular which whisks guests down to the beach. Although facing directly onto a busy street, the hotel is carved into the rocks of the steep hillside so that the rooms are staggered up many levels, a situation that provides intriguing nooks and crannies for small terraces, intimate little gardens laced with fragrant blossoms, and even a swimming pool. The decor has an old-fashioned, somewhat tired look which is fortunately relieved by a few pieces of antique furniture that add a bit of interest. The bedrooms vary in personality—some are much more attractive than others. However, all are air-conditioned, have direct-dial telephone, radio, television, mini-bar, and either a terrace or balcony. You will certainly not be disappointed if you are lucky enough to snare a room such as number 12—a real gem with a colorful tiled floor, antique brass bed, an attractive writing desk, and, most wonderful of all, French doors which open to a secluded terrace with a romantic view of the sea. When the weather is warm, breakfast is served outside in the garden with a memorable, sweeping vista of the dramatic coastline.

VILLA FIORITA
Manager: Vincenzo Manganaro
Via Luigi Pirandello, 39
98039 Taormina, Sicily, Italy
Tel: (0942) 24 122 Fax: (0942) 62 59 67
24 rooms, Double: Lire 150,000
Open all year
Credit cards: all major
No restaurant, breakfast only
On the eastern coast of Sicily

Although only a few kilometers down a twisting road from the colorful, medieval hilltop town of Erice, Valderice cannot compete in old-world charm with its neighbor. But don't be discouraged as you drive through the congested town, because as you take the road S187 east toward Castellammare, you are once again in the countryside and will see on your right the Baglio Santacroce—an appealing small, family-run hotel built into a rustic stone farmhouse dating back to 1636. The thick exposed stone walls, tiled floors accented by hand-woven rugs, and simple furnishings of the guestrooms are in harmony with the original structure. No two bedrooms are alike, yet all are attractive and have antique headboards and chairs fashioned from olive wood. Nestled on the terrace to the side of the hotel is a small, pretty swimming pool—a welcome retreat after a day of sightseeing. From the pool, the view to the west is interrupted a bit by modern buildings, but the vista straight ahead to the sea is outstanding. The hotel portion of the Baglio Santacroce has a charming antique ambiance, but the style changes completely in the newly built restaurant which wraps around the front of the hotel. Here the mood is jarred by starkly modern decor, but the sweeping view over the olive and lemon trees out to the sea is beautiful. The restaurant features Mediterranean-style cooking, specializing in freshly caught fish.

BAGLIO SANTACROCE
Owners: Cusenza Family
1 km E of Valderice on S187
91019 Valderice (TP), Sicily, Italy
Tel: (0923) 89 11 11 Fax: (0923) 89 11 92
25 rooms, Double: Lire 140,000
Open all year
Credit cards: all major
Restaurant open daily
1 km E of Valderice, 80 km SW of Palermo

If you would like to combine your sightseeing of Siena with a luxury resort, then the Certosa di Maggiano might be just your cup of tea. This is an expensive hotel, but delightful and unique. Outside, the hotel looks quite ordinary—just a wall facing the road—but when you step inside it is a fairyland. It doesn't resemble a hotel in the slightest: and it is no wonder, for the hotel is built into the restored ruins of a 700-year-old Carthusian monastery. As you enter the arcaded courtyard you can almost see the ghosts of monks, their dark robes flowing, silently walking beneath the vaulted roof of the cloisters. On three sides of the courtyard are arranged the guestrooms, the lounges, the game rooms, the library, the bar, and the exquisite dining room. The fourth side of the courtyard is formed by a small church. The guestrooms are spacious and pleasant, but not outstanding in decor. However, the public rooms are smashing, with antiques galore, all of the finest quality. Another bonus: there is a beautiful pool in the gardens that is never crowded since this is such a tiny hotel. There are so few people around, that it truly is like being a guest on a private estate.

CERTOSA DI MAGGIANO
Manager: Anna Recordati
Via Certosa, 82/86
53100 Siena, Italy
Tel: (577) 28 81 80 Fax: (0577) 28 81 89
5 rooms,, 12 suites Double: Lire 500,000
Suite: Lire 700,000–850,000
Open all year
Credit cards: all major
Restaurant
2 km E of Siena, near the Porta Romana gate
USA Rep: Relais & Chateaux 212-856-0115

The Locanda dell'Amorosa makes a wonderful base for exploring the hilltowns south of Florence. It is very accessible since it is located in Sinalunga which is just a few minutes from the expressway between Rome and Florence. From the Locanda dell'Amorosa it is an easy drive to such sightseeing delights as Siena, Pienza, Orvieto, Todi, and Assisi. However, it is not location alone which makes this hotel so perfect: there is far more. Truly, the Locanda dell'Amorosa would be marvelous if there were nothing nearby—in fact, the hotel is a tiny town a few kilometers south of Sinalunga, approached along a road lined by a majestic row of cypress trees. Park your car and enter the walls of the 14th-century medieval town where you are greeted by an enormous plaza with its own little church—exquisite inside with its soft pastels and its lovely fresco of the Madonna holding the Christ child. To the right of the main entrance to the courtyard are the stables which have been converted to a beautiful restaurant whose massive beams and natural stone-and-brick walls are original and tastefully enhanced by arched windows, thick wrought-iron fixtures, and wooden tables. Soon to be opened is a new wine bar, Enoteca, with a large selection of wines. The guestrooms, located in a separate building to the left of the main entrance, are tastefully appointed with a few antiques and matching bedspreads and draperies. The rest of this tiny village spreads out behind the main square and the buildings are used for other purposes—including the production of wine. The hotel is hoping to add a swimming pool.

LOCANDA DELL'AMOROSA
Manager: Carlo Citterio
53048 Sinalunga (SI), Italy
Tel: (0577) 67 94 97 Fax: (0577) 63 20 01
17 rooms, Double: Lire 330,000–530,000
Closed January 10 to March 8
Credit cards: all major
Restaurant closed Mondays
80 km S of Florence, 45 km E of Siena

What a sense of impending grandeur you experience as you wait for the giant metal gates of the Villa Cortine Palace to swing open. Inside, the road winds and curves impressively past fountains and statues, flower gardens and mighty trees, until you reach the summit where the Villa Cortine Palace reigns. This beautifully situated villa has been expanded so that the original wing now boasts a new section which appears to have more than doubled the size of the original castle. Some of the remodeling has a too-modern feel: one rather wishes that perhaps more of an old-world ambiance could have been preserved. However, in the old section of the villa, which is to the left as you enter the lobby, the rooms still maintain their grandeur with incredibly ornate furniture, soaring ceilings, and stunning paintings. Upstairs the guestrooms are large and are decorated with color-coordinated drapes, chairs, and bedspreads. What leaves absolutely nothing to be improved upon are the gardens—what a gorgeous sight: they are absolutely awe-inspiring. The villa is surrounded by graveled walkways that wind in and out amongst the fountains, ponds, statues, and glorious rose gardens, all overlooking the lovely Lake Garda.

VILLA CORTINE PALACE HOTEL
Manager: Roberto Cappelletto
25019 Sirmione (BS), Italy
Tel: (030) 99 05 890 Fax: (030) 91 63 90
55 rooms,, 2 suites Double: Lire 440,000–560,000*
Suite: from Lire 850,000*
*3-night minimum
Open April to November
Credit cards: all major
Restaurant open daily
Park setting–overlooks Lake Garda
127 km E of Milan, 35 km W of Verona
USA Rep: JDB Associates 800-346-5358

Located about an hour's drive south of Milan's Linate airport, the Locanda del Lupo makes a convenient stop if you plan to drive directly south toward Florence. Soragna is a sleepy little town in the countryside whose main point of interest is a walled, medieval fortress. Around the central plaza buildings of great character are interspersed with modern construction. The Locanda del Lupo, built in the 18th century by the noble Meli Lupi family, is easy to find—just a block off the plaza. The inn is best known as a gourmet restaurant: there is a series of beautiful dining rooms with gleaming copper hanging from whitewashed walls, terra-cotta floors, dark beamed ceilings, antique clocks, and 17th-century oil paintings. To the left of the reception area is a cozy bar and, beyond, a formal living room furnished in antiques. A flight of stairs leads to the guestrooms whose old-world ambiance is enhanced by beamed ceilings, tiled floors, and thick walls. Each bedroom is individually decorated and exudes a refined, country-house atmosphere. Authentic antique furnishings (including fine wooden chests and wrought-iron bedsteads) impart a feeling of quality. *NOTE:* From the Milan-Bologna expressway, take the Fidenza exit and follow signs to Soragna.

LOCANDA DEL LUPO
Manager: Elisabetta Dioni
Via Garibaldi 64
43019 Soragna (PR), Italy
Tel: (0524) 69 04 44 Fax: (0524) 69 350
46 rooms, Double: Lire 216,000
Suite: Lire 286,000
Closed August
Credit cards: all major
Restaurant open daily
100 km S of Milan, 118 km N of Bologna

The Grand Hotel Excelsior Vittoria has a superb location high on the cliff overlooking the port and bay of Sorrento and surrounded by an orange grove and park of about four acres with a swimming pool. You enter the hotel, a grand old villa with a real old-world atmosphere, through a formal gate which is just a short stroll from the center of town. The furnishings, for the most part, continue the antique mood. The Excelsior Vittoria is a good place to splurge and reserve one of the superior rooms with a view of the sea. The ceilings in some of the reception rooms and in the marvelous airy dining room have gorgeous frescoed designs. The terraces and gardens surrounding the hotel offer wonderful views, as do the bedrooms which face the bay. When we first saw the Grand Hotel Excelsior Vittoria there was a gracious, though faded, elegance to the hotel giving it a slightly worn look. However, this magnificent villa has since been lovingly restored under the guidance of Lidia Fiorentino, the owner's wife, carefully retaining the unique turn-of-the-century mood. Staying here will certainly delight anyone who loves the feeling of reliving the grandeur of days gone by in a villa by the sea.

GRAND HOTEL EXCELSIOR VITTORIA
Owners: Fiorentino Family
Manager: Mario Damiano
Piazza Torquato Tasso, 34
80067 Sorrento (NA), Italy
Tel: (081) 80 71 044 Fax: (081) 87 71 206
125 rooms, Double: Lire 395,000–510,000
Suite: Lire 580,000–1,000,000
Open all year
Credit cards: all major
Restaurant open daily
48 km S of Naples, 250 km S of Rome
USA Rep: JDB Associates 703-684-3834

It was love at first sight as I drove up the long graveled road through forest and vineyard and suddenly caught my first glimpse of the Borgo Pretale, a tiny cluster of weathered stone buildings nestled next to their medieval watchtower. My first impression was more than justified—this small inn is truly paradise. There is absolute serenity and beauty here with nothing to mar its perfection. Civilization seems far away as the eye stretches over a glorious vista of rolling hills forested with oaks, juniper, and laurel, interspersed with square patches of vineyards. But although this small village is seemingly remote, it is only a short drive south of Siena, thus a perfect hideaway from which to enjoy the magic of Tuscany. Although the buildings seem rustic, this tiny hotel, tucked into a 12th-century hamlet, offers some of the finest accommodations in all of Italy. Each room is a showplace of fine country antiques and splendid designer fabrics, blended together with the artful eye of a skilled decorator. Every piece is selected to create a sophisticated yet rustic elegance. The lounge beckons guests to linger after dinner by the roaring fire. A path leads to a groomed tennis court and farther on to a swimming pool on a hillside terrace. *NOTE:* Pretale-Sovicille is not on any map we could find. The closest town on the Hallwag map is Rosia, which is about 5 kilometers southeast of Borgo Pretale.

BORGO PRETALE
Manager: Daniele Rizzardini
53018 Localita Pretale-Sovicille (SI), Italy
Tel: (0577) 34 54 01 Fax: (0577) 34 56 25
33 rooms, Double: Lire 320,000–384,000
Open mid-March to mid-November
Credit cards: all major
Restaurant open daily
18 km SW of Siena on Rte 73

The walled hilltown of Spoleto is a must on any trip to Umbria. What Spoleto has that is so outstanding is its Bridge of Towers (*Ponte delle Torri*), an absolutely awesome feat of engineering. Built in the 13th century on the foundations of an old Roman aqueduct, this bridge, spanning a vast crevasse, is supported by ten Gothic arches that soar into the sky. Built into the hillside, the Hotel Gattapone (a mustard-yellow building with dark-green shutters) provides a box-seat location to admire this architectural masterpiece. As you enter, there is a cozy reception area. To the left is a bright, sunny lounge with modern black-leather sofas, a long black-leather bar, very pretty deep-blue walls, large pots of green plants, an antique grandfather clock, and, best of all, an entire wall of glass which provides a bird's eye view of the bridge. To the right of the reception area, steps sweep down to another bar and lounge where breakfast is served. This room is even more starkly modern, with deep-red wall coverings. The newer wing of the hotel houses the superior-category bedrooms, each with a sitting area and large view windows. In the original section of the hotel the bedrooms are smaller, but also very attractive and every one has a view. Tucked below the hotel is a sunny terrace. Although most of the hotels in this guide have more of an antique ambiance, the Gattapone is highly recommended—a special hotel offering great warmth of welcome and superb vistas.

HOTEL GATTAPONE
Owner: Dr. Pier Hanke Giulio
Via del Ponte, 6
06049 Spoleto (PG), Italy
Tel: (0743) 22 34 47 Fax: (0473) 22 34 48
13 rooms, Double: Lire 200,000–300,000
Open all year
Credit cards: all major
No restaurant, breakfast only
Located 130 km N of Rome, 48 km S of Assisi

As you twist up the steep narrow road from Spoleto toward Monteluco, you will see on your left an appealing, ochre-colored villa just peeking out from a dense cloak of trees. The setting looks so fabulous that you will hope this is your hotel. It is, and you won't be disappointed. The Eremo delle Grazie is an astounding property—truly a living museum, with history simply oozing from every nook and cranny. The property has been the home of the Lalli family for many years, but its roots date to the 5th century to a small religious grotto, where pious men lived, which is now behind the bar. From its humble beginnings, the religious importance of this little cave grew and in the 15th and 16th centuries one of Italy's important cardinals called Eremo delle Grazie home (his bedroom is now one of the guestrooms). The cardinal knew how to live in comfort—his cave was not carved in the rocks, but painted onto his bedroom walls. One of my favorite places in Eremo delle Grazie is the tiny, incredibly beautiful, vaulted chapel with beautifully preserved 15th-century paintings of the life of Mary. Another favorite is the splendid terrace with a sweeping view of the glorious Umbrian landscape. Just below the hotel, a swimming pool is tucked onto a terrace. According to Signor Lalli, Michelangelo was once a guest at Eremo delle Grazie. In his letter to Vasari, Michelangelo wrote that he left part of his heart at Eremo delle Grazie. You will too.

EREMO DELLE GRAZIE
Owner: Professor Pio Lalli
06049 Monteluco, Spoleto (PG), Italy
Tel: (0743) 49 624 Fax: (0743) 49 650
11 rooms, Double: Lire 350,000–450,000
Open all year
Credit cards: none accepted
Restaurant open daily during high season
3.5 km E of Spoleto, 124 km N of Rome

The road to the Pensione Stefaner winds up a tiny mountain valley in the heart of the Dolomites. The road is spectacular. As we rounded the last curve before St. Zyprian (San Cipriano) the valley opened up and there spread before us was a sweeping vista of majestically soaring mountains. Across soft-green meadows painted with wildflowers and dotted with tiny farm chalets soared an incredible saw-toothed range of gigantic peaks. A tiny church with a pretty steeple added the final touch of perfection to the already idyllic scene. There are many places to stay in this region—none are glamorous resorts, but rather small family-run pensions. One of our favorites is the Pensione Stefaner, an attractive, chalet-style hotel with flower-laden balconies. There is a smattering of antiques, but most of the furniture is new. The hotel is efficiently and warmly managed by the young, attractive Villgrattner family. Signora Villgrattner is a genuinely gracious hostess and her husband (the chef) provides wonderful home-cooked meals for the guests. The simple bedrooms, some of which have balconies with mountain views, are all impeccably tidy. *NOTE:* Tiers is called Tires on some maps. The town of St. Zyprian (San Cipriano) rarely shows up on any maps, but it is just 3 kilometers east of Tiers.

PENSIONE STEFANER
Owners: Villgrattner Family
39050 Tiers-St. Zyprian (BZ), Italy
Tel & fax: (0471) 64 21 75
15 rooms, Double: Lire 260,000–340,000*
*Rate includes breakfast and dinner
Closed mid-November to mid-December
Credit cards: none accepted
Restaurant open daily, for guests only
NE Italy in Dolomites
17 km E of Bolzano, 3 km E of Tiers

Le Tre Vaselle is a very sophisticated inn located in the small wine town of Torgiano which is very near Assisi. The decor of the hotel is that of a lovely country manor. The owners are the Lungarotti family, famous for their production of superb wines: Signor Lungarotti owns all of the vineyards around Torgiano for as far as the eye can see. The hotel probably evolved to fill the need for a place for business associates and friends to stay when visiting the vineyards. The accommodations are extremely comfortable and have all the amenities of a large city hotel. The most amazing aspect of Le Tre Vaselle is that it has stunning conference rooms furnished in antiques with intimate adjacent dining rooms. The Lungarotti family has thought of everything: to keep the wives happy while their husbands are in meetings, the hotel schedules cooking classes in one of the most professional kitchens I have ever seen. The Lungarottis also have a private wine museum that would be a masterpiece anywhere in the world. Not only do they have an incredible and comprehensive collection of anything pertaining to wine throughout the ages, but the display is a work of art. The museum alone would be worth a detour to Le Tre Vaselle.

LE TRE VASELLE
Owners: Lungarotti Family
Manager Giovanni Margheritini
Via Garibaldi, 48
06089 Torgiano (PG), Italy
Tel: (075) 98 80 447 Fax: (075) 98 80 214
61 rooms, Double: from Lire 290,000
Open all year
Credit cards: all major
Restaurant open daily
17 km SW of Assisi, 158 km N of Rome

The Baia Paraelios is an absolutely delightful hotel tucked onto the spur of land that juts from the toe of Italy near the ancient port of Tropea. The hotel is actually a resort which follows the contours of the hillside from the highway down to the beach. The reception office is located at the top of the hill and the mood is set from the moment you register. The small office is tastefully decorated with plants and charming old prints on the walls and the personnel in the office are gracious and warm in their welcome. The rooms are all bungalows artfully terraced down the hill to capture the best view possible from each. Midway down is a lovely pool and at beach level you find a beautiful dining room and a comfortable, inviting lounge. The bungalows each have one or more bedrooms, a sitting room, and a deck or patio. The decor is simple but in excellent taste, with tiled floors and earth tones used throughout. One of the most beautiful white-sand beaches I saw in Italy stretches invitingly in front of the complex. The Baia Paraelios makes a nice stop along your route south—not only will you have the benefit of a lovely break in your travels, but also the nearby ancient town of Tropea, which hangs on the cliffs above a beautiful bay, is fun to explore.

BAIA PARAELIOS
Owner: Adolfo Salabe
88035 Parghelia, Tropea (CZ), Italy
Tel: (0963) 60 03 00 Fax: (0963) 60 00 74
70 bungalows, Double: Lire 380,000–660,000*
*Rate includes all meals
Open May 10 to September 25
Restaurant open daily
Southern Italy–near tip of toe
420 km S of Naples, 5 km N of Tropea

The Stella d'Italia is located in San Mamete, a tiny, picturesque village nestled along the northern shore of Lake Lugano, just a few minutes' drive from the Swiss border. The hotel (which has been in the Ortelli family for three generations) makes an excellent choice for a moderately priced lakefront hotel. Mario Ortelli, an extremely cordial host, showed us throughout the hotel which has two adjoining wings, one quite old and the other a new addition. My choice for accommodation would be in the original part which has more old-world ambiance—the rooms I saw here were very pleasant, with large French windows opening onto miniature balconies capturing views of the lake. The lounges and dining room have a few antique accents, but are basically modern in decor. The nicest feature of the hotel is the superb little lakefront garden—in summer this is where all the guests spend their time. Green lawn, fragrant flowers, lacy trees, and a romantic vine-covered trellised dining area make this an ideal spot for whiling away the hours. Steps lead down to a small pier from which guests can swim. Another interesting feature for golf enthusiasts is that there are several golf courses within an easy drive from the hotel—one of these (near the town of Grandola) is one of the oldest in Italy. The ferry dock for picking up and dropping off passengers is adjacent to the hotel.

STELLA D'ITALIA
Owner: Mario Ortelli
San Mamete
Lake Lugano, 22010 Valsolda (CO), Italy
Tel: (0344) 68 139 Fax: (0344) 68 729
36 rooms, Double: Lire 165,000
Open April to September
Credit cards: all major
Restaurant open daily
Lakefront hotel
8 km E of Lugano, 100 km N of Milan

The Pensione Accademia is enchanting—a fairytale villa with delightful gardens and a romantic canal-side location. The hotel has a fabulous setting on an oasis of land almost looped by canals. In front is a beautiful, completely enclosed, secret garden whose walls are so heavily draped with vines that it is not until you discover black iron gates that you see steps leading down to the villa's own gondola landing. As you leave the garden and enter the wisteria-covered palazzo, you come into a spacious old-fashioned parlor with reception desk on the left. A staircase leads upstairs where some of the guestrooms are located in the original villa and others, connected by a hallway, in a portion of the hotel borrowed from an adjacent building. No two of the guestrooms are alike, but none are decorator-perfect—they are like guestrooms in a private home. Some of the bedrooms in the front have canal views, but are noisier than those looking over the garden. The hotel management has an ongoing program of renovations. The only hitch to this picture of perfection is that your chances are slim of snaring a room in this romantic hideaway— the hotel is so special that loyal guests reserve their own favorite room for the following year as they leave. Spring and fall are most heavily booked—your chances are better in July and August when the prices are even a little lower.

PENSIONE ACCADEMIA
Owner: Giovnna Salmaso
Manager: Massimo Dunato
Dorsoduro 1058
3123 Venice, Italy
Tel: (041) 52 37 84 6 Fax: (041) 52 39 15 2
26 rooms, Double: Lire 225,000
Open all year
Credit cards: all major
No restaurant, breakfast only
Near the Accademia boat stop

The Hotel Flora is reached down a tiny lane, just off one of the main walkways to St. Mark's Square: a secluded hideaway, protected from the bustle of the city yet conveniently close to all the action. At the end of the tiny alley the doors open into a small lobby, beyond which is an enchanting small garden, an oasis of serenity with white wrought-iron tables and chairs surrounding a gently tinkling fountain. Potted plants, small trees, and lacy vines complete the idyllic scene. The hotel encloses the garden on three sides: doors open to the right to a dear little bar and the breakfast room. The lounges are Victorian in mood with dark furniture. The bedrooms vary greatly in their size and decor, but all have antique furnishings and Victorian-style wallpaper covers many of the walls. There is definitely an old-world atmosphere. There is no restaurant at the hotel, which is absolutely no problem since Venice abounds with wonderful places to dine. Breakfast, of course, is served to guests. Signor Romanelli, who owns this small hotel, personally sees that his guests are well taken care of. The Hotel Flora is a favorite of many travelers to Venice. Although it is a relatively simple hotel and would not appeal to those looking for deluxe accommodations, the Hotel Flora is a rare find for those who want a relatively inexpensive place to stay in the heart of Venice that combines a superb location, warmth of welcome, and charm.

HOTEL FLORA
Owner: Roger Romanelli
Calle larga 22 Marzo, 2283/a
30124 Venice, Italy
Tel: (041) 52 05 844 Fax: (041) 52 28 217
44 rooms, Double: Lire 280,000
Open all year
Credit cards: all major
No restaurant, breakfast only
3-minute walk from St. Mark's Square

If you love opulent elegance, and if cost is of no consequence to you, the Gritti Palace is an excellent choice for your hotel in Venice. The location is marvelous—just a short walk from St. Mark's Square yet far enough removed to miss the city's noise and summer mob of tourists. With careful planning, you can be entirely insulated in a private and very special world from the moment you arrive until you reluctantly depart. If you take a private motor launch from the airport or the Piazza Roma, you can descend stylishly at the deluxe little private pier in front of the hotel where porters will be waiting to whisk you to your room to be pampered and spoiled. All at a price, of course. The Gritti Palace is expensive—but then what would you expect when staying in the 15th-century palace of the immensely wealthy Venetian Doge, Andrea Gritti? The Gritti Palace has a charming terrace on the bank of the Grand Canal where you dine in splendor and watch the constant stream of boat traffic. The lobby and lounge areas open off the terrace and are grandly decorated with antiques. The bedrooms are large and very fancy in decor, and those that face the canal are presented with a 24-hour show.

HOTEL GRITTI PALACE
Manager: Paolo Danieli
Campo Santa Maria del Giglio, 2467
30124 Venice, Italy
Tel: (041) 79 46 11 Fax: (041) 52 00 942
99 rooms, Double: Lire 732,600–897,600
Open all year
Credit cards: all major
Restaurant open daily
Near St. Mark's Square
USA Rep: Luxury Collection 800-325-3589

The Hotel La Fenice et Des Artistes, although not inexpensive, costs less than many other hotels that do not offer nearly its charm. The lobby is small, but seems spacious since there are two small garden patios that open from it. Here guests sit in the late afternoon for a cup of tea or an aperitif before dinner. Doors to the right lead to a club-like lounge and an intimate bar. The reception area is a triangle connecting the original building on the right with a newer wing on the left. Both sections are nice and most of the rooms are air conditioned—a welcome relief on a hot day. The bedrooms are not large, but adequate, each room color-coordinated with a different wallpaper, setting the theme. Within a few blocks there is a fabulous choice of appealing places to dine. Taverna La Fenice, one of the oldest and most elegant restaurants in Venice, is incorporated into the old wing of the hotel. The fascinating La Fenice Theater, one of the oldest and most beautiful theaters in Europe, is just around the corner—most conveniently located for music lovers.

HOTEL LA FENICE ET DES ARTISTES
Manager: Dante Appollonio
Campiello de la Fenice, S. Marco 1936
30124 Venice, Italy
Tel: (041) 52 32 333 Fax: (041) 52 03 721
75 rooms, Double: Lire 230,000–295,000
Open all year
Credit cards: all major
Restaurant (separate management) open daily
Near La Fenice Theater

A fellow travel writer first recommended the Locanda Sturion to us as an intimate hotel where, with only 11 rooms, each guest is known by name and given personal attention. We quite agree that for a reasonably priced hotel, just a three-minute walk from the Rialto Bridge, the Locanda Sturion has a definite appeal. If you have a problem climbing stairs, be aware that the hotel is not at street level. You ring a bell and the receptionist unlocks the front door which leads to a very long flight of white marble steps. At the top is another door and then a small reception area. Just beyond is one of the nicest features of this small hotel, an intimate parlor-like breakfast room with red brocaded walls, cozy tables with pretty carved chairs, a Venetian glass chandelier, and, on the end wall, a series of three large windows overlooking the Grand Canal. What a wonderful place to eat breakfast and start your day! The guestrooms are all similar in decor, with an old-fashioned look. I don't think they are original antiques, but good copies of antique wooden headboards are used throughout. One of the most attractive rooms is number 1—a spacious room with windows overlooking the Grand Canal. Although not on the canal, room 8 is also very large and attractive. If you choose the Locanda Sturion, you will not be the first to enjoy its hospitality: the hotel dates back to the 13th century when it was built as an inn by the Doge of Venice to house itinerant merchants.

LOCANDA STURION
Manager: Sergio Fragiacomo
San Polo, 679, Calle del Sturion
30125 Venice, Italy
Tel: (041) 52 36 243 Fax: (041) 52 28 378
11 rooms, Double: Lire 180,000–260,000
Open all year
Credit cards: AX, VS
No restaurant, breakfast only
3-minute walk to the Rialto Bridge

At first glance the exterior of the Pensione Seguso appears quite bland: a rather boxy affair without much of the elaborate architectural enhancements so frequently evident in Venice. However, the inside of the pension radiates warmth and charm, with Oriental rugs setting off antique furniture and heirloom silver service. The hotel is located on the left bank of Venice—across the Grand Canal from the heart of the tourist area, about a 15-minute walk to St. Mark's Square (or only a few minutes by ferry from the Accademia boat stop). For several generations the hotel has been in the Seguso family who provide a homelike ambiance for the guest who does not demand luxury. In front there is a miniature terrace harboring a few tables set under umbrellas. Several of the bedrooms have views of the canal (although these rooms are the noisiest due to the canal traffic). Remember this is a simple pension, with most of the rooms sharing a bathroom: if you are looking for the amenities offered by a hotel, the Pensione Seguso would not be for you. However, the most pleasant surprise is that the value-conscious tourist can stay at the Pensione Seguso with breakfast and dinner included for what the price of a room alone would cost in most hotels in Venice. The Seguso has an elevator—handy if you have a problem with stairs.

PENSIONE SEGUSO
Owners: Seguso Family
Grand Canal Zattere, 779
30123 Venice, Italy
Tel: (041) 52 86 858 Fax: (041) 52 22 340
36 rooms, Double: Lire 268,000–283,000*
*Rate includes breakfast and dinner
Open all year
Credit cards: all major
Restaurant open daily, for guests only
10-minute walk from the Accademia boat stop

The Hotel Cipriani was founded by the late Giuseppe Cipriani, who during his lifetime became almost a legend in Venice. This beloved man, who founded the internationally famous Harry's Bar in Venice, had a dream of building a fabulous hotel within easy reach of St. Mark's Square and yet far enough away to guarantee seclusion and peace. He bought 3 acres on the island of Giudecca and with the financial assistance of some of his prestigious friends, such as Princess Briget of Prussia and the Earl of Iveagh (head of the Guinness brewing company in Dublin), he accomplished his dream—an elegant Venetian palace-style hotel. The Cipriani is the perfect hotel for those of you who must have a pool, for it is the only hotel with a pool in Venice. And what a pool—it is Olympic size and surrounded by beautiful gardens. The splendor continues inside where the lounges are tastefully decorated in whites and beiges and the bedrooms are large and elegant. Since our last visit, seven super deluxe apartments, some overlooking St. Mark's Square, have opened in the renovated Palazzo Vendramin adjacent to the hotel. We have not yet been able to inspect this new addition, but it looks beautiful in the pictures. You truly have the best of all worlds at the Cipriani—you are at a superior resort yet only minutes from the heart of Venice in the private launch that waits to whisk you, any time of the day or night, to St. Mark's Square.

HOTEL CIPRIANI
Manager: Dr. Natale Rusconi
Isola della Giudecca, 10
30123 Venice, Italy
Tel: (041) 52 07 744 Fax: (041) 52 03 930
105 rooms, Double: Lire 850,000–1,200,000
Palazzo Vendramin: Double: Lire 1,600,000–2,900,000
Open all year
Credit cards: all major
Restaurant open daily
On Giudecca Island
U.S.A Rep: Relais & Chateaux 212-856-0115

If the idea of being close to Venice and yet near a beach and casino appeals to you, then perhaps you should consider a hotel located on the Lido, a small island opposite St. Mark's Square. A 15-minute boat ride and a short taxi trip brings you to the Albergo Quattro Fontane, a charming inn which reminds me more of a French country home than an Italian villa. It has a white stuccoed exterior with gabled roof, green shutters, and vines creeping both over the door and around some of the small balconies. To the left of the main building is a lovely courtyard whose privacy is established by another wing of the hotel, giving the garden a cozy, walled-in effect. Inside the hotel there is an ambiance of a country home with antiques cleverly used throughout the lounges. The beach is only a short distance away and the Albergo Quattro Fontane can make arrangements for you to reserve a private beach cabana when you arrive at the inn. The cost per day will vary, depending both upon the location and the comparative luxury of the cabana you choose. The beach is wide and the water inviting and clear, although the sand is not as fine and white as we have seen on some of the beaches in southern Italy. It is quite an experience to sample the interesting hierarchy of the Italian beach system.

ALBERGO QUATTRO FONTANE
Manager: Bente Bevilacqua
Via 4 Fontane
30126 Lido of Venice
Venice, Italy
Tel: (041) 52 60 22 7 Fax: (041) 52 60 72 6
68 rooms, Double: from Lire 330,000
Open end of April to October 20
Credit cards: all major
Restaurant open daily
On the Lido, across from Venice

The tiny island of Torcello is located about 50 minutes from Venice by boat. This lovely, sleepy little island is usually considered a short stop for the tour boats as they ply their way among the maze of little islands surrounding Venice. But for those who want to linger on Torcello, where they can be close to Venice yet feel out in the country, there is a deluxe inn owned by the Cipriani family. This small inn, the Locanda Cipriani, is well-known to knowledgeable gourmets as a fantastic restaurant. Many arrive every day from Venice just to dine, and depart never knowing that upstairs this restaurant also has guestrooms. The inn is very simple, much more like a small farmhouse than a deluxe hotel. Inside there is a rustic, cozy dining room and outside a beautiful dining terrace surrounded by gardens brilliant in summer with all varieties of flowers. There are only a few bedrooms—all are suites. Breakfast and dinner are included in the room rate. This is an expensive inn, but an elegant hideaway for relaxing and dining royally in a beautiful country setting. Many famous guests have already discovered this oasis—including Ernest Hemingway, who came here to write. I think you will share his belief that the Locanda Cipriani Torcello is a very special place.

LOCANDA CIPRIANI TORCELLO
Owner: Carla Cipriani
Manager: Bonifacio Brass
30012 Isola Torcello
Venice, Italy
Tel: (041) 73 01 50 Fax: (041) 73 54 33
5 suites: Lire 520,000*
*Rate includes breakfast and dinner
Closed November 4 to March 15
Credit cards: all major
Restaurant closed Tuesdays
Island location
Reached by boat from Venice

The Hotel Gabbia d'Oro, superbly positioned in the heart of romantic Verona, is truly a gem. From the moment you step inside you are surrounded by an understated elegance. Although this is a very deluxe hotel, there is no feeling of stiff formality—your welcome is genuinely warm and friendly. Just off the spacious reception area is a cozy lounge with massive beamed ceilings, ancient stone walls, fine antiques, and handsome old prints in gold frames. Beyond the lobby is an intimate bar with rich wood paneling set off to perfection by chairs upholstered in cheerful cherry-red fabric. There is also a lovely, quiet, inner garden courtyard where on occasion intimate concerts are held. The guestrooms are individually decorated, reflecting exquisite taste: antiques abound and rich color-coordinating fabrics are used throughout. Nothing has been spared to make each room beautiful. The standard bedrooms are very pretty, but if you can afford to splurge, opt for one of the junior suites which are much more spacious. It is such a pleasure to see a new hotel emerge after renovation that reflects so beautifully the authentic rich heritage of the original building. The Hotel Gabbia d'Oro truly captures the romance of Verona. Although excellent restaurants abound in Verona, the hotel offers a buffet and pre-theater restaurant, exclusively for guests. Also, in summer, private, elegant dinners can be arranged with advance notice.

HOTEL GABBIA D'ORO
Manager: Camilla Balzarro
Corso Porta Borsari 4/A
37121 Verona, Italy
Tel: (045) 80 03 060 Fax: (045) 59 02 93
27 rooms, Double: from Lire 390,000
Suites: Lire 1,020,000
Open all year
Credit cards: all major
Restaurant open on request, for guests only
Located in the heart of Verona

The entrance to the Hotel Victoria is starkly modern—almost with a museum-like quality. The white walls, white ceiling, white floors, and an enormous skylight are softened by green plants. At first glance I was disappointed since I had heard so many glowing reports of the merits of this small hotel. However, the mood begins to change as you enter the reception area with its Oriental carpets and by the time you arrive in the lounge area, there is a definite move toward an antique ambiance. Here you find original heavy ancient wooden beams and one of the original stone walls exposed, leather chairs, and some lovely antique tables. The bedrooms are extremely modern and beautifully functional with good reading lights, comfortable chairs, and excellent bathrooms. The Victoria actually dates back centuries and the new hotel is built within the shell of an ancient building. The architect even incorporated some of the archaeologically interesting finds of the site into a museum in the basement level. When the hotel is not full and all of the tables are not needed, special "windows" open up on the floor of the bar and the museum below is lit so that you can study the artifacts as you enjoy an aperitif.

HOTEL VICTORIA
Owner: Signor Andrea Tamborini
Manager: Signora Giusy Loro
Via Adua, 8
37121 Verona, Italy
Tel: (045) 59 05 66 Fax: (045) 59 01 55
75 rooms, Double: Lire 284,000–350,000
Open all year
Credit cards: all major
No restaurant, breakfast only
In the heart of Verona
USA Rep: Harry Jarvinen 800-876-5278

The Hotel Turm belongs to the Romantik hotel chain. Just being a member of this exclusive club indicates the hotel is pretty special because, to become a member, the inn must have the owner personally involved in the management and the interior must have an antique ambiance. The Hotel Turm has an especially attractive little dining room with vaulted whitewashed ceilings and chalet-style rustic wooden furniture. There are a few antiques in the hallways and lounges. The bedrooms are simple, but very pleasant, with light-pine furniture and fluffy down comforters on the beds. There is a swimming pool on the terrace where one can swim or lounge while gazing out to the little town and the mountains beyond and there is even a small indoor pool. The Hotel Turm dates back to the 13th century and Signor Pramstrahler takes great care to maintain touches of the old-world charm with antique chests, cradles, chairs, and ancient artifacts. *NOTE:* Völs is called Fié on some maps.

ROMANTIK HOTEL TURM
Owners: Pramstrahler Family
Fié allo Sciliar
1-39050 Völs am Schlern
Sudtirol (BZ), Italy
Tel: (0471) 72 50 14 Fax: (0471) 72 54 74
24 rooms, Double: Lire 170,000–278,000
Closed November 3 to December 20
Credit cards: MC, VS
Restaurant closed Thursdays
16 km E of Bolzano, 7 km S of Siusi (Seis)
USA Rep: Euro-Connection 800-645-3876

MAPS

Regions of Italy

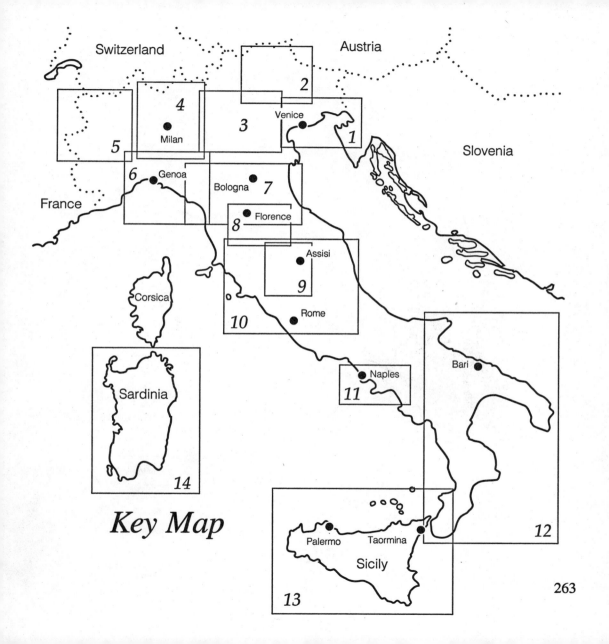

Switzerland

Austria

2

Venice

3

4

Milan

1

Slovenia

5

France

6
Genoa

Bologna

7

8
Florence

Assisi

9

10

Rome

Corsica

Bari

Sardinia

Naples

11

14

12

Key Map

Palermo

Taormina

Sicily

13

263

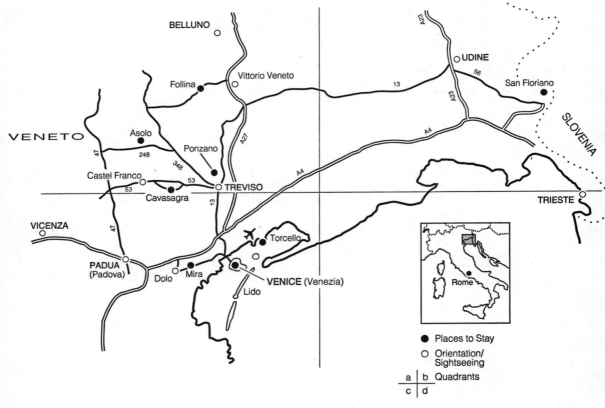

Map 1

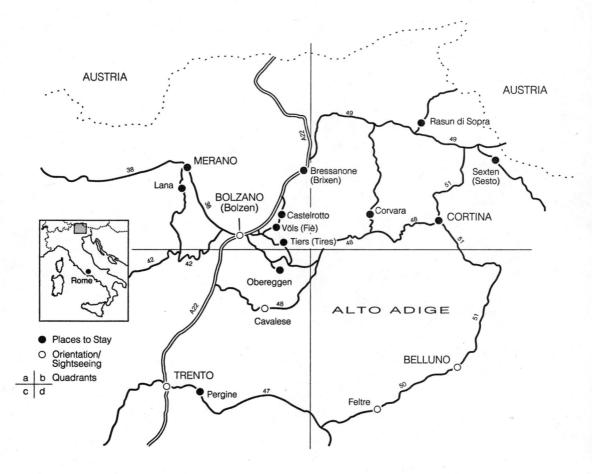

AUSTRIA

AUSTRIA

38   MERANO

Lana

BOLZANO
(Bolzen)

Castelrotto
Völs (Fiè)
Tiers (Tires)

Bressanone
(Brixen)

49

49

Rasun di Sopra

51

Sexten
(Sesto)

Corvara

48

CORTINA

51

Rome

42

42

Obereggen

48

Cavalese

ALTO ADIGE

51

A22

Places to Stay

Orientation/
Sightseeing

a | b   Quadrants
c | d

TRENTO

Pergine

47

BELLUNO

50

Feltre

Map 2

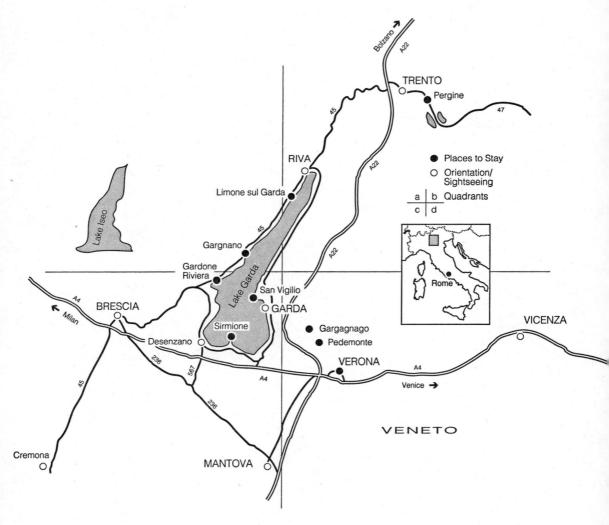

Map 3

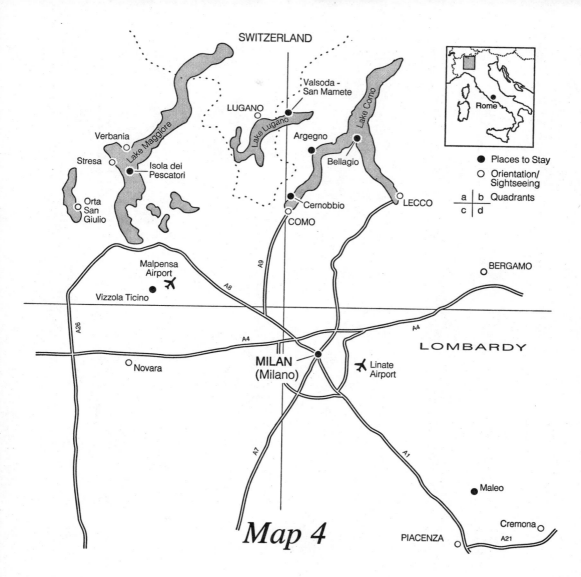

SWITZERLAND

Valsoda -
San Mamete

LUGANO

Lake Lugano

Argegno

Bellagio

Lake Como

Verbania

Lake Maggiore

Stresa

Isola dei
Pescatori

Orta
San
Giulio

Cernobbio

COMO

LECCO

Rome

● Places to Stay
○ Orientation/
    Sightseeing

a	b
c	d

Quadrants

Malpensa
Airport

BERGAMO

A9

Vizzola Ticino

A8

A26

A4

LOMBARDY

A4

Novara

MILAN
(Milano)

Linate
Airport

A7

A1

Maleo

Map 4

Cremona

PIACENZA

A21

267

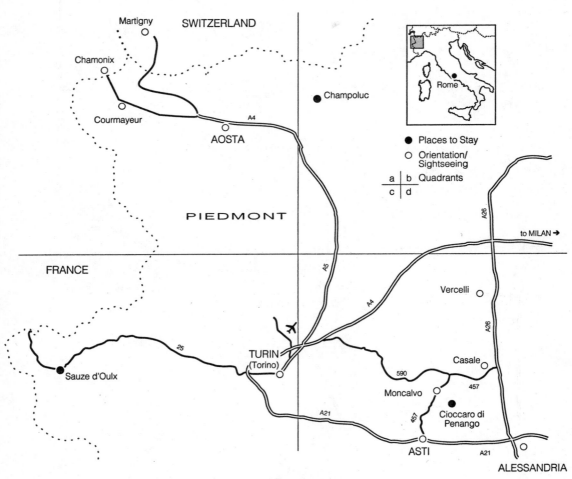

Map 5

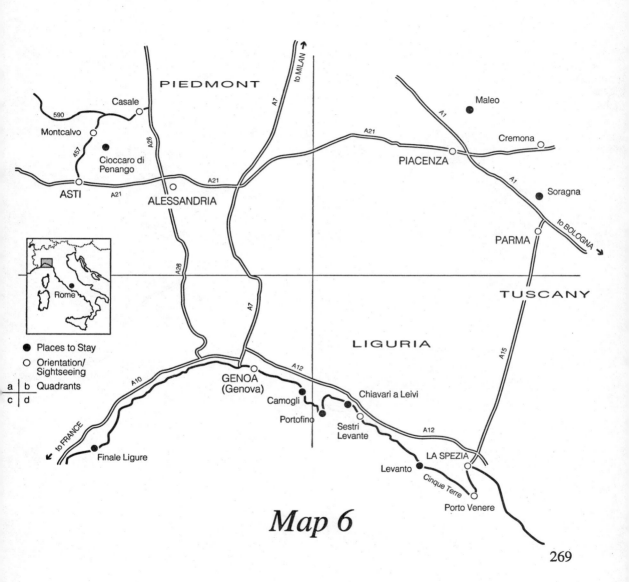

PIEDMONT

Casale

590

Montcalvo

457

Cioccaro di
Penango

ASTI   A21

A26

ALESSANDRIA

A7

to MILAN

A21

Maleo

Cremona

A1

PIACENZA

A1

Soragna

to BOLOGNA

PARMA

TUSCANY

A26

A7

LIGURIA

A15

Places to Stay

Orientation/
Sightseeing

a | b   Quadrants
c | d

A10

to FRANCE

GENOA
(Genova)

A12

Camogli

Portofino

Chiavari a Leivi

Sestri
Levante

A12

La SPEZIA

Finale Ligure

Levanto

Cinque Terre

Porto Venere

Rome

Map 6

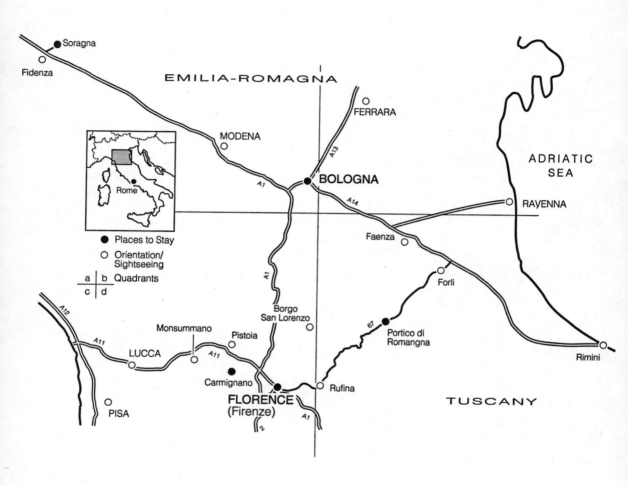

Map 7

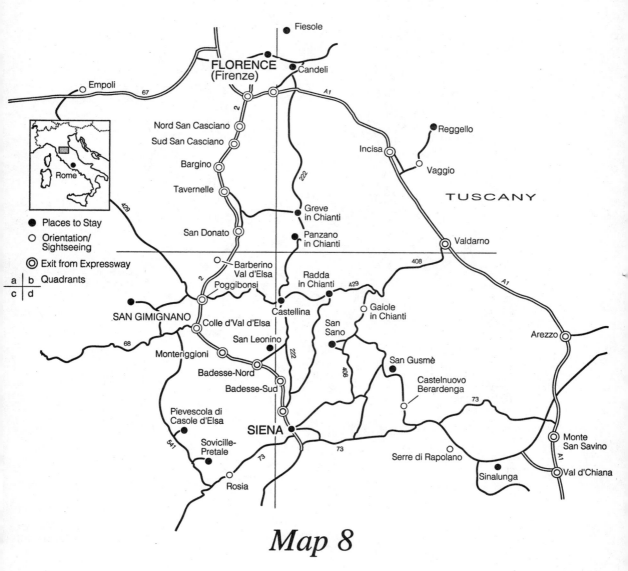

Map 8

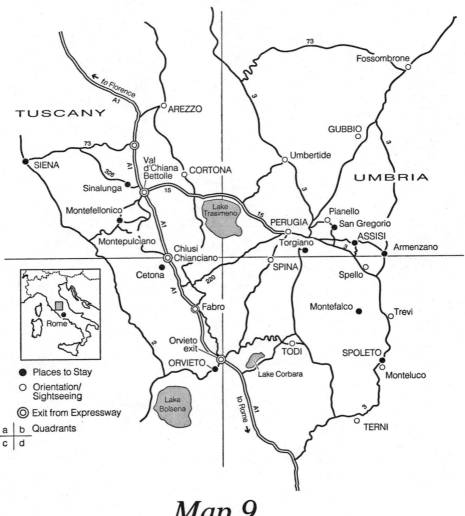

TUSCANY

← to Florence
A1

AREZZO

73
A1

SIENA

326

Val
d'Chiana
Bettolle

CORTONA

Sinalunga

15

Montefellonico

A1

Montepulciano

Chiusi
Chianciano

Cetona

220

A1

Fabro

2

Orvieto
exit

ORVIETO

Lake
Bolsena

Rome

73

Fossombrone

GUBBIO

3

Umbertide

UMBRIA

3

Lake
Trasimeno

15

PERUGIA

Pianello

San Gregorio

ASSISI

Torgiano

3

Armenzano

SPINA

Spello

Montefalco

Trevi

TODI

SPOLETO

Lake Corbara

Monteluco

to Rome
A1

3

TERNI

Rome

● Places to Stay

○ Orientation/
  Sightseeing

◎ Exit from Expressway

a	b
c	d

Quadrants

Map 9

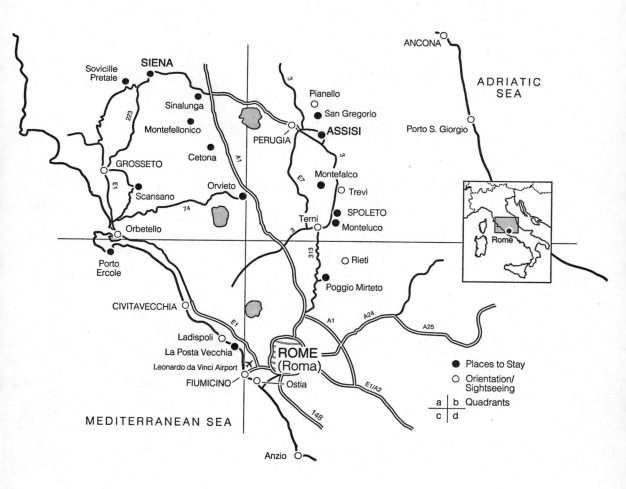

Map 10

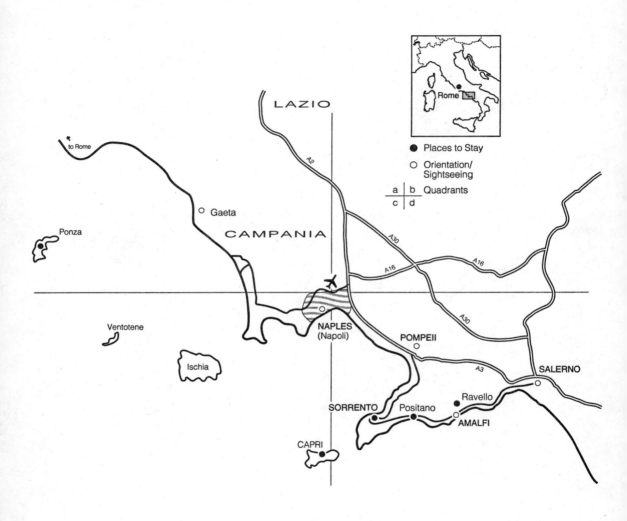

Map 11

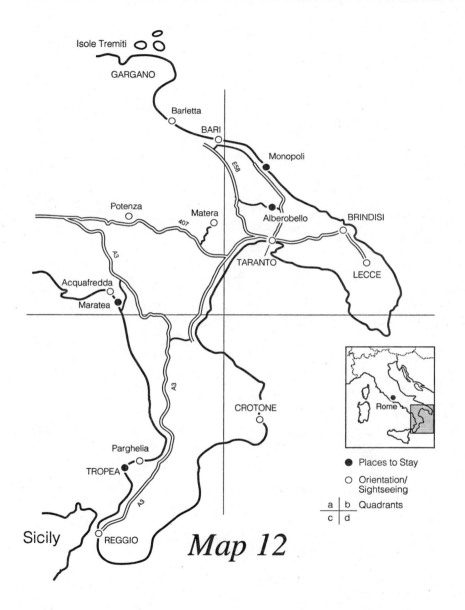

Isole Tremiti

GARGANO

Barletta

BARI

E55

Monopoli

Potenza

Matera

407

Alberobello

BRINDISI

TARANTO

LECCE

Acquafredda

A3

Maratea

A3

CROTONE

Parghelia

A3

TROPEA

Sicily

REGGIO

Map 12

Rome

● Places to Stay

○ Orientation/
   Sightseeing

| a | b | Quadrants |
| c | d | |

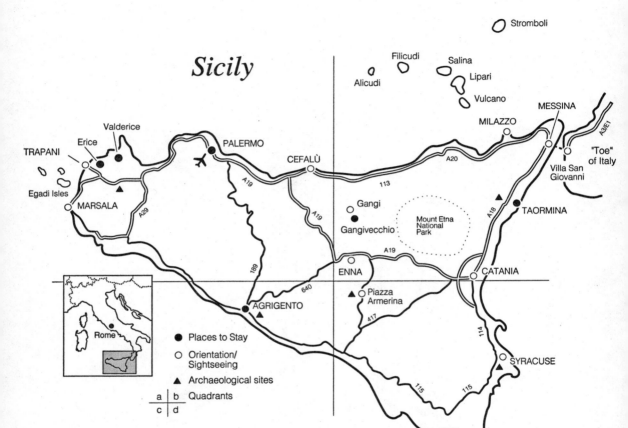

Sicily

Stromboli

Filicudi

Salina

Alicudi

Lipari

Vulcano

MESSINA

MILAZZO

TRAPANI

Valderice

Erice

PALERMO

CEFALÙ

"Toe"
of Italy

A3/E1

Egadi Isles

A20

Villa San
Giovanni

MARSALA

A19

113

Gangi

Mount Etna
National
Park

TAORMINA

A29

A18

A19

Gangivecchio

A19

Rome

189

ENNA

CATANIA

640

AGRIGENTO

Piazza
Armerina

114

● Places to Stay

417

○ Orientation/
Sightseeing

115

SYRACUSE

▲ Archaeological sites

115

a	b
c	d

Quadrants

Map 13

Sardinia

PORTO CERVO

OLBIA

SASSARI

597

ALGHERO

131

131

NUORO

Rome

537

ORISTANO

● Places to Stay
○ Orientation/Sightseeing

a	b	Quadrants
c	d

131

CARBONIA

CAGLIAR

Map 14

Index

C

M

Q

R

W

SEAL COVE INN—LOCATED IN THE SAN FRANCISCO AREA

Karen Brown Herbert (best known as author of the Karen Brown's guides) and her husband, Rick, have put 19 years of experience into reality and opened their own superb hideaway, Seal Cove Inn. Spectacularly set amongst wild flowers and bordered by towering cypress trees, Seal Cove Inn looks out to the ocean over acres of county park: an oasis where you can enjoy secluded beaches, explore tidepools, watch frolicking seals, and follow the tree-lined path that traces the windswept ocean bluffs. Country antiques, original watercolors, flower-laden cradles, rich fabrics, and the gentle ticking of grandfather clocks create the perfect ambiance for a foggy day in front of the crackling log fire. Each bedroom is its own haven with a cozy sitting area before a wood-burning fireplace and doors opening onto a private balcony or patio with views to the distant ocean. Moss Beach is a 35-minute drive south of San Francisco, 6 miles north of the picturesque town of Half Moon Bay, and a few minutes from Princeton harbor with its colorful fishing boats and restaurants. Seal Cove Inn makes a perfect base for whale-watching, salmon-fishing excursions, day trips to San Francisco, exploring the coast, or, best of all, just a romantic interlude by the sea, time to relax and be pampered. Karen and Rick look forward to the pleasure of welcoming you to their hideaway by the sea.

Seal Cove Inn, 221 Cypress Avenue, Moss Beach, California 94038, USA
Telephone: (415) 728-7325   Fax: (415) 728-4116

We Love to Hear from Karen Brown's Readers

ACCOLADES: We'd love to hear which accommodations you have especially enjoyed—even the shortest of notes is greatly appreciated. It is reassuring to know that places we recommend meet with your approval.

COMPLAINTS: Please let us know when a place we recommend fails to live up to the standards you have come to expect from Karen Brown. Constructive criticism is greatly appreciated. We sometimes make a mistake, places change, or go downhill. Your letters influence us to re-evaluate a listing.

RECOMMENDATIONS: If you have a favorite hideaway that you would like to recommend, please write to us. Give us a feel for the place, if possible send us a brochure and photographs (which we regret we cannot return). Convince us that on our next research trip, your discovery deserves a visit. All accommodations included in our guides are ones we have seen and enjoyed. Many of our finest selections are those that readers have discovered—wonderful places we would never have found on our own.

Please send information to:

KAREN BROWN'S GUIDES
Post Office Box 70
San Mateo, California 94401, USA
Telephone: (415) 342-9117 Fax: (415) 342-9153

Be a Karen Brown's Preferred Reader

If you would like to be the first to know when new editions of Karen Brown's guides go to press, and also to be included in any special promotions, simply send us your name and address. We encourage you to buy new editions and throw away the old ones so that you don't miss a wealth of wonderful new discoveries or run the risk of staying in places that no longer meet our standards—you'll be glad you did. We cover the miles searching for special places so that you don't have to spend your valuable vacation time doing so.

Name _____

Street _____

Town _____ State _____ Zip _____

Telephone _____ Fax _____

Please send information to:

KAREN BROWN'S GUIDES
Post Office Box 70
San Mateo, California 94401, USA
Telephone: (415) 342-9117   Fax: (415) 342-9153

HIDDEN TREASURES OF ITALY
Reservation Request Form

Name(s) of traveler(s):_____

Total number in party: _____   Number of children: _____   Ages: _____

Address: _____

_____

Tel: _____

Fax: _____

B&B name and location: _____

Second choice: _____

Type of accommodation: single _____   double _____   triple _____   apt._____

Dates desired: (Arrival) _____   (Departure) _____

Number of nights: _____

Meal plan: B&B _____   half board _____   full board _____   does not apply _____

Special Requests:

Hidden Treasures of Italy, 934 Elmwood Avenue, Wilmette IL 60091, USA
Tel: (847) 853-1312 Fax: (847) 853-1340

HIDDEN TREASURES OF ITALY

Hotel/Bed & Breakfast Booking Service

You may conveniently reserve any of the bed and breakfasts in this guide through Hidden Treasures of Italy's booking service. Car rentals and special interest tours (cooking classes, wine and garden tours, or horseback riding excursions) for small groups can also be arranged. Simply copy (as many times as necessary) and fill out the reservation-request form opposite this page and fax or mail it along with a $35 booking fee per reservation to:

HIDDEN TREASURES OF ITALY
934 Elmwood Avenue
Wilmette, IL 60091, USA
Tel: (847) 853-1312 Fax: (847) 853-1340
From Europe: Tel & fax: (Italy) 39-6-3052537

Upon confirmation of your request(s), exact rates with current exchange rate will be quoted and full prepayment by check, Visa or MasterCard will be required within 15 days from the date of notification. After receipt of payment, a written voucher will be issued to you to present to the hotel upon arrival. A **two-night minimum** stay is required per hotel/bed and breakfast.

CANCELLATION AND CHANGE POLICY
We will do our best to accommodate changes in dates or hotel choice, however this can never be guaranteed. Each additional request will require a supplementary $35 booking fee. Full refund of prepayment (excluding the booking fee) will be given up to 30 days prior to arrival date. No refund will be made within 30 days of your arrival. Booking fee is refundable **only** in the case where neither first nor second choices are available.

Cancellation insurance is strongly recommended

CLARE BROWN has many years of experience in the field of travel and has earned the designation of Certified Travel Consultant. Since 1969 she has specialized in planning itineraries to Europe using charming small hotels in the countryside for her clients. The focus of her job remains unchanged, but now her expertise is available to a larger audience—the readers of her daughter's country inn guides. Clare lives in Hillsborough, California, with her husband, Bill.

BARBARA TAPP, the talented artist who produces all of the hotel sketches and delightful illustrations in this guide, was raised in Australia where she studied in Sydney at the School of Interior Design. Although Barbara continues with freelance projects, she devotes much of her time to illustrating the Karen Brown guides. Barbara lives in Kensington, California, with her husband, Richard, their two sons, Jonothan and Alexander, and daughter, Georgia.

JANN POLLARD, the artist responsible for the beautiful painting on the cover of this guide, has studied art since childhood, and is well-known for her outstanding impressionistic-style watercolors which she has exhibited in numerous juried shows, winning many awards. Jann travels frequently to Europe (using Karen Brown's guides) where she loves to paint historical buildings. Jann lives in Burlingame, California, with her husband, Gene.

NOTES

USA Order Form

Please ask in your local bookstore for KAREN BROWN'S GUIDES. If the books you want are unavailable, you may order directly from the publisher.

Austria: Charming Inns & Itineraries $16.95

California: Charming Inns & Itineraries $16.95

England: Charming Bed & Breakfasts $15.95

England, Wales & Scotland: Charming Hotels & Itineraries $16.95

French Country Bed & Breakfasts $15.95

France: Charming Inns & Itineraries $16.95

Germany: Charming Inns & Itineraries $16.95

Ireland: Charming Inns & Itineraries $16.95

Italy: Charming Bed & Breakfasts $15.95

Italy: Charming Inns & Itineraries $16.95

Spain: Charming Inns & Itineraries $16.95

Swiss Country Inns & Itineraries $16.95

Name _____ Street _____

Town _____ State _____ Zip _____ Tel _____

Credit Card (MasterCard or Visa) _____ Exp _____

Add $4 for the first book and 50 cents for each additional book for postage & packing. California residents add 8.25% sales tax. Order form **only** for shipments within the USA. Indicate number of copies of each title; send form with check or credit card information to:

KAREN BROWN'S GUIDES
Post Office Box 70, San Mateo, California, 94401
Telephone: (415) 342-9117 Fax: (415) 342-9153